FIRST CLASS CITIZENSHIP

Also By Michael G. Long

God and Country:
Diverse Perspectives on Christianity and Patriotism
(with Tracy Wenger Sadd)

Billy Graham and the Beloved Community:
America's Evangelist and the Dream of Martin Luther King, Jr.

Against Us, but for Us:
Martin Luther King, Jr. and the State

FIRST CLASS CITIZENSHIP

THE CIVIL RIGHTS LETTERS OF JACKIE ROBINSON

EDITED BY MICHAEL G. LONG

TIMES BOOKS HENRY HOLT AND COMPANY NEW YORK

Times Books
Henry Holt and Company, LLC
Publishers since 1866
175 Fifth Avenue
New York, New York 10010
www.henryholt.com

Distributed in Canada by H. B. Fenn and Company Ltd.

Permissions credits are listed on pages 341–42.

Library of Congress Cataloging-in-Publication Data

Robinson, Jackie, 1919–1972.
First class citizenship : the civil rights letters of Jackie Robinson / edited by Michael G. Long.—1st ed.
p. cm.
Includes bibliographical references and index.
ISBN-13: 978-0-8050-8710-9
ISBN-10: 0-8050-8710-9
1. Robinson, Jackie, 1919–1972—Correspondence. 2. African American baseball players—Correspondence. 3. African Americans—Civil rights. I. Long, Michael G. II. Title.
GV865.R6A4 2007
796.357092—dc22
[B] 2007018621

Henry Holt books are available for special promotions and premiums. For details contact: Director, Special Markets.

First Edition 2007

Designed by Kelly Too

Printed in the United States of America

1 3 5 7 9 10 8 6 4 2

For Jackson,
who deserves his own page

I think I've been much more
aggressive since I left baseball.

—Jackie Robinson

CONTENTS

EDITOR'S INTRODUCTION

"Have you seen the Jackie Robinson file?"

I was conducting research on President Richard Nixon at the National Archives in Laguna Beach, California, when the archivist Paul Wormser approached my desk with that beautiful question.

It was December 2005, and while the Robinson file was beyond my immediate research topic, I could not resist the delicious temptation.

"I have not," I replied. "But I'd like to."

Paul quickly returned with the file, and for the next several hours I was just spellbound, completely immersed in digesting and copying a significant body of letters between Robinson and Nixon.

The topics ranged from the personal to the political—from shared lunches to Eisenhower's race politics—but most of them centered on Robinson's hard-hitting efforts to advance a civil rights agenda within the Republican Party in the 1950s and 1960s.

I was hooked because this was a Jackie Robinson I did not know. Growing up in central Pennsylvania in the 1970s, I had been exposed to benign biographies that depicted him as a smiling second baseman—a nice young man who had "turned the other cheek" when facing those who were furious about Branch Rickey's experiment of breaking the color barrier in Major League Baseball.

Of course, the elementary-school books offered the standard statistics, too, and so I also learned that even while enduring countless taunts, this smiling young man had earned a remarkable .311 career batting average and helped to lead the Brooklyn Dodgers to six National League pennants and one World Series championship.

Call it truncated history—and part of the reason for my shock and delight as I plowed through the Nixon-Robinson correspondence.

Here, at last, was a Jackie Robinson far beyond the baseball diamond.

An angry black man who grabbed a pen and wrote rage-filled letters about segregation and discrimination. A fiery prophet who rebuked politicians for telling African Americans to exercise patience and forbearance when pursuing their constitutional rights. A fervent patriot committed to using his celebrity status and considerable resources to overcome the racial divide *right now* so that his children would have a brighter, bolder future.

It was as if I was meeting a new—or perhaps another—Jackie Robinson.

At first I was not sure what to do with the letters, but after returning to my hotel and watching yet another television program on athletes "gone bad," I resolved to share that precious file with the wider world. We deserve a much better role model from professional sports, I thought, and who better than Jackie Robinson?

Within the week I asked Rachel Robinson, Jackie's widow, for permission to publish the letters, and she kindly agreed. But as I continued my research at archives across the country, especially at the Library of Congress, which holds the Jackie Robinson Papers, I began to crave a bigger project.

The letters to Nixon were a good start, but Robinson wrote civil rights letters to so many major historical figures (Malcolm X, Barry Goldwater, Martin Luther King, Jr., John F. Kennedy, Hubert Humphrey, Adam Clayton Powell, Jr., Nelson Rockefeller) and about so many controversial topics (black power, the Vietnam War, divisions within the civil rights movement). And his letters sparked substantive replies that reflected America's running conversation about politics and race and economics. How could I not share all these letters, too? I went back to Rachel, who has long touted Jackie as an informal civil rights leader, and she graciously agreed to the wider project.

Her generosity is to our benefit, because the more clearly we can hear Jackie Robinson's voice from beyond the baseball diamond, the better we will understand the complicated history of race and politics in the United States, the more deeply we will sense our successes and failures to establish equal justice under law, and the fairer we will be when assessing the rich legacy of this American icon.

Other scholars and writers have come to this realization long before I have, and Alfred Duckett, Sharon Robinson, Arnold Rampersad, Jules Tygiel, and David Falkner have led the way in introducing us to Jackie Robinson's life after his retirement from baseball. But their efforts notwithstanding, the general public has largely ignored or dismissed Robinson's civil rights advocacy beyond the playing field, preferring instead to focus on the bright smile of a youthful baseball player. At best we will occasionally recall his understandable hostility toward fellow players, umpires, and the media during the latter days of his baseball career. But this fiery image, just like his civil rights legacy, has been far from enduring.

Perhaps it has been safe and convenient for us to picture Robinson as the tolerant, clean-cut ballplayer who gently helped to integrate professional sports in the United States. But however comfortable it may be, our collective focus on the first part of his baseball career is utterly unfair to the Jackie Robinson who loudly criticized the practices and policies of racist America, devoted countless hours to civil rights fundraising and rallies, twisted the arms of politicians hungry for black votes and yet fearful of a white backlash, and encouraged young African Americans who have since become well-known veterans in the ongoing battle for civil rights.

This is the Jackie Robinson you will discover in the pages ahead. You will soon see that the only object mightier than a bat in his right hand was a ballpoint pen, and that in the struggle for civil rights he wielded his pen with remarkable talent and energy.

While he lavished eloquent praise on those who sought to overcome racial segregation and discrimination (for example, Lyndon Johnson and the Freedom Riders of the 1960s), Robinson also wrote scorching letters to anyone who dared to differ with his vision of fair play for African Americans (for example, Barry Goldwater and Adam Clayton Powell, Jr.).

By turns affectionate and direct, incisive and incendiary, the letters provide us with a fresh opportunity to encounter Robinson anew, this time in his own words—largely unfiltered and uncensored, and sometimes just plain unbelievable.

It is not always easy to understand this prophet with pen in hand. Robinson's passion for civil rights was complicated and nuanced. A natural maverick, he charted his own course, offering his support to Democrats and Republicans, questioning the tactics of civil rights leaders already in conflict with one another, and challenging the nation's leaders to fulfill the promises of democracy and capitalism.

Robinson's maverick spirit created a good number of enemies along the way. Malcolm X and his followers depicted him as an "Uncle Tom" perfectly suited to clean up after his "white bosses," and the Nixon administration identified him as a threat significant enough to warrant a written report from J. Edgar Hoover—even as Robinson offered to help the Nixon team.

Taken together, Robinson's letters and their replies provide us with new insight into the conversations that both created and weakened the civil rights movement. Above all else, however, these rich letters complete our picture of Jackie Robinson—a Hall of Fame baseball player, to be sure, but also an extraordinary political powerhouse and a civil rights leader in his own right, who personified the "first class citizenship" that he demanded for *all* Americans, and who, to the day of his death, fiercely competed against anyone who would stand in his way.

A NOTE ON THE TEXT

In editing Jackie Robinson's letters, I have made minimal changes to correct misspellings, typographical errors, and run-on sentences. Because I wish to preserve the compelling cadence found in these letters, all of my changes are "silent"; they are not marked by the use of brackets or [*sic*]. Robinson and his fellow letter writers were not grammarians by any stretch of the imagination, but they were careful enough to make sure, with the help of assistants, that their letters were easily readable, if not thoroughly enjoyable.

Robinson occasionally relied on ghostwriters for his many projects. The playwright William Branch wrote Robinson's column for the *New York Post*, and Alfred Duckett, a public relations expert, wrote Robinson's column for the *New York Amsterdam News*. But in each of these instances, the ghostwriter collaborated closely with Robinson to be sure that the words reflected his ideas, and Robinson himself reviewed everything that went out under his name so that he could stand behind it. Duckett also helped Robinson to craft letters, and his handwork is especially detectable in the rhetorical flourishes of several letters from 1963 onward; a good example of his work is the August 1964 letter from Robinson to Barry Goldwater. It is also likely that Evelyn Cunningham, a former reporter for the *Pittsburgh Courier*, played a major role in helping Robinson draft correspondence during the late 1960s, when she and Duckett worked on Robinson's staff during his employment with Governor Nelson Rockefeller of New York.

Although he was a devoted letter writer, Robinson did not compose letters about every aspect of his civil rights work, let alone every major civil rights issue, or all the personalities he encountered, and if there are apparent gaps in the book, it is most likely because I could find no letters that he wrote on the subject. Sometimes, rather than sitting down to write a letter, Robinson would just pick up the phone. Nevertheless, I do not claim to have exhausted all possible sources for Robinson's extant letters; he was incredibly prolific, and he wrote to hundreds of everyday citizens.

Finally, my research assistants and I could not locate several important letters—some written by Robinson, some received by him—to which Robinson and his correspondents refer in the pages ahead; these letters are simply not in the obvious places of the archives where one would expect to find them.

FIRST CLASS CITIZENSHIP

1

FAITH IN DEMOCRACY

· 1946–1956 ·

ROBINSON TO RALPH NORTON

Jackie Robinson broke baseball's color barrier on August 28, 1945, when he signed a letter of agreement that bound him to the Brooklyn Dodgers. Two months later, on October 23, Branch Rickey, general manager of the Dodgers, offered Robinson a formal contract to play for the Montreal Royals, the Dodgers' top farm team. In this handwritten letter to Ralph Norton, an acquaintance from his days at Pasadena Junior College, Robinson writes of his tryout in Florida the following spring.

March 12, 1946

Hello Ralph,

I too remember the good old days at P.J.C. and I remember you from the Chronicle. It was nice hearing from you and I do appreciate your well wishes. It would be really nice hearing from the fellows you mentioned, and I am sure that if we get encouraging letters such as yours it is going to be tough keeping us off the club. I would appreciate hearing more from you and I will keep you informed as to our progress. So far it has been a real pleasure playing here with the fellows. Everyone has been so nice and they have given us help along the way. I did not expect any trouble but I also did not expect to be welcomed as I have. It reminds me of the days at P.J.C. when all the fellows used to block and clear the way so I could run with the ball. We have met a couple that have resented us, but only a sharp eye could tell. All I can say is if we make the club, it will be on our own merit. If not it will be due to the fact that the many ballplayers Montreal has are better than we are. Our manager Clay Hopper has been very helpful and is giving us every chance possible. If you hear from Glick, Vanderweer or Shatford give them my regards.

Sincerely,
Jackie

NORMAN THOMAS TO ROBINSON

Robinson made his major-league debut with the Brooklyn Dodgers on April 15, 1947, and among his ardent supporters that year was Bernice Franklin, the owner of a general store near Tyronza, Arkansas. "I live in a small all-Negro town," she wrote Robinson. "We go to Memphis for all our amusements, but there is no greater thrill than a broadcast of the Dodgers baseball game . . . right now the farmers are gathering [at the store] for your game this afternoon." Another fan was Norman Thomas, leader of the Socialist Party of America, six-time candidate for the presidency, and advocate for racial justice and world peace. Throughout 1947 Robinson agreed to follow Rickey's biblical admonition to "turn the other cheek," and Thomas was pleased with this nonviolent strategy.

September 23, 1947

Dear Mr. Robinson:

Now that the Dodgers have won the pennant, it is very appropriate, I think, to thank you not only for what you did in the pennant race but for what you have done for the colored race and for the fraternity which ought to characterize our mutual relations. You have performed a real service to our country and in general to a world which must learn to honor men for what they are and do regardless of race.

I am writing on the letterhead of an organization interested in the kind of world relations that will bring peace, and I rather think its members would share my feeling about your contribution to the kind of attitude on which peace depends.

Sincerely yours,
Norman Thomas

ROBINSON TO ADMIRER

Not all fan mail was as high-minded as Norman Thomas's, and the following is Robinson's reply to a troubled young woman who had written of her love for him. The letter reveals Robinson's quick and easy appeal to moral principles—an appeal that would become characteristic of his civil rights letters.

October 15, 1947

Dear Miss [editor's deletion]:

Ordinarily I wouldn't even consider answering a letter like yours, but I believe you need to get straightened out on a few things. A girl as attractive and intelligent as you sound certainly should have no difficulty in finding the right man and creating a sound, honest life together in marriage. You are suffering from some kind of mental delusion that can bring you nothing but trouble and unhappiness and my advice is to get interested in some kind of work outside your daily routine in the office.

When I married Mrs. Robinson, I exchanged vows to love, honor and cherish her for the rest of my life. "Honor" means just that to me, and any sneaking, skulking escapade would destroy the very thing that enables me to hold my head up high.

Just in case you might want to write me again, I must inform you that all my mail is opened at the Brooklyn baseball club offices and then forwarded to me.

Yours in reproof,
Jackie Robinson

LESTER GRANGER TO ROBINSON

By now a celebrity athlete, Robinson appeared before the House Un-American Activities Committee (HUAC) on July 18, 1949, as it held hearings on African American loyalty to the United States. Of special concern to the committee was a remark reportedly made by Paul Robeson, the internationally renowned singer and actor, about the possibility of a war between the United States and the Soviet Union. "It is unthinkable," Robeson allegedly stated, "that American Negroes would go to war on behalf of those who have oppressed us for generations against a country which in one generation has raised our people to the full dignity of mankind." In his widely publicized testimony, Robinson characterized Robeson's remark as "very silly," adding that African Americans would "do their best to help their country stay out of war; if unsuccessful, they'd do their best to help their country win the war—against Russia or any other enemy that threatened us." Lester Granger, executive director of the National Urban League, praises Robinson in the following letter. Near the end of his life, however, Robinson expressed regret for appearing before HUAC.

July 19, 1949

Dear Robbie:

Together with hundreds of thousands of other Americans in New York City and throughout the country, I was inordinately proud when I picked up the papers last night and this morning and read the reports of your appearance before the House Committee on Un-American Activities. I don't need to tell you what impression you made on the public generally.

One report stressed the dignity and sincerity with which you made your statement. In nutshell form, you have stated the case for the American Negro in such a way as to send it around the world in quarters where no other such expression would have received any notice at all. This should be a matter of great pride to you and your wife, even while you realize that there will be sharp criticism and some underhand attacks coming from left-wing or uninformed sources.

I am now an old hand at the business of receiving public criticism as well as approbations. I have learned that praise never lasts as long as I would like, but also that criticism is never important when it is delivered by dishonest or uninformed people.

The Communist group is exceptionally skilled at kicking up a row that seems to be out of all proportion to their actual numbers among our population. They can fill Madison Square Garden for a rally. They can recruit a hundred people to send a thousand telegrams and letters. They can magnify the squeak of a mouse to the point where it seems like the roar of a lion.

I hope that you will expect this kind of result and not be at all disturbed when it occurs. For your information, after the radio and evening newspapers made their comments last night, I circulated for five hours among bars and grills, sidewalk groups and neighbors and friends. It was remarkable that in not one single case did I receive from any person to whom I talked anything but praise for the way in which you had expressed yourself. My experience may have been exceptional in its absence of any criticism, but I am confident that it was typical in its overwhelming preponderance of approval for your point of view.

You have rendered a service to our people which will be gratefully regarded for many years to come. On behalf of the National Urban League and the millions of Americans who believe in what we are trying to do, I want to thank you for your service.

I hope to improve upon the acquaintanceship—or, I hope, friendship—which we have developed in our contacts. Please give Mrs. Robinson my warm regards.

Sincerely yours,
Lester B. Granger

ROBINSON TO BRANCH RICKEY

Robinson considered Rickey to be the father he never had, and he was disappointed when Rickey sold his ownership interest in the Dodgers in 1950 and became general manger of the Pittsburgh Pirates. Robinson refers to Rickey's tenure as general manager of the St. Louis Cardinals in the 1930s and early 1940s.

No date [November 1950]

Dear Mr. Rickey,

I have been intending to write for about a month now and it seems that finding the right words comes hard as I will attempt at this time to put them down.

It is certainly tough on everyone in Brooklyn to have you leave the organization but to me it's much worse, and I don't mind saying we (my family) hate to see you go but realize that baseball is like that and anything can happen. It has been the finest experience I have had being associated with you, and I want to thank you very much for all you have meant not only to me and my family but to the entire country and particularly the members of our race. I am glad for your sake that I had a small part to do with the success of your efforts and must admit it was your excellent guidance that enabled me to do it. Regardless of what happens to me in the future, it all can be placed on what you have done and, believe me, I appreciate it.

I don't know the circumstances that caused you to sell, but I am smart enough to know that a person does not sell a growing thing unless there is some misunderstanding some place. But I do want to wish you and your family the very best of everything and sincerely hope that you are able to bring to Pittsburgh just what you did to Brooklyn and St. Louis. I hope to end my playing in Brooklyn as it means so very much, but if I have to go any place I hope it can be with you.

My wife joins me in saying thanks very much, Mr. Rickey, and we sincerely hope that we can always be regarded as your friends and whenever we need advice we can call on you as usual regardless of where we may be.

My very best wishes to you and yours and a hope for your continued success.

Sincerely yours,
Jackie

BRANCH RICKEY TO ROBINSON

December 31, 1950

Dear Jackie:

It is not at all because of lack of appreciation that I have not acknowledged your good letter of some time ago. Neither your writing and sending the letter, nor its contents, gave me very much surprise. I have observed that you have learned long ago that most things, good or bad, just don't happen to people by accident. Your thoughtfulness in the field of so-called unimportant things has doubtless led to much of your success. Anyhow, the fact that you wrote the letter, and particularly the things you said in it, not only meant very much to me, and was, as I have said, deeply appreciated, but it also revealed why you have come to so much deserved distinction.

I hope the day will soon come when it will be entirely possible, as it is entirely right, that you can be considered for administrative work in baseball, particularly in the direction of field management.

I do not know of any player in the game today who could, in my judgment, manage a major league club better than yourself. I recently made this statement in the presence of several writers in the course of various remarks, but I have looked in vain for the reporting of the statement.

Very often during these holidays, I have thought of you and Rachel and the family. I choose to feel that my acquaintanceship with you has ripened into a very real friendship, growing out of our facing and trying to solve common problems and our continuous record of seeing eye to eye in practically all of these problems that faced us.

I do not suppose that our paths will probably parallel again in any close fashion, but I do want you and Rachel to know that always I, and, indeed the family, will have a constant and lasting interest in your welfare and happiness.

As I have often expressed to you, I think you carry a great responsibility for your people, and I am sure that you sense the duties resting upon you because of that responsibility, and I cannot close this letter without once more admonishing you to prepare yourself to do a widely useful work, and, at the same time, dignified and effective in the field of public relations. A part of this preparation, and I know you are smiling, for you have already guessed my oft repeated suggestion, is to finish your college course meritoriously, and get your degree. It would be a great pleasure for me to be your agent in placing you in a big job after your playing days are finished. Believe me always.

Sincerely yours,
Branch Rickey

JOHN D. ROCKEFELLER III TO ROBINSON

Robinson and his Dodgers teammate Roy Campanella worked together as counselors at the Harlem branch of the YMCA. They also supported the Y by soliciting funds from the Rockefeller family, a longtime benefactor of African American causes.

January 18, 1951

Dear Mr. Robinson:

My son and I enjoyed very much our recent talk with you. I was especially interested to hear about the work you and Mr. Campanella are doing in furthering the boys work program of the Harlem Y.M.C.A.

Because of my appreciation not only of the importance of this program but also of the part you personally are playing in it, it gives me real pleasure to send you the enclosed cashier's check drawn to the order of the Harlem Branch as a contribution toward the expense of this program during the current year. Since the Rockefeller Brothers Fund gives to the Y.M.C.A. of the City of New York, my brothers and I have not felt that we could normally contribute to branches of the "Y" within the city. Because of this you will understand, I am sure, my asking that this gift be reported as having come from an anonymous source.

In writing this letter I don't feel that it is complete without an expression of sincere admiration and appreciation of those principles for which you stand personally in American life.

Sincerely,
John D. Rockefeller

"THE TRAVELERS" TO ROBINSON

On the day he received this letter, and aware of this threat against his life, Robinson slugged a home run in the first game of a doubleheader at Crosley Field, home of the Cincinnati Reds. The Dodgers swept the twin bill, 10–3 and 14–4, and the threat proved idle.

No date
[received May 20, 1951]

We have already got rid of several like you. One was found in river just recently. Robinson, we are going to kill you if you attempt to enter a ballgame at Crosley Field.

The Travelers

"DODGER HATER" TO ROBINSON

This letter is yet another example of the many death threats that Robinson received throughout his baseball career. Arnold Schuster, referenced below, had identified the bank robber William Sutton following the robbery of a Queens bank in 1950, and two years later, shortly before the beginning of Sutton's trial, Schuster was murdered on the streets of Brooklyn. It is unclear whether the author of the following letter is disturbed by Robinson's skin color, athletic prowess, or both. But there was no attempt to kill Robinson, and the Dodgers won the pennant in 1953.

September 15, 1953

Dear Mr. Robinson,

[FBI deletion] was warned *not* to win the pennant. But he did anyhow, and he won't be in St. Louis. Well that's bad cause *you* are going to get it. Remember what happened to Arnold Shuyster in Brooklyn in 1952? Well Wed. nite Sept. 15 you *die*. No use crying to the cops. You'll be executed gangland style at Busch stadium.

Dodger Hater

ROBINSON TO DWIGHT EISENHOWER

On November 23 Rachel and Jackie Robinson attended the fortieth anniversary dinner for the Anti-Defamation League of B'nai B'rith in Washington, D.C. President Dwight D. Eisenhower, the keynote speaker at the televised event, made a special effort to shake Robinson's hand just after delivering his speech.

November 25, 1953

Dear Mr. President:

I want to take this opportunity to let you know how very much it meant to me to be able to meet you briefly at the dinner in Washington Monday night.

It was a great privilege for me to appear on a program in which the President of the United States took part. It was equally great for me to experience the warmth and sincerity of your handshake in the midst of such an illustrious group of Americans.

My wife and I will always remember our experience that night. It is events like this that make us certain our faith in democracy is indeed justified.

Very sincerely yours,
Jackie Robinson

DWIGHT EISENHOWER TO ROBINSON

November 30, 1953

Dear Mr. Robinson:

Thank you very much for your nice note. In answer, may I say only that you represent to me and to many Americans one more evidence that our democracy, in which we have so much pride, is indeed in our country a workable, living ideal. All of us are grateful to you for the courage on your part required to demonstrate this.

With best wishes to you and Mrs. Robinson,

Sincerely,
Dwight D. Eisenhower

ROBINSON TO MAXWELL RABB

The following letter is early evidence of Robinson's lifelong efforts to advance the cause of civil rights through affordable housing—and to make money in business beyond the baseball diamond. Here he seeks assistance from Maxwell Rabb, secretary to the Eisenhower cabinet, in securing a federal mortgage for a New York City housing project for minorities. The project never reached completion.

November 15, 1954

Dear Mr. Rabb:

Thank you for your letter. I am sorry it did not reach here until I was in Washington, and that I was unable to contact you.

I was very interested in Mr. Alan Paton's story in the *Saturday Evening Post*, where he said, "The Negroes today are no longer saying let my people go, but let my people in." He was referring to the tremendous need there is for Minority Housing, and his article spurred my writing you again. I am sure you must know how important this field is, and I feel that it's an obligation that should be fulfilled. It also seems that besides being a real necessity it would serve as a big public relations job.

I do hope that I can get a favorable reaction from you on this matter as it is extremely important to the retention of our site which we had approved sometime ago. I know the housing situation is a precarious one right now, but I don't believe anyone could find anything but praise for the Administration for relieving this serious strain.

I have been in touch with the Urban League, and they feel also that you would be doing a fine thing if something could be arranged. They have given me their wholehearted support, and it's the encouragement that I needed from this end. Now if we can only get the Administration's support a badly needed project could be under way.

Sincerely yours,
Jackie Robinson

ROBINSON TO AVERELL HARRIMAN

In October 1955 shots were fired at the home of Reverend Joseph A. DeLaine, a local civil rights activist who had organized parents to fight for equal treatment for African American students in Clarendon County, South Carolina. DeLaine's efforts—which had helped spur one of the lawsuits of Brown v. Board of Education*—led to threats against his life, and because he returned fire in the October 1955 incident, local authorities charged him with assault and battery, with intent to kill. DeLaine protested his innocence, claiming to have fired only at the car of the assailant, and fled to New York. Here Robinson lobbies New York governor Averell Harriman to protect DeLaine from extradition proceedings. DeLaine avoided extradition and became the founding pastor of an African Methodist Episcopal church in Buffalo, New York.*

December 6, 1955

Dear Governor Harriman:

As you know, there is much concern in the City of New York, and in the Harlem community, in particular, about the future fate of Rev. Joseph A. DeLaine, "fugitive" from Clarendon County, South Carolina.

At this time, in many areas of the South, there is great unrest and unsettlement, which is part of the death throes of a great social evil. We are sure that in time, the spirit embodied in the Constitution of the United States will prevail in all sections of the country; however, it is important now that we be vigilant in guarding against flagrant miscarriages of justice that will hurt not only the innocent victims, but also the perpetrators.

As an American citizen and as a human being concerned about the welfare of all people, I am writing to urge you not to sign extradition papers for Rev. Joseph A. DeLaine. I believe that he is worthy of sanctuary, and that of all states, the Empire State, New York, should provide a haven for a very courageous man whose only crime was being born a Negro and attempting to protect his person, his family and his home.

I feel confident that you will give this matter every consideration, and that justice and the spirit of the true American democratic way of life will prevail with you as you make your decision.

Very sincerely yours,
Jackie Robinson

ROBINSON TO CAROLINE WALLERSTEIN

David and Caroline Wallerstein, close friends of the Robinsons, resided in Chicago, where David was president of the largest movie-theater chain in the Midwest. In the following letter to Caroline, Robinson refers to his ongoing salary negotiations with E. J. "Buzzie" Bavasi, the general manager of the Dodgers, and to Martin Stone, Robinson's new financial adviser. Robinson was looking forward to life beyond the diamond at this point, and he expresses hope for a future in sports broadcasting. He was already doing a local television sports show in New York City with the sportscaster Marty Glickman, and he was hoping that it would become a national program. Glickman was no stranger to racial discrimination himself; twenty years earlier he was a star runner at Syracuse University and had been selected to compete in the 400-meter relay at the 1936 Olympic Games in Berlin. At the last minute, however, U.S. track officials pulled him and another Jewish runner from the competition, apparently in deference to the host—Adolf Hitler.

January 3, 1956

Dear Caroline,

Well, the new year has arrived and I'm looking forward to it, although at this time I'm not sure what is to happen. I was to talk with Buzzie last week but he came up sick. I don't know if it was a legit sickness but he put our meeting off anyway. I had a long talk with Marty Stone the other day, and he was telling me not to give in to their wishes and that's what my plan is. I'm not sure whether I'll be playing next year or not so I am looking for other things. I also want to thank both you and Dave for your interests. I am sure you must know that most networks are not ready yet, and I believe it's a shame because I am certain most people are. Our program at NBC has the highest local sports rating and it's creating considerable talk not only with the people but the station. I am fairly certain that NBC is about ready to do something . . . but regardless of that I have the feeling it's only fear that holds them back. I am doing a spot with Marty Glickman and we work very well together. I am as sure as anything that this sort of a program would go just as well on a larger scale as it does over the local station, and it will also in my opinion create a good deal of good public relations value . . .

Since the World Series pictures have been previewed there has been a lot more talk about the steal of home and my play all around. Dick Young and Mike Gaven both gave me tremendous credit for the series, and it made the old boy feel good. I guess we really live for good writeups, but not at the sacrifice of our principles. Each week on our program we try to bring this out, and Marty Glickman usually throws a provocative question at me and, believe me, we say what we believe. Because of this I have made many friends, and I really hope everyone understands some of my reasons. I know also that because of my outspokenness some don't like it, but nevertheless I'll always say what I believe. I'll take the true friends like you and your family, and in the end I believe most people will realize just as you do some of our reasons . . .

Always,
Jackie

ROBINSON TO WILLIAM KEEFE

Bill Keefe, sports editor for the Times-Picayune *of New Orleans, had written an editorial suggesting that Robinson's behavior was the catalyst for a new Louisiana law that criminalized interracial sports.*

July 23, 1956

Dear Mr. Keefe:

I am in receipt of a clipping in which you make reference to me in connection with the passage of the athletic segregation bill in Louisiana.

I am writing you, not as Jackie Robinson, but as one human being to another. I cannot help, nor possibly alter what you think about me. I speak to you only as an American who happens to be an American Negro and one who is proud of that heritage.

We ask for nothing special. We ask only that we be permitted to live as you live, and as our nation's constitution provides. We ask only, in sports, that we be permitted to compete on an even basis and, if we are not worthy, then the competition shall, per se, eliminate us. Certainly you, and the people of Louisiana, should be capable of facing such competition.

Myself, and other Negroes in the majors, stop in hotels with the rest of the club in towns like St. Louis and Cincinnati. These hotels have not gone out of business. No investment has been destroyed. The hotels are, I believe, prospering. And there has been no unpleasantness.

I wish you could see this as I do, but I hold little hope. I wish you could comprehend how unfair and un-American it is for the accident of birth to make such a difference to you. I assume you are of Irish extraction. I have been told that, as recently as fifty years ago, want ads in newspapers carried the biased line "Irish and Italians need not apply" in certain sections of our country. This has been forgotten, or at least overcome.

You call me "insolent." I'll admit I have not been subservient, but would you use the same adjective to describe a white ballplayer—say Ted Williams, who is, more often than I, involved in controversial matters? Am I insolent, or am I merely insolent for a Negro (who has courage enough to speak against injustices such as yours and people like you)?

I am deeply regretful that Louisiana has taken this step backward . . . because your sports fans, and I believe there are many fine persons among them, will be deprived of top attractions because of it . . . not for the Negro in Louisiana who will, because of your law, be deprived of the right of free and equal competition—but because of the damage it does to our country.

I am happy for you, that you were born white. It would have been extremely difficult for you had it been otherwise.

Sincerely yours,
Jackie Robinson

HERBERT LEHMAN TO ROBINSON

The platform hearings on civil rights at the 1956 Democratic National Convention pitted opponents to integration against civil rights activists, including the liberal senator Herbert Lehman of New York. The liberals were dealt a blow on August 16 when the convention rejected a platform plank that promised implementation of Supreme Court decisions prohibiting segregation in transportation and public schools—including the landmark ruling in Brown v. Board of Education. *Eleanor Roosevelt moderated the contentious convention debate, and although the final language did not mention* Brown, *the Democratic platform declared that the Supreme Court was the final authority on civil rights issues, and it condemned the use of violence in racial matters.*

August 21, 1956

Dear Jackie:

Thanks very much indeed for your telegram of August 16th, which reached me at the Convention in Chicago. It was very thoughtful of you to wire me and I greatly appreciate it.

I was of course disappointed that our minority report on civil rights was not adopted at the Convention. Had it been possible to secure a roll call vote, I think we would have had a very good chance of winning. Regardless of our defeat, I think the fight which we made was very worthwhile and will be of much use in the future. I am very confident that within a reasonably short time the whole country will recognize that every man, woman and child, regardless of race, color or religion, must receive all their rights and liberties guaranteed by our constitution and by our statutes.

Thank you again very much indeed for your telegram.

With kind personal regards, I am

Yours very sincerely,
Herbert H. Lehman

I have long been one of your fans and I watch the Dodger games on T.V. as often as possible.
HL

BRANCH RICKEY TO ROY WILKINS

In December 1956 the National Association for the Advancement of Colored People (NAACP) presented Robinson with the Spingarn Medal, an annual award for distinguished achievement. At the luncheon held in his honor, Robinson stated: "Today marks the high point in my career. To be honored in this way by the NAACP means more than anything that has happened to me before. That is because the NAACP, to me, represents everything that a man should stand for: for human dignity, for brotherhood, for fair play." In the following telegram to Roy Wilkins, executive director of the NAACP, Branch Rickey commends Robinson yet again.

December 7, 1956

The National Association for the Advancement of Colored People is to be congratulated for giving this signal recognition to Jackie Robinson. Not very many folks really appreciate how well he has done in a very hard but challenging assignment. It was important that I choose an understanding partner in the baseball innovation. But it was also equally important that the man should sense understandingly the responsibility that he carried for his whole race. I think he has pioneered both jobs with high satisfaction. Frankly the honor you are bestowing has been long deserved. Therefore my heartiest congratulations to the NAACP and then of course you will please extend to Robbie my heartfelt felicitations.

Branch Rickey

HAROLD HOWLAND TO ROBINSON

Harold Howland, a staff member of the U.S. State Department's International Educational Exchange Service, invites Robinson to become a goodwill ambassador for the United States. Like Robinson, the State Department recognized that racial segregation and discrimination damaged the international credibility of the United States, especially in developing countries. Howland wrote this letter the day after it was announced that the Dodgers had traded Robinson to their crosstown rivals, the New York Giants. Three weeks later, Robinson would announce his retirement from baseball. There is no evidence to suggest that he accepted Howland's invitation.

December 14, 1956

Dear Jackie:

I'd like to refer to our earlier exchange of letters and simply say that we in the State Department still feel that you could do a lot of good in winning respect and understanding for our country if you were to take on a trip abroad to meet informally with youth groups and sports enthusiasts.

We would of course handle all the details of travel and cover your expenses. We would need about a month to work out the details of the trip, so if and when you can see your way clear to take on a goodwill trip abroad for your country please give me a call, collect. As you know, Bob Mathias, Sammy Lee, Jesse Owens, Bob Richards are some of the outstanding American athletes who have won immeasurable respect for the United States. We think you are of the same caliber, hence our continuing hope that you can find a month or two to visit abroad. I realize you have just returned from Japan as a member of the Dodger team, but what we have in mind is developing a program about you to a number of countries in South America.

Best wishes for a successful season with the Giants.

Sincerely yours,
Harold E. Howland

2

FROM FAITH TO FRUSTRATION

· 1957 ·

BROOKS LAWRENCE TO ROBINSON

Shortly after receiving the NAACP award, Robinson accepted the position of vice president of personnel at Chock Full O' Nuts, a chain of coffee shops owned by William Black and staffed mostly by African Americans. Robinson's acceptance of the position reflected a variety of factors: his difficult relationships with Buzzie Bavasi and Walter O'Malley (owner of the Dodgers), his diminishing athletic abilities, his ongoing discontent with racism in baseball, and his emerging hope to break color barriers in American business and commerce. Major League Baseball teams were not completely integrated at the time of his retirement (the Philadelphia Phillies, Detroit Tigers, and Boston Red Sox were still all-white), but Rickey's innovation had led to the recruitment of numerous black players, including Brooks Lawrence, who began his baseball career as a pitcher with the Negro leagues and then broke into Major League Baseball in 1954, playing with the St. Louis Cardinals and the Cincinnati Reds.

No date
[postmarked January 18, 1957]

Dear Jackie,

I have been reading a number of articles on your retirement and this one that I am enclosing is by far the best. I am sorry to hear that you retired but I can definitely see your point. It is always hard, however, to watch the great ones go. But always better to go when they are on top as you were. I am writing this letter to congratulate you on your new position. Do as good a job there as you did on the diamond and everything will be fine. I know you can and my best wishes are with you. I am also writing this to express my sincere gratitude for the job that was done by you while playing. You opened the door for me and others who followed you, and when you opened it you threw it wide open. You gave to us a new way of life for which we will be eternally grateful. Thanking you again and sending all my best wishes. Best wishes also to your family.

Sincerely,
Brooks Lawrence

P.S. Besides that I don't have to pitch to you *no more!*

ROBINSON TO MARTIN LUTHER KING, JR.

Less than a month after retiring from baseball, Robinson began a national speaking tour to help raise money and solicit members for the NAACP. In the following letter, which was probably drafted by Gloster Current, national director of branches for the NAACP, Robinson enlists the support of Martin Luther King, Jr., whose leadership of the bus boycott in Montgomery, Alabama, had earned his praise in an earlier letter to Rachel. "The more I read about the Montgomery situation," Robinson had written, "the more respect I have for the job they are doing."

King had just been elected president of the Southern Christian Leadership Conference (SCLC)—a civil rights organization that cooperated and conflicted with the NAACP throughout the 1950s and 1960s—but he found Robinson difficult to deny. "Although my schedule is extremely busy at this time," King replied, "I will do all within my power to make time for such a magnificent task." This exchange marks the first collaborative effort between King and Robinson, but there is no available evidence to suggest that King offered any significant help to the NAACP campaign.

February 11, 1957

Dear Reverend King,

I consented with pleasure to become the National Chairman of the 1957 NAACP Freedom Fund Campaign because I believe in the progress of the Association and in the bright promise of the American way of life.

The NAACP has stood out for me as the tireless champion of the rights and well-being of the Negroes of America. It is even more than that; it is the champion of all Americans who cherish the principles on which this country was founded.

I would be honored and grateful if you were to become a member of the National Advisory Committee to aid me in reaching the 1957 goal of one million dollars. All over the world our American dollars are fighting for freedom for all men; here at home we seek a fund to make democracy real for our largest minority group. I am certain that with your inspiration and advice as a committee member we cannot help but go over the million-dollar goal. The demands upon you will be few. We wish your consent to serve and to have your name listed on a special campaign letterhead and otherwise publicized.

We expect to have one meeting of the committee as soon as it is constituted and no more than one other meeting later in the year, but you will be kept advised of the campaign as it moves along.

The NAACP is an old, established organization which, from its formation in 1909, has had both white and colored people as members and officers. It has carried forward its program in the courts, in all legislatures, and through public education. This 1957 campaign is part of an intensified effort to make emancipation an actual fact by the centennial of the Emancipation Proclamation in 1963.

I know that with your help we will win our goal in 1957. In the language of baseball, I ask you to join my team and help hit a million-dollar home run for freedom in 1957. Roy Wilkins, our executive secretary, joins me in hoping that we will hear from you at your earliest convenience so that our letterhead can go to press.

Very sincerely yours,
Jackie Robinson

GLOSTER CURRENT TO ROY WILKINS

Robinson had an occasionally stormy relationship with his former teammate Roy Campanella, and in this NAACP memorandum Current writes that Robinson was disturbed over Campanella's alleged reference to "forced integration"—a phrase popularized by those who opposed legislative efforts to accomplish desegregation. The memorandum offers an inside look at Robinson's role within the NAACP. Current refers to Henry Moon, the director of public relations for the NAACP, and John Morsell, the NAACP's assistant executive secretary.

March 18, 1957

A few days ago Jackie Robinson called and was greatly disturbed over a story in the *Daily News* quoting Campanella. Mr. Campanella, in Miami, made some reference to "forced" integration. Both Mr. Moon and I suggested to Jackie that the most effective answer would be to include, in a prepared text, a carefully worded statement in his next address dealing with the topic of "forced" integration, and pointing out how he and others feel about this viewpoint, without specifically mentioning Campanella.

To this end, I would like to suggest that Mr. Moon or Dr. Morsell prepare for Jackie a one or two-page statement which he could weave into his Richmond address March 31st. I also suggested, and Mr. Moon concurred, that the text of his Richmond speech be prepared in advance in order that the fullest possible newspaper coverage might be obtained.

Using Jackie as a spokesman in this manner will give us an opportunity to get across to much of the southern public our views at this time when there are several things which we wish to get across to many persons whom we are seeking to convince of the correctness of our position.

ROBINSON TO RICHARD NIXON

Robinson first met Richard Nixon during the 1952 Republican National Convention in Chicago. Introduced by Harrison McCall, a prominent Republican from California, Nixon shared his memory of the first time he had encountered Robinson—at a 1939 football game between UCLA and the University of Oregon. According to McCall, "Nixon then proceeded to describe an unusual play which occurred in that game and Jackie Robinson recalled immediately the play Nixon referred to, even though it had occurred several years before, and proceeded to explain to Nixon the reason back of the play. I said to Nixon as we walked away that, while Robinson had undoubtedly met a lot of notables during his career, nevertheless I was sure there was one person he would never forget." Neither Robinson nor Nixon would forget. Impressed with Nixon's anticommunism as well as his occasional pro–civil rights statements, Robinson began to quote Nixon in his NAACP speeches, and the two began to write a series of letters that continued until Robinson's death in 1972. Here Robinson praises Nixon for speaking out against U.S. racism during a recent trip to Africa.

March 19, 1957

My Dear Mr. Nixon:

I was delighted to read Earl Mazo's dispatch from Addis Ababa, Ethiopia, published in the *New York Herald Tribune* of March 13, 1957, in which he quoted your telling refutation of anti-American charges made by the Communists.

It was most reassuring to have you speak out in the heart of Africa so the peoples of that continent and of the world should know that "We shall never be satisfied with the progress we have been making in recent years until the problem is solved and equal opportunity becomes a reality for all Americans."

I am sure that in this statement you express the sentiment of the vast majority of the American people who wish to see an end to racial discrimination and segregation. As you indicated, much remains to be done but progress has been made, especially in recent years, and we are confident that this progress will continue at an accelerated pace until this evil is entirely eliminated from American life.

I know that you realize that in the tasks that lie ahead all freedom-loving Americans will want to share in achieving a society in which no man is penalized or favored solely because of his race, color, religion or national origin. In this endeavor you have my best wishes and steadfast cooperation.

Sincerely yours,
Jackie Robinson

RICHARD NIXON TO ROBINSON

March 22, 1957

Dear Jackie,

As you can imagine, there were a number of letters on my desk when I returned to the office today after an absence of three weeks. I can assure you, however, that there were none which meant more to me than your thoughtful letter of March 19.

It is a privilege to be working along with someone like yourself to achieve the important objective of guaranteeing equal opportunity for all Americans, and your expression of approval will be a constant source of strength and encouragement to me.

I hope that our paths will cross one of these days so that we will have a chance for a personal chat and, in the meantime, this note brings my very best wishes to you.

Sincerely,
Richard Nixon

ROBINSON TO MARTIN LUTHER KING, JR.

Unlike other civil rights leaders at the time, Robinson publicly supported Eisenhower as a proponent of the civil rights movement, especially after the president had spoken in favor of civil rights legislation in the 1956 presidential campaign. Robinson's enthusiastic defense of Eisenhower began to soften, however, when the president refused to make a public statement following the January 10 bombing of several homes and churches of civil rights activists in Montgomery, Alabama. No doubt aware of Robinson's call for a presidential statement, Martin Luther King, Jr. invited Robinson to speak at a mass rally marking the end of a campaign to rebuild the scorched churches. Although he declines the invitation in the following letter, Robinson later chaired a campaign to rebuild black churches that were bombed in Albany, Georgia, in 1962.

April 24, 1957

My dear Reverend King:

It is with sincere regret that I find it impossible to come to Montgomery during the month of May. I have read with mounting concern of the attacks upon our churches in your city. There is no cause more deserving of support than the campaign for funds to rebuild these structures.

As you know, I have just recently undertaken a new job with the Chock Full O' Nuts chain in this city. The responsibilities attendant thereon make it virtually impossible for me to leave my office during the week. Most of my weekends for the past several months have been occupied with filling speaking engagements in behalf of our Fight for Freedom campaign.

I know you will understand my inability to be with you. If the campaign continues during the summer and into the fall, perhaps we may be able to arrive at a mutually convenient date for me to visit Montgomery.

Be assured of my desire to be of service. I remain,

Sincerely yours,
Jackie Robinson

ROBINSON TO DWIGHT EISENHOWER

In a May 9 White House memorandum Maxwell Rabb recommended that Eisenhower make time for a "brief hello" during Robinson's May 14 trip to Washington, D.C., to receive an award from the Washington Interfaith Committee. "Ordinarily," Rabb wrote, "I would not recommend something like this, but in view of Jackie Robinson's strong support of the President, it might be worth considering the possibility of taking advantage of his presence to make a few friends." While still supportive, Robinson delivers a subtle jab at the president in the following letter, when he states that he is "greatly encouraged by the statements from members of your official family." Robinson was pleased that Nixon and Sherman Adams, special assistant to Eisenhower, had recently made strong pro–civil rights statements, but he also continued to be troubled by Eisenhower's own public reticence.

May 15, 1957

Dear Mr. President,

Thank you for taking time from your very busy schedule to give me another big thrill.

After talking with Mr. Rabb, I have a much better understanding of your thinking in the field of race relations and am more positive than ever that your leadership will help us succeed in our efforts to eliminate the acts of violence and prejudice here.

Ours has been a long and difficult battle. But we are greatly encouraged by the statements from members of your official family. I'm sure this is due to your leadership and the tremendous respect they all have for you. There is no question in my mind that, with your continued efforts, the battle will be won and much of the prestige which racial problems are causing us to lose will be regained and preserved.

Respectfully,
Jackie Robinson

ROBINSON TO MAXWELL RABB

Robinson lobbies Rabb for a statement by Eisenhower about ongoing violence against civil rights activists. Robinson's reference to "ideas you have in mind" is unclear.

May 15, 1957

Dear Mr. Rabb:

I'm sure you must know how appreciative I am of your kindness to me during my visit to Washington. To have someone as busy as you take time away from his schedule to be so nice gives me a deep sense of gratitude. If ever I can do anything for you, please don't hesitate to call on me.

I am having a meeting with Mr. Roy Wilkins later today and I assure you I'll do all in my power to see that nothing happens to interfere with the ideas you have in mind.

If you have an opportunity, I hope you can get an expression from President Eisenhower condemning violence. Such a statement would give us a great deal of encouragement and would certainly give me the necessary material for my comments about the President when I'm at my NAACP meetings.

Please give my regards to your lovely family. It was a pleasure to meet them.

Sincerely,
Jackie Robinson

PS: If it's possible for us to get a couple of the pictures taken with the President, it would be appreciated.

DWIGHT EISENHOWER TO ROBINSON

May 21, 1957

Dear Mr. Robinson:

It was good to see you the other day and to receive your friendly letter.

Your approval of our efforts to achieve equality of opportunity is very gratifying. As you know, problems which touch upon human values present deep-seated emotional difficulties. It is our hope that we can continue to foster a moral climate within which the forces of informed good will operate effectively in an atmosphere of democracy.

Sincerely,
Dwight D. Eisenhower

MARTIN LUTHER KING, JR. TO ROBINSON

Tensions over fund-raising had begun to surface between the SCLC and the NAACP during the early days of the Montgomery bus boycott in the winter of 1955–1956, especially when King wrote Wilkins a letter accusing the NAACP of raising money "in the name of our movement." The following letter, which reflects King's sensitivity about fund-raising conflicts, suggests that Robinson was unaware of any tension between the two civil rights leaders in 1957. King refers to the NAACP's Fight for Freedom Fund (FFF).

June 12, 1957

Dear Mr. Robinson:

This is to acknowledge receipt of your letter of May 23. Contents have been noted with care. I feel that the FFF dinner honoring Branch

Rickey, Sr., and Duke Ellington can be an epic making affair. It is certainly a marvelous idea.

Ordinarily I would be more than happy to serve on the dinner committee. Because of the diminishing funds of the Montgomery Improvement Association I will have to undertake a money raising campaign for the association in the early Fall. I do not feel that it would be good psychology to attempt to raise money for both groups simultaneously. In the light of this I must decline your gracious invitation to serve on the Dinner Committee. Please know that I regret this very deeply. I am sure that you can understand the problem that I am confronting. Please know that my non-acceptance is not due to a lack of interest, but to the basic commitment to the Montgomery community.

Although it will not be possible for me to serve directly on the committee, you can be assured that I will lend my support at any other point that it is possible.

It was good seeing you in Washington on Friday. I considered it a great honor to receive an honorary degree with you.

You have done a great work for the race and the nation and all people of good will are indebted to you for your contribution. Mrs. King joins me in sending best regards. Please give our warm regards to your charming wife.

Very sincerely yours,
M. L. King, Jr.

ROBINSON TO RICHARD NIXON

Criticism of Nixon's civil rights record received considerable publicity during the 1956 presidential campaign, and one of the most vocal critics was Senator Lehman, who used a nationwide radio broadcast to highlight anti–civil rights votes cast by Nixon in the House and Senate. "Today," Lehman stated, "Nixon says he is all for civil rights. Which is the truth—the record of his actual votes or his present campaign speeches? Which Richard Nixon would sit in the White House if something happened to President Eisenhower—the anti–civil rights Nixon, or the pro–civil rights Nixon? Who knows? Nobody knows. Let's not take a chance." Robinson was familiar with this type of criticism, and in this letter he invites Nixon to respond to the charges. E. Frederic Morrow, referenced below, was Robinson's good friend and one of the few African Americans employed in the Eisenhower White House, serving as an administrative officer for special projects.

June 25, 1957

My dear Mr. Vice President:

I hope you will not consider me presumptuous, but I feel I must write you about a matter that has been bothering me of late. I have taken note of your speeches and your reports to President Eisenhower on Asia and Africa, and I have developed a deep sense of appreciation for your constant efforts to provide a greater measure of justice for Negro Americans and all others. I have not hesitated to express my feelings to my friends so I have become involved in heated discussions with some of them. They ask, "How can you support Nixon after the poor civil rights record he had in the Senate? Can't you see he's making these speeches now with his eye on the presidency in 1960?"

I have expressed my belief in your sincerity and have quoted Fred Morrow to support my beliefs. My friends say, naturally, that Mr. Morrow is "saying what he has to say."

I am sure you understand that I am not active in partisan politics and do not write either as a Republican or Democrat but as a person seeking reassurance in his beliefs.

Sincerely yours,
Jackie Robinson

RICHARD NIXON TO ROBINSON

July 12, 1957

Dear Jackie:

This is just a note to thank you for your letter of June 25. I appreciate the sincerity and candor with which you wrote.

Since you were a star player for the Brooklyn Dodgers, I know you realize that anyone who is in the public eye is subject to comment on all kinds of matters. One simply learns to roll with the punches and keeps trying to do as well as one can.

The matter of assuring equal opportunities for all is one of the most important and far-reaching problems facing this nation. Not only is our position a concern domestically, but the decisions made and steps taken are under constant scrutiny abroad. The enactment of Civil Rights legislation is a positive action that can be taken toward living up to our ideals. I believe that we will see passage of Civil Rights legislation during this session of Congress.

It was thoughtful of you to write me and I hope you will not hesitate to do so again.

With every good wish,

Sincerely,
Richard Nixon

ROBINSON TO MAXWELL RABB

Robinson expresses disappointment with comments that Eisenhower made in his July 17 news conference. On July 16 the president had issued a written statement thanking the Senate for taking up his civil rights legislation. "I hope," Eisenhower had stated, "that Senate action on this measure will be accomplished at this session without undue delay." At his July 17 press conference, however, he added: "I personally believe if you try to go too far too fast in laws in this delicate field, that has involved the emotions of so many millions of Americans, you are making a mistake. I believe we have got to have laws that go along with education and understanding. And I believe if you go beyond that at any time, you cause trouble rather than benefit."

July 19, 1957

Dear Mr. Rabb:

I am really in a muddle, and I don't know exactly what to do.

I believe you know my position and my feeling toward the Administration, and I really want to continue to believe as I have. I know it may not make a great deal of difference to anyone down there how I feel, but being the guy I am, I must know that I am being honest with myself when I speak up as I have been doing.

All of us were so proud to have our faith vindicated by the President in his stand on Monday when he issued a prepared statement expressing his desires and beliefs, and then we were knocked spinning by his press conference at what appeared to be a complete about face.

The President, all the senators and everyone else must know that we are not asking for any special favors and would not want any kind of legislation that would cause trouble, but we do feel that where it is necessary, there should be legislation.

All over the world oppressed people are crying and getting their freedom, yet in what is supposed to be the world's greatest Democracy, many of our responsible leaders appear to be unduly influenced by the few bigots who fear the universal acceptance of civil rights.

I have been trying to understand and have sought answers to questions. Can you help?

Sincerely yours,
Jackie Robinson

ROBINSON TO RICHARD NIXON

After the Senate passed the jury trial amendment to its version of the 1957 civil rights bill—which effectively undermined the voting rights provision—Nixon characterized the move as "a vote against the right to vote" and pledged to fight for a more effective bill.

August 2, 1957

My dear Mr. Vice President:

Thanks for the position you took in behalf of all Americans. I assure you that as an individual I and many others will never forget the fight you made and what you stand for. The Negro is finally realizing the power of unity, and the defeat by a few bigots who were able to carry enough influence to defeat a measure that in just a small way insured a little freedom for people that have been hoping for a chance in a country we are all so proud of—I am sure this will unite us even more.

I assure you, we will not forget those of you with enough courage to stand by your conviction, nor will we forget the others.

Sincerely yours,
Jackie Robinson

RICHARD NIXON TO ROBINSON

August 8, 1957

Dear Jackie:

It was most thoughtful of you to write as you did on August 2. Although the Senate vote on August first was most discouraging, you can be sure that I shall continue to do everything I can to see that a more effective bill than the watered-down version which was approved by the Senate on Wednesday night is eventually passed.

So that I can more adequately respond to your letter of June 25, I have been having a study made of my voting record in the House and Senate. This should be completed in the next few days and I will send it to you.

The next time you are down this way I hope you can stop by the office for a visit because I would enjoy the opportunity of discussing with you some of the issues in which we are mutually interested.

With every good wish,

Sincerely,
Richard Nixon

ROBINSON TO FREDERIC MORROW

Civil rights activists debated whether to seek a presidential veto of the watered-down civil rights bill passed by Congress, especially because segregationist senators had gutted the voting rights provision. While Wilkins and King agreed to accept the bill, Robinson used this telegram to lobby Morrow for a veto. On September 9 Eisenhower signed the Civil Rights Act of 1957, the first civil rights legislation in more than eighty years.

August 12, 1957

Am opposed to civil rights bill in its present form. Have been in touch with a number of my friends. We disagree that half loaf better than none. Have waited this long for bill with meaning. Can wait a little longer unless House amends bill. Hope the President will veto it. We sincerely appreciate the many true Americans who insist on equal rights for all.

Jackie Robinson

RICHARD NIXON TO ROBINSON

The following memorandum, drafted by his staff, is Nixon's response to Robinson's June 25 concerns about the vice president's civil rights convictions. The memorandum also compares Nixon's civil rights record with John Kennedy's. FEPC, noted below, refers to the Fair Employment Practices Commission.

August 13, 1957

MEMORANDUM

The Vice President has had unprecedented experience in international affairs during the last five years. He has been a participating member of the National Security Council and has presided over its meetings in the absence of the President on various occasions. He has visited 40 countries, representing this nation, which has been of great importance in the development of friendship and understanding of the United States position among the uncommitted peoples in the world who will be decisive in the years ahead, e.g., his visits to Southeast Asia and Africa. He has been instrumental in formulating as well as interpreting the foreign policy of this Administration which has brought peace to the world and a reasonable chance for peace in the future.

The contrast in the foreign policy field between the Vice President and Senator Kennedy is most striking. Senator Kennedy's most recent venture into foreign policy was to issue a statement concerning the relationship of Algeria to France. This statement caused widespread reaction against the United States in France and was even repudiated by Adlai Stevenson, the 1956 Democratic nominee for President.

On civil rights the position of the Vice President has been unequivocal. His whole legislative career and his action as Vice President have proved him to be a firm opponent of discrimination. In his approach to civil rights matters, he has always advocated a positive program, disregarding the extremist views on both sides. For instance, he opposed a compulsory FEPC on a Federal level but has worked tirelessly to use the influence of the Federal Government to eliminate areas of discrimination. The Vice President is Chairman of the President's Committee on Government Contracts which has been most effective in fighting job discrimination.

Senator Kennedy's position on the Civil Rights proposals during this session of the Congress has been characterized by opportunism and an obvious desire to obtain the Democratic nomination for President in 1960. While professing to be a strong supporter of Civil Rights on certain occasions, in the real tests on this issue, Senator Kennedy joined the forces opposed to any civil rights legislation on three important occasions.

He voted against amending the Senate rules so that the filibuster, which killed so much civil rights legislation through the years, could be curbed. The Vice President, in marked contrast, handed down an historic opinion that the Senate has the power to change its rules so that filibusters could be curbed.

The Senator voted against adopting the procedure to place the House Bill on the Senate Calendar, supporting a point of order raised by Senator Russell, which would have referred the House Bill to the Senate Judiciary Committee headed by Senator Eastland.

Finally, Senator Kennedy supported the amendment requiring a trial by jury in criminal contempt cases in the enforcement of civil rights legislation. The position assumed by the Senator in all of these crucial decisions can be interpreted as a calculated appeal to the delegates from Georgia, Mississippi, South Carolina and the other Southern states in the 1960 Democratic National Convention.

Significantly, Senator Kennedy did not take part in the debate on civil rights but sat on the sidelines hoping to be spared any brickbats which would come from exerting leadership in this area.

ROBINSON TO RICHARD NIXON

August 28, 1957

My dear Mr. Vice President:

Frankly, Mr. Nixon, I haven't been too concerned with your past record one way or the other. What you do and say is the important thing.

We are all very proud of what you are doing. As far as I am concerned, a man's motives don't mean a thing as long as he is attempting to do good. We sincerely believe that is your intention, and we heartily endorse it.

I would be pleased to meet with you any time that you may find it possible.

Sincerely yours,
Jackie Robinson

AVERELL HARRIMAN TO ROBINSON

Robinson wrote to Harriman about the Little Rock crisis, which had begun on September 4 when Arkansas governor Orval Faubus enlisted the National Guard to help block nine African American students from enrolling at all-white Central High School.

September 8, 1957

Dear Jackie:

Thank you for your letter. I fully share your concern over recent events in Arkansas. They not only violate the constitutional rights of American citizens, but are damaging our prestige around the world. This seriously weakens our leadership in the fight against communism.

I earnestly hope that Governor Faubus now realizes that he has been badly advised; that he will reverse his stand and support the federal court order.

The use of the National Guard, which is largely supported by federal funds, to defy, rather than uphold, our federal constitution is a precedent which must not be permitted to stand.

I am sending the text of your letter and my reply to the President in order that he may know that he has the support of the people of New York in taking effective action in this constitutional crisis with which our nation is confronted.

Averell Harriman,
Governor of New York

ROBINSON TO DWIGHT EISENHOWER

On September 10 President Eisenhower called for "patience" when addressing the Little Rock crisis before a group of Rhode Island Republicans, and here Robinson criticizes the president's plea for patience and lobbies for the use of executive powers in advancing civil rights.

September 13, 1957

My dear Mr. President:

A few days ago I read your statement in the papers advising patience. We are wondering to whom you are referring when you say we must be patient. It is easy for those who haven't felt the evils of a prejudiced society to urge it, but for us who as Americans have patiently waited all these years for the rights supposedly guaranteed us under our Constitution, it is not an easy task. Nevertheless, we have done it.

It appears to me now, Mr. President, that under the circumstances the prestige of your office must be exerted. A mere statement that you don't like violence is not enough. In my opinion, people the world over would hail you if you made a statement that would clearly put your office behind the efforts for civil rights. As it is now, you see what the Communist nations are doing with the material we have given them.

I am aware, Mr. President, this letter expresses a mood of frustration. It is a mood generally found among Negro Americans today and should be a matter of concern to you as it is to us.

Very respectfully yours,
Jackie Robinson

ROBINSON TO DWIGHT EISENHOWER

Faubus withdrew the National Guard from Central High School on September 23, allowing a white mob to terrorize the African American students, attack reporters covering the crisis, and vandalize school property. After the mob ran with impunity once again on September 24, Eisenhower ordered the deployment of the 101st Airborne Division of the U.S. Army to Central High School.

September 25, 1957

My dear Mr. President:

Please accept my congratulations on the positive position you have taken in the Little Rock situation. I should have known you would do the right thing at the crucial time.

May God continue giving you the wisdom to lead us in this struggle.

Very respectfully yours,
Jackie Robinson

ROBINSON TO LOUIS SEATON

In this letter to Louis Seaton, vice president of personnel at General Motors, Robinson threatens public action in response to news reports about discriminatory hiring practices.

November 4, 1957

Dear Mr. Seaton:

In reply to your letter of October 29, I would like to know how you would explain the article in the Southwest edition of the *Wall Street Journal*, the October 25 issue, where your General Manager of the Atlanta plant bluntly states, "When we moved into the South, we agreed to abide by local custom and not hire Negroes for production work. This is no time for social reforming in that area, and we're not about to try it." The article further states that the plant employs only a few Negroes, mainly for janitorial work.

There is a great deal of concern in the Negro community over this remark, and I feel like so many of my friends when they say a statement of policy as expressed in your letter is meaningless unless it is enforced. We have heard of the trouble in Cleveland, in Tarrytown, New York, and in Michigan, where like the Southern Negro worker, employment is limited to menial jobs, and in most cases they are not upgraded according to skills.

I, like many of my friends, are General Motors users now, but it appears to me I can't continue to buy the product of a prejudiced company if it is proven to be prejudiced. From the article in the papers, this appears to be the policy at General Motors.

Personally, I am not at all satisfied with Mr. Anderson's statement, simply because it seems to have been blatantly violated.

I am joining with the other Negroes that have been informed of this practice to explore the direction we must take. I sincerely hope we don't have to make a public appeal in this regard, but I am certain there has to be some action taken.

Very truly yours,
Jackie Robinson

ROBINSON TO WALTER REUTHER

Robinson also contacts Walter Reuther, president of the United Automobile Workers, about General Motors. Reuther asked his staff to send Robinson a report on the matter, and the report indicated that while there had been some progress in the hiring of blacks for production jobs, the union was unsuccessful in securing white-collar jobs for African American workers. There is no evidence that Robinson led a boycott against General Motors.

November 7, 1957

Dear Mr. Reuther:

I am enclosing a carbon of the letter I wrote to Mr. Seaton of General Motors.

I felt that before we made a public appeal I should write and inform you we intend to act on this matter.

It is my opinion, Negroes should not buy any of this company's product unless some action is taken by them. With this market as competitive as it is, we don't have to spend our dollars where we can't earn them.

I would appreciate your comments in this regard.

Have followed your wonderful work. I want to wish you continued success.

Very truly yours,
Jackie Robinson

ROBINSON TO RICHARD NIXON

Shortly after passage of the Civil Rights Act of 1957, Robinson praises Nixon for his record and criticizes Attorney General William Rogers for announcing in a December 9 press conference that the Eisenhower administration favored a "cooling off" period and that it would not seek new civil rights legislation in 1958.

December 24, 1957

My dear Mr. Vice President:

I am certain you know my position in regards to politics. Being neither a Republican nor a Democrat, I am able to look at the man and go from there. I have been and am impressed with you and the position you have taken, and I feel I can say this and express to you my concern and you will understand my reasoning.

I had felt the Republicans were doing the things that would enable me in good conscience to say they are for me. Then, I read what Mr. Rogers had to say, and I wondered. I do know his statements have not helped our thinking, and because of my respect for you, felt I must say that in the circle I am in, people are wondering.

I believe most Americans are near enough to our democratic ideals to be persuaded by our leaders. Mr. Rogers had an adverse affect, and I am sure you must be aware of it. I hope we have all progressed to the point we do not allow one person to be the spokesman for all, but the feeling is he spoke for the Republicans when he said we will do nothing more. We cannot stop now; there has been too much progress, but everyone knows there is a long, long way to go.

I sincerely hope you understand my feelings in this regard.

Sincerely yours,
Jackie Robinson

3

AGAINST PATIENCE

· 1958 ·

ROBINSON TO CHESTER BOWLES

Robinson had invited Chester Bowles, the former Democratic governor of Connecticut, to an NAACP dinner honoring Branch Rickey and Duke Ellington, but Bowles had sent his regrets. Bowles was the first governor to abolish segregation in the National Guard and earned a national reputation for his commitment to civil rights.

January 15, 1958

Dear Mr. Bowles:

Please excuse my delay in writing to you. I can't tell you how impressed we were and are with you and the things you stand for. It's a refreshing feeling listening to you and understanding what a real man stands for. In all my travels you are the only person in public life that I inquired about that received nothing but praise. I hope that whatever your ambitions are, they will be fulfilled.

I am certain you are aware of the success of the dinner, and the thing that impressed me most was that 80% of the people attending were Negroes. Tell Mrs. Bowles the Negro is beginning to take the lead. The dinner, in my opinion, was just an expression of this position. If we have the dinner this year, I hope you will be able to attend. We will give you a notice in plenty of time this year.

This battle for civil rights is taking a definite turn. It's due to the many Chester Bowleses we have around that are not afraid of what the future holds. If we can lick this fear, I am certain we can lick the problem of racial tension.

My best to your family. It's nice knowing people like you. It certainly gives us all a great deal of encouragement.

Sincerely,
Jackie Robinson

RICHARD NIXON TO ROBINSON

January 23, 1958

Dear Jackie:

I wish to express my appreciation for your letter of December 24 emphasizing the need for continued progress in the field of civil rights.

First of all, I want to assure you that there is no intention on the part of the Administration to discontinue its wholehearted efforts to achieve the goal of human dignity and equality of opportunity for all Americans.

As you know, the battle for equal rights, in which we are both so interested, has many different and yet related aspects. When Bill Rogers indicated that the Administration did not intend to press for additional civil rights legislation in this current session of Congress, his statement by no means meant that there was any intention of relaxing our efforts to reach the ultimate objective of equal opportunities for all our citizens.

The civil rights legislation which was adopted after long debate and much opposition during the last session was the first in 82 years. At a time when every bit of support was needed to achieve a stronger bill, there was, as you will recall, disagreement among and lack of support from many individuals and groups which previously had been most vocal in this struggle. That is one of the reasons why there appears to be little possibility that additional civil rights legislation could be enacted in the present session.

This realistic appraisal, however, does not mean that we should become discouraged. Although the Act passed by the Congress was considerably weaker than that originally proposed by the President, its passage was an important milestone in American history.

I do not believe our citizens will have an opportunity to appraise properly this epochal action until the Civil Rights Commission is sufficiently organized to enforce the provisions of the Act. I think you will agree that it would be well to know how effective the present law is going to be before attempting to pass further legislation.

Another aspect of the total problem which I know you recognize is that the activities of the Civil Rights Commission will serve as an educational process in winning wider acceptance of civil rights legislation generally.

While all great movements of reform started slowly and encountered bitter opposition, they soon gathered an irresistible momentum and gained rapid acceptance. I fervently believe this will be the case in the battle for equal rights.

Incidentally, may I express my deep appreciation for your generous public comments on my work in this field. I hope we can continue to work together for our common objective.

With kind regards,

Sincerely,
Richard Nixon

ROBINSON TO RICHARD NIXON

February 5, 1958

My dear Mr. Vice President:

I read your letter with care and deep concern. While I know that Rome was not built in a day, I think you will agree that I have shown some patience throughout the years with the slow progress made in the field of civil rights. Nevertheless, I am convinced that those of us who are earnestly concerned about the problems of civil rights and integration must measure progress not in terms of how much progress we have made recently but how far we have yet to go before we achieve full first class citizenship for the Negro. Until we do give him all the rights to which he is entitled under the constitution, we cannot hope to successfully forestall the propaganda emanating from those we refer to as non-Democratic countries. Moreover, top Negro leadership which attempts to meet this propaganda, no matter how insincere the basis for this propaganda is, will be repudiated by the Negro masses if they attempt to justify the thought of a "breathing spell" in the fight for integration at a time the total Negro South and the best elements of the white South are looking to the government for leadership and protection from disaster at the hands of the representatives of the White Citizens Council and white office holders in the South who are determined that the Supreme Court's mandate will not be obeyed in our lifetime.

Finally, I must say I have come to the conclusion that the fight for integration is not being played with gentlemen who observe the rules of cricket. In this fight no holds are barred; therefore, I respectfully suggest that it seems to me in a fight with the enemy we cannot tell them in advance, as Mr. Rogers did, that we will allow a breathing spell and if all turns out well we will go forward. We must if we are to win this fight put all people on notice who indicate that they will defy the Supreme law of the land that we on the other hand will maintain a ceaseless and continuing effort to make the mandate of the Supreme Court a reality in our lifetime.

Sincerely yours,
Jackie Robinson

CHESTER BOWLES TO ROBINSON

Bowles seeks Robinson's help in his budding campaign for the Democratic nomination for the U.S. Senate. Jackie and Rachel had built a home in Stamford in 1954, but not before encountering discrimination from white home owners and real estate brokers. Bowles refers to his wife "Steb," Dorothy Stebbins Bowles.

February 10, 1958

Dear Jackie:

Many thanks for your nice letter. I thought that you and I had agreed to operate on a first name basis? I'm sticking with the "Jackie" only on the condition that you also drop the Mr. Otherwise, I shall have to revert to "Mr. Robinson"!

I can't tell you how much I appreciate your letter. Anyone who has been in public life as long as I have is bound to get discouraged and frustrated sometimes and to feel that all things that you feel are most important are impossible of fulfillment. Then along comes a nice letter like yours which makes everything appear a little more possible after all.

May I add that I know of very few people who have contributed over the last ten or fifteen years to ease the situation which has always seemed to me the primary disgrace of our democracy. Under the most difficult circumstances you have conducted yourself with extraordinary tact, courage, understanding and skill, and our country is the better for what you and your wife have done and are doing.

A lot of people will try to turn the discrimination issue into a political football during the coming years and there will be the usual double talk from Republicans and Democrats alike. However, I for one feel that the Democratic Party must go far beyond the Republican approach which is to treat this as a "legal issue on which the Supreme Court has spoken." It must be tackled for what it really is—a *moral* issue between those who believe in the dignity of man and those who believe in the dignity of some men.

I just finished writing an article for the *Saturday Evening Post* which will appear in the March 1st issue on the similarity between what Gandhi did in South Africa and India and the big task that remains to be done here in America. I have discussed the extent to which the Gandhian methods are applicable here along the lines of Martin Luther King's efforts in Montgomery.

I will see that you get a copy just as soon as it is off the press and I earnestly hope that you will like it. If you do feel that it's constructive I will deeply appreciate it if you will send a few copies where you feel they will do the most good. I am certain, for instance, that if you send reprints to some of the political leaders here in Connecticut it could be very helpful to my own efforts to get the Senate nomination. Your name is a very influential one in your home state.

Many thanks again, Jackie, for your nice note and do give my warm regards to your wife whom Steb and I were so happy to meet, and whom we are looking forward to seeing again with you.

My warmest regards.

Sincerely,
Chester Bowles

RICHARD NIXON TO ROBINSON

March 12, 1958

Dear Jackie:

Since receiving your letter of February 5 I have had several discussions of the problems in which we are mutually interested with Bill Rogers and others in the Administration.

I hope the next time you happen to be coming to Washington you can give us some advance notice because I would welcome the opportunity of talking with you personally with regard to some of the problems we face in this field.

With every good wish,

Sincerely,
Richard Nixon

CHESTER BOWLES TO ROBINSON

April 7, 1958

Dear Jackie:

The campaign for the Senate nomination here in Connecticut is now in full swing. I have been hard at work for the last many weeks calling on delegates throughout the state to work up the necessary support.

My announcement came late because I agreed to wait until Dick Lee, the able young Mayor of New Haven, decided whether to run or not. He had expected to make his decision in November but it didn't finally come out until February and this meant delay.

However, I think we are now caught up and it looks as though we have at least a 50-50 chance for the nomination. The chances for election are excellent.

As you know, there are now nearly 100,000 Negro citizens in Connecticut which probably means about 35,000 voters. This is a powerful bloc and could easily swing an election in one direction or another.

The older members of this group are very familiar with what I did when I was governor, i.e., we made Connecticut the first state to abolish segregation in the National Guard; introduced tough anti-discrimination legislation in all housing to which the state government gave assistance, either direct or indirect; created a really vigorous Civil Rights Commission; made a survey on discrimination in regard to entrance requirements among the state universities which did a great deal to break down the racial bars in Connecticut private educational institutions; etc.

But this was eight years ago and since then we have been more closely connected with foreign affairs in most peoples' minds. A new group of Negro citizens has come into our state who is less directly familiar with what I have done here.

A good strong statement from you, as a resident of Stamford, which could be sent out to each of the 850 delegates would be enormously helpful. If you can see your way clear to writing one I will be deeply appreciative and I am sure Leonard Gross would be willing to help us get it reproduced and mailed.

If you are willing to do this, Jackie, I suggest that the best approach would be a forthright one, i.e., that in the days of Roosevelt most Negroes voted for the Democratic candidates because Roosevelt was so obviously concerned with their economic problems and fought so persistently to ease them.

However, in the last few years there has been a sharp shift by the Negro voters away from the Democrats because the party as a whole has not taken a clear-cut position on civil rights. The Negro voters next fall will judge the Democrats by the candidate they select for the Senate.

You might then say that my record is clear to every thoughtful Negro citizen in the United States ever since I entered public life 20 years ago; that Negro voters throughout America know that Connecticut has an opportunity to send someone to Washington who understands the civil rights issue and is prepared to stand up and be counted; and that anything less than a sweeping majority for me at the Democratic state convention will be a source of bewilderment to the Negro voters not only in America but throughout the United States, etc. You might mention the fact that Purtell, the Republican candidate, has had a good voting record on this issue although he has not been very active. You would know how to say this in your own persuasive way as a Connecticut citizen.

I have been pleased by the fact that the Democratic Negro leaders in such cities as Hartford have been among the first to come out and support me. One of them, Boce Barlow, the first Negro judge in Connecticut and a recent graduate of the Harvard Law School, is a person I know you would particularly enjoy meeting sometime. Perhaps we can get you together with him and some other Connecticut people who you and your wife might like to know at our house when things die down a bit.

I do hope, Jackie, that you can see your way clear to do this. If for any reason you cannot, please do not hesitate to say so.

With my warmest regards to you and your nice wife.

Sincerely,
Chester Bowles

ROBINSON TO MAXWELL RABB

Robinson criticizes Gamal Abdel Nasser, the pro-socialist and anti-colonialist leader of Egypt, and volunteers to host a radio program that would air in Ghana with the purpose of undermining Nasser's influence and emphasizing "the positive side of Negro progress" in the United States. Rabb replied on May 8: "[Your] suggestion about helping supply Ghana with program material makes a great deal of sense to me and I think it is a suggestion that should be pursued by the State Department with great dispatch and urgency. I am, therefore, taking this matter up immediately with the appropriate people in the State Department calling attention to your communication and to your suggestion. I am sure we will have an answer in the very near future." There is no available evidence that Robinson recorded a weekly program for Ghana.

No date [April 1958]

I was listening yesterday to a radio broadcast which reported that the State of Ghana is on the air in Africa with a new and powerful radio voice. The report indicated that the Ghana station is presently operating under a power of 20,000 watts and is considering increasing its strength to as much as 100,000 watts. This will make Ghana an equal voice in Africa with Nasser's station in Egypt; and since Nasser is continuously beaming anti-American propaganda to the Africans, Ghana represents the hope for democratic expression. As I understand it, Ghana's broadcasts are in English and in French.

A thought occurred to me that perhaps I can be of some help in supplying Ghana with program material which would help to overcome the anti-American sentiments emanating from the Nasser-controlled broadcasting. I would be willing to record in this country a program each week which would summarize the news from the United States, the positive side of Negro progress. This could essentially be a reportorial job with an emphasis on opportunity under a democratic system, and an honest account of racial advancement. Indeed, it may be that I would have to point out some of the problems which exist in order to be completely fair. But on the other hand, the over-all effect would be positive.

I would suggest that in addition to whatever narrative I would contribute, there might be a weekly interview with some outstanding person related, of course, to the subject of race relations. These interviews would include not only outstanding Negroes in the United States but persons of various races and religions.

It strikes me too that if there were sufficient interest, I might also spearhead a drive to incorporate a separate program—or perhaps a feature within my own program—where a Nat "King" Cole or Cab Calloway or Louis Armstrong would act as a kind of disc jockey to feature popular music either of current vogue or in the jazz genre.

This idea appeals to me because I feel that it is important that we state our side to the people of Africa. Perhaps I can use the publicity which surrounded my career to good advantage. I know that the Africans are familiar with my name and sports record and what is more, there are many people abroad who are aware of my stand on Civil Rights. Indeed, I have had a good deal of correspondence from Africa over the last several months.

If America is to have a voice in Africa it should come from a Negro, and I am willing to do my part. It may be that I will need some help with the writing of the material and the production of the show, but I certainly do not ask for any assistance other than facilities and personnel. It occurs to me that the "Voice of America" might be interested, or if you think it advisable, it could be done on direct negotiations with the government of Ghana.

I am writing to you obviously because I do not know how best to proceed. At the same time I recognize your sympathy with the general objective I have in mind so that your good offices can be used to expedite matters and to lead the way.

Will you give this some thought and lend me your direction? I'd be most grateful.

With sincere personal regards, I remain

Cordially,
Jackie Robinson

ROBINSON TO CHESTER BOWLES

Although he refuses to "mix politics" in this reply to Bowles, Robinson would campaign full-time for Richard Nixon two years later. Thomas Dodd, Bowles's opponent in the 1958 primary, won the Democratic nomination and then defeated the incumbent senator, William Purtell.

May 1, 1958

Dear Chet:

I have torn up many letters in answer to yours of April 7th. If I felt I could mix politics, I don't know of a person I would rather go all out for over you.

I have had many discussions as to the advisability of my doing as you asked, and it was always the same results—at this time stay as much away from politics as you can.

Please understand the respect and admiration I have for you and why I have to refuse to do something I want to do.

Please give my regards to your wife and family. My wife feels exactly as I do, and she hopes you understand.

Sincerely,
Jackie Robinson

ROBINSON TO DWIGHT EISENHOWER

On May 12 Robinson attended the Summit Meeting of Negro Leaders in Washington, D.C. In his keynote speech about racial conflict, Eisenhower stated that "there are no revolutionary cures" and once again called for "patience and forbearance."

May 13, 1958

My dear Mr. President:

I was sitting in the audience at the Summit Meeting of Negro Leaders yesterday when you said we must have patience. On hearing you say this, I felt like standing up and saying, "Oh no! Not again."

I respectfully remind you, sir, that we have been the most patient of all people. When you said we must have self-respect, I wondered how we could have self-respect and remain patient considering the treatment accorded us through the years.

17 million Negroes cannot do as you suggest and wait for the hearts

of men to change. We want to enjoy now the rights that we feel we are entitled to as Americans. This we cannot do unless we pursue aggressively goals which all other Americans achieved over 150 years ago.

As the chief executive of our nation, I respectfully suggest that you unwittingly crush the spirit of freedom in Negroes by constantly urging forbearance and give hope to those pro-segregation leaders like Governor Faubus who would take from us even those freedoms we now enjoy. Your own experience with Governor Faubus is proof enough that forbearance and not eventual integration is the goal the pro-segregation leaders seek.

In my view, an unequivocal statement backed up by action such as you demonstrated you could take last fall in dealing with Governor Faubus if it became necessary, would let it be known that America is determined to provide—in the near future—for Negroes—the freedoms we are entitled to under the constitution.

Respectfully yours,
Jackie Robinson

DWIGHT EISENHOWER TO ROBINSON

June 4, 1958

Dear Mr. Robinson:

Thank you very much for taking the time to write me some of the thoughts you had after the meeting of the Negro leaders here in Washington. While I understand the points you make about the use of patience and forbearance, I have never urged them as substitutes for constructive action or progress.

If you will review my talk made at the meeting, you will see that at no point did I advocate a cessation of effort on the part of individuals, organizations, or government, to bring to fruition for all Americans, the employment of all the privileges of citizenship spelled out in our Constitution.

I am firmly on record as believing that every citizen—of every race and creed—deserves to enjoy equal civil rights and liberties, for there can be no such citizen in a democracy as a half-free citizen.

I should say here that we have much reason to be proud of the progress our people are making in mutual understanding—the chief buttress of human and civil rights. Steadily we are moving closer to the goal of fair and equal treatment of citizens without regard to race or color.

This progress, I am confident, will continue. And it is gifted persons such as yourself, born out of the crucible of struggle for personal dignity and achievement, who will help lead the way towards the goals we seek.

Sincerely,
Dwight D. Eisenhower

ROBINSON TO DWIGHT EISENHOWER

Robinson suggests a meeting between the president and "responsible Negro leadership." Two weeks later, on June 23, Eisenhower met with Martin Luther King, Jr. (SCLC), A. Philip Randolph (Brotherhood of Sleeping Car Porters), Roy Wilkins (NAACP), and Lester B. Granger (National Urban League).

June 10, 1958

My dear Mr. President:

I was very pleased at the contents of your letter and extremely happy about your personal tribute to me. However, my concern isn't for personal achievements but for the accomplishment of our nation and the part 17 million loyal Negro Americans can play in bringing about equality for all Americans.

We have a great stake in our country's development, and we are in a period where teamwork and cooperation will determine the progress we continue to make.

It is with this thought in mind, I respectfully request your giving consideration to having a meeting with Negro leaders in an effort to further our progress of mutual understanding. Unfortunately, too many Negro leaders and Negro masses misinterpret your statement about patience. They consider that you favor patience alone rather than patience backed up when necessary with law enforcement.

It is my view that a meeting by you with responsible Negro leadership in the near future would help clarify and advance the cause of equal rights for all of our citizens and thus eliminate some of the unfavorable propaganda used by our enemies abroad.

Respectfully yours,
Jackie Robinson

ROY WILKINS TO ROBINSON

In defiance of a state fair-housing statute, Levitt & Sons excluded blacks from residing in Levittown, New Jersey, a newly constructed community. Robinson joined Wilkins and others in protest of the discriminatory practice, and in 1960 the Supreme Court dismissed an appeal that would have allowed the New Jersey Levittown Corporation to continue defying the fair-housing statute. In the pointed letter below, Wilkins seeks to school Robinson in the way of politics.

July 22, 1958

Dear Jackie:

Attached is the copy of my letter to Mr. Samuel Williams, President of the New Jersey State Conference of Branches.

Even though I know its content very well, I nevertheless have read it again since your comment in Cleveland that you had "heard" that I had written a letter to our New Jersey people, urging them to "ease up" on the Levitt organization.

In this business of human relations, with the interplay of politics, organizational chess moves, human egos, intra-organizational strivings, etc., it is often helpful to the general cause to run down a rumor promptly (especially if checking sources that are available) rather than accept it at face value.

I have no means of knowing who told you that I had written a letter instructing our New Jersey people to "ease up" on Levitt, but immediately after our conversation in Cleveland, I went directly to Mr. Williams and inquired whether he had received any such impression from my letter. He said he had not and that on the contrary he interpreted it as an affirmation of our regular policy and a warning not to pay attention to anything except a definitive act on the part of the Levitt organization reversing its announced policy.

Sincerely,
Roy Wilkins

ROBINSON TO JAMES HAGERTY

Bayard Rustin, arguably the most important tactician of the civil rights movement, enlisted Robinson, Coretta Scott King, and Harry Belafonte to lead the 1958 Youth March for Integrated Schools in Washington, D.C. In the following letter Robinson thanks James Hagerty, the White House press secretary, for showing interest in the march and lobbies for Eisenhower to welcome the young marchers. But Robinson was unsuccessful. A racially integrated group of students presented their petition at the White House gate, and a guard denied the group's request to meet with Eisenhower or any other White House official.

October 15, 1958

Dear Mr. Hagerty:

Just wanted to let you know how much I appreciated your interest and concern in our Youth March.

I have given this a great deal of thought and feel more strongly than ever that we will make a great contribution to our American way of life. If handled right and received right by the people in Washington, we will be saying to the world that certainly we have our problems with people, but they are in the minority. The majority of people feel as these thousands of youngsters of all races and creeds that are here today feel. I believe it will have a great impact on the people of the world seeing white and Negro children of all ages and faiths walking hand in hand peacefully demonstrating their belief in our democratic way of life.

I believe President Eisenhower can make a lasting impression by welcoming us in the same manner in which we are marching. Together we can say to the world, only in America can a demonstration like this be made.

Sincerely,
Jackie Robinson

4

PROFILES IN QUESTION

· 1959 ·

ROBINSON TO FREDERIC MORROW

Speaking before the Seventh Annual Republican Women's Conference on April 14, Fred Morrow stated: "The basic failure of the party to recognize Negro-Americans as first-class citizens, with all the hopes and aspirations that go with this role in American life, is the primary contributing factor to the party's failure to attract and to hold the Negro voters' loyalty." Morrow also claimed that neglect of the African American vote had caused the Republican defeat in the 1958 national elections and would lead to the same result in the 1960 presidential election—unless "soul-searching" leaders became responsive to the needs of African American voters. The following letter includes one of the few criticisms that Robinson directed at Nixon in 1959.

April 15, 1959

Dear Fred:

Of course, you know I agree with what you are alleged to have said before the Republican Women's Conference. I am certain you know how much I respected Mr. Nixon for the number of fine things he has said in the past. His voice has been silent lately, and he has to bear the burden along with other Republican leaders.

Congratulations on your speech. I sincerely believe you have done the Republican Party a great service. If they don't heed your advice, they are certainly hurting themselves.

Sincerely yours,
Jackie Robinson

ROBINSON TO JOHN KENNEDY

With the assistance of the ghostwriter and playwright William Branch, Robinson became a syndicated columnist for the New York Post, *a leading liberal newspaper, in April 1959. The column appeared three times a week and addressed any subject of his choosing, usually politics and sports. On May 8, just a few weeks into the new venture, Robinson aired his concerns about "the records of all the leading contenders" for the 1960 presidential election. "I'm remembering, too," he wrote, "the votes that Sen. Kennedy and some other Northern 'liberals' cast to send the 1957 Civil Rights Bill back to committee in a Southern-engineered attempt to kill any action by Congress to help Southern Negroes gain the equal voting rights promised them by the Constitution nearly 90 years ago. And I'm wondering just what was said by and to this same Senator behind closed doors at the Southern Governors' Conference that resulted in his emerging as the fair-haired boy of the Dixie politicians." Kennedy responded to these concerns in a personal letter, and below is Robinson's reply.*

May 25, 1959

My dear Senator Kennedy:

If you did not attend the Southern Governors' Conference, the press certainly played up an appearance unjustly. I recall vividly reading of the conference and of the endorsement by the Southern Governors.

Because I spoke of the incident in my column does not mean I do not consider you a very capable man. All of the people we have talked with recognize what you have done and with the exception of your vote to send the 1957 Civil Rights Bill back to Committee, we respect your position. However, regardless of the number of people who voted with you on this bill, for the sake of some 17 million Negro Americans, I do not feel this particular action was in the best interest of all concerned.

As far as Mr. Wilkins is concerned, I still remember the N.A.A.C.P. conference in Detroit where in his speech to the delegates Mr. Wilkins urges us not to forget Senator Kennedy when and if he tried for a national office. I am told you know of this speech, so I need not go into it further.

Senator Kennedy, I assure you I was pleased to get your letter. Your concern about what you feel is unfair certainly adds to the respect I have for you. Yet, I must be honest with you. If our research turns up anything that we feel is against the best interest of all the people, we intend to speak out against it. I am interested, just as you are, in seeing that democracy works for all people and as long as I have a voice, I intend speaking out against what I feel is an injustice.

This will be in the field of politics, employment, education and any of their related fields.

I want nothing more than is given to all Americans, and because I believe the Negroes' stake in America is very strong, I and many Negroes I know intend to press for equal opportunity. Until this end is obtained, sir, I don't believe our democracy can work completely. I am sure you have to agree the Negro has proven his loyalty to our country. It is now time for our country to prove its loyalty to the Negro as well.

I am well aware of the great number of liberal white people who have contributed greatly toward the progress we have made. Your contribution being among them, but Senator Kennedy, can we measure the progress we have made or do we look at the distance we have to go?

Sincerely yours,
Jackie Robinson

JOHN KENNEDY TO ROBINSON

Kennedy assures Robinson that his 1957 vote was not anti–civil rights and that he favored a defeated provision—Title III—which would have given the Justice Department the right to sue in cases of school desegregation.

June 18, 1959

Dear Mr. Robinson:

Thank you very much for your friendly response and for your frank exchange of views regarding the need for equal rights for all of our citizens. As I pointed out in my original letter, I believe that we share a deep concern and agree that there are important areas where we have not yet fulfilled the promise of democracy.

Let me just assure you again that I did not attend the Southern Governors' Conference and that I played no personal part, directly or indirectly, in its deliberations.

I also want to reaffirm the reasons for the vote in 1957 to send the Civil Rights bill back to the Judiciary Committee. I cast this vote, as did Senator Morse and others, on the clear understanding that we would vote to discharge the bill from Committee after ten days. There were ample votes to discharge the bill after that time. Though I thoroughly appreciated the reasons which motivated the majority of the Senate in bypassing the Committee, I did feel that it could create an unfortunate precedent for other types of legislation. I also feel, though this is a matter of judgment, that this vote was a chief reason for the defeat on the floor of Title III, which I considered then and still consider a vital part of any comprehensive civil rights law.

I am enclosing a copy of the letter which I received from Roy Wilkins this past fall as well as a brief resume of my legislative record in civil rights.

Again, best thanks for the letter. I know that we agree fully on the need for further progress both through the law and through the good will of individual citizens.

Sincerely,
John F. Kennedy

ROBINSON TO CHESTER BOWLES

After failing to win his bid for the Senate, Bowles was elected to the House of Representatives. He and Robinson continued to correspond, and here Robinson criticizes John Kennedy for meeting with Alabama governor John Patterson, who endorsed Kennedy shortly after their private conversation. "I think Kennedy is going to win," Patterson declared. "And I think he is a friend of the South." It was an endorsement that led some African Americans, including Representative Adam Clayton Powell, Jr. of New York, to question whether Kennedy had cut a deal with the governor. Robinson echoes Powell's criticism, questions whether Senator Hubert Humphrey of Minnesota can win the Democratic nomination, and refers to a meeting with Tom Mboya, a leading figure in Kenya's transition to political independence.

July 14, 1959

Dear Mr. Bowles:

First, let me congratulate you on the fine job you are doing. It was good reading the comments in the press regarding the respect the senior Congressmen have for a man they consider a freshman in Congress. I am certain, however, it's because they know the great work you have done in the past.

I recognize this as being rather presumptuous. However, I am going to ask anyway. I have been greatly impressed by Senator Humphrey and greatly disappointed in Senator Kennedy. If Humphrey gets the nomination, I go for the Democrats; if it's Kennedy, every effort will be turned to the Republican nominee.

I cannot move the barrier that was placed before me from the breakfast Kennedy had with Gov. Patterson of Alabama and from the Governor's later statement that he is for Kennedy because he is a friend of the South. How can we as Negroes condone this in light of the declared attitude of Patterson and southerners of his kind? This may be only to get the nomination, but I don't feel I can take the chance. If you were in my shoes, could you?

On the other hand, I have just the opposite feeling for Senator Humphrey. He impresses me as being a man you can trust to do what is right by all the people. He has been forthright and honest in my eyes. What I would ask in regard to Senator Humphrey is, does he seem to have much of a chance, and what do you think of my evaluation?

Please give my regards to Mrs. Bowles. It was good seeing her at the meeting for Mr. Tom Mboya.

Again may I wish you continued success. If you don't mind my saying so, we need more Bowleses in our Congress and Senate.

Sincerely yours,
Jackie Robinson

P.S. I hope you do not mind my writing in this manner. If this isn't ethical, I will understand your not being able to give me your opinion. If on the other hand you care to, I will keep it as confidential as you would want me to do.

CHESTER BOWLES TO ROBINSON

August 20, 1959

Dear Jackie:

Please forgive this belated reply to your frank and thoughtful letter about Hubert Humphrey, Jack Kennedy and the coming election.

I am deeply convinced that 1960 may be the most decisive election in our lifetime.

We simply have to find ways to steadily eliminate racial discrimination, expand our economy more rapidly and get our relations with the world on a more affirmative and understanding basis. No President in history will face a challenge as great as Mr. Eisenhower's successor.

I am interested in what you say about Hubert Humphrey and Jack Kennedy. I have known Hubert perhaps longer than anyone in Congress and I have the greatest admiration for him.

Since the 1948 Convention when I actively supported his successful efforts for a stronger Civil Rights plank in the Democratic platform, I have admired his courageous leadership on a wide variety of issues. If Hubert is elected he will make an outstanding President. He has character, dedication, ideas and energy. I am proud to have worked with him and to consider him a close personal friend.

Having said this I must add that I also have the same kind of respect for Jack Kennedy and that this respect has been growing the more I see of him.

I can understand why you reacted strongly to Governor Patterson's statement. I have no knowledge of the motivations or the angles that may be involved on Patterson's part. However, I have talked to Jack at length about discrimination as a national problem and segregation as a Southern problem, and he has not only said the things I hoped he would say but he said them in a way that carried very great conviction.

The most important thing to me is that in recent years Jack Kennedy has grown fast and in the right direction. He started with an excellent mind, with sympathy and understanding for people and, I believe, with a high degree of personal integrity. One of the best indications of his general outlook is the remarkable group of young liberals who are working for him in the most devoted way.

You mentioned, Jackie, that in the event of a Kennedy nomination you would vote for the Republicans. It seems to me that one of the biggest problems we all face is understanding the real differences between the two parties.

The Republicans do a lot of talking about civil rights around election time. But I have sat here in the House and watched them as a body under tight leadership maneuver with the worst of the Southern Democrats to kill our chances for meaningful civil rights legislation.

Their whole legislative position is based on an economic coalition between the Republican party, with a handful of exceptions, and the

Southern Democratic right wing. As long as this coalition stays together, the Republicans can continue to slow down or stop liberal legislation like public housing, slum clearance, minimum wages and much more.

This alliance can be kept in good working order only as long as the Republican leaders and most Republican members agree to pay the price of supporting Southern maneuvering to block civil rights bills, amend them, or water them down until they become meaningless.

Let me give you an example of how they operate. The first housing vote that came up in the House this year was a bad bill which would have done very little to build new houses or clear slums. This was the Herlong bill.

The Republican leadership knew that the only way to get it passed was to gain the support of Southern Congressmen. Therefore, a large majority of Republicans voted against a Powell amendment that would have outlawed discrimination across the board in any federally backed housing. Nevertheless, we defeated the bill.

The next day we brought out the really good bill. An anti-discrimination amendment for public housing was proposed this time by the Republicans who so recently had voted against it. This time they all voted for it in an unrecorded teller vote.

This effort of course was to make the bill unattractive to the Southerners and therefore to kill it. It was a very dramatic moment when the four Negro members of the House—all Democrats—asked to be the first to be counted *against* the anti-discrimination amendment because they knew it was being used in a cynical effort to kill public housing and slum clearance. . . .

If you could watch such day-to-day maneuvers here in Washington, I'm sure you would agree with me that a Northern Democrat who is basically liberal, such as Humphrey, Kennedy, or Stevenson, offers our *only* hope for major legislative progress on a Civil Rights issue.

Although there are some fine people in the Republican Party who are very clear on this question, they are a very small minority of the Republican Party leadership. And it is the Old Guard Republicans, tied totally to the most reactionary forces in the South, who are the controlling factor in the Eisenhower Administration.

If any Republican is elected in 1960, this group will control his Administration precisely as they do now—because they hold the political power.

I agree fully in your enthusiasm for Hubert Humphrey. He is a wonderful person who would make a great President. However, I earnestly hope you will reconsider your views on Jack Kennedy. I think I know him well and I have not the slightest doubt that as President he would perform outstandingly on this question, which is so important to you, to me, and to many others.

If you are coming to Washington some time soon, I hope you will let me know. I would like to have you meet Jack Kennedy and talk with him. I took the liberty of asking his office to send me his most recent civil rights statements and they are enclosed.

Many thanks, Jackie, for writing me as you did. Incidentally, you and I once made a deal to drop these "Mr." formalities. Now you go and break our agreement!

Please give my best regards to your wife.

Sincerely,
Chester Bowles

ROBINSON TO CHESTER BOWLES

Once again Robinson draws attention to Kennedy's apparent alliance with the governor of Alabama, this time citing Patterson's criticism of Paul Butler, chair of the Democratic National Committee (DNC), for his announcement that he would ask the DNC to adopt a rule ensuring that state delegations—and their home organizations—would support the candidates nominated at the convention. Worried that a liberal might win the nomination, Patterson and other southern legislators called for Butler's resignation.

While questioning the wisdom of supporting a party whose prominent members obstructed civil rights legislation in 1957, Robinson continues to praise Democratic senator Hubert Humphrey. At the end of the year, in his December 14 column, Robinson offered a glowing assessment. "In my conversations with Sen. Humphrey," he stated, "I've learned that human rights and human dignity are uppermost in his thinking."

August 26, 1959

Dear Chet:

It was awfully nice hearing from you. I think you know I am sincerely interested in the questions I asked of you and would like very much to look at Senator Kennedy in a different light. Your endorsement changes my feelings considerably. However, the Senator has been too willing to accept the favors of Patterson, and until we are certain what goes on in these meetings, it's hard to have confidence in him as a candidate. I wish he would give me a reason to think otherwise.

I recognize as true what you say about the coalition of Republicans and Southern Democrats, but it appears that every committee is headed by an Eastland or some other Dixiecrat who seems to have power over a great many people. I am reminded of the way Speaker Rayburn wielded his gavel at the Convention, how Senator Johnson, although I have heard some very favorable comments about him, has acted on many issues. With all these people heading up committees with great influence and power, I can't help but look for someone who is willing to say publicly the right things. I wish Senator Humphrey had more of a chance as he says things as if he really means them, and everything carries a punch. If a candidate expects to be popular, he cannot take the middle of the road. Either he is for or against an issue, and to be looked upon favorably one must be willing to accept criticism from one source or another.

Why did Kennedy send for Patterson? It seems on every issue involving civil rights Patterson is most vocal against them. The present issue with Paul Butler finds Patterson yelling the loudest. Yet, Kennedy has accepted him, and Patterson keeps saying Kennedy is a friend of the South. A truly good candidate must be a friend of the South as well as a friend of the North, East and West, but it's difficult for me or my friends to see how he can be a friend of the kind of South that Patterson represents. This is too close to the kind of friendship Eisenhower has, and I hope we don't have to have four more years of this kind of leadership. It appears to me we need the forthrightness of a Truman, and so far Humphrey is the only one who has given it.

Kennedy can change my thinking by merely being empathetic in that all the people are deserving of the things our Constitution guarantees. He need not push for anything special, only be firm in his statement, and if Patterson objects let him know it's his duty to represent all the people regardless of race or creed.

I have spoken with friends of Kennedy's from Boston. They agree with your feeling about him but feel he does not have to walk so gingerly on issues involving the North or South.

I still feel we need more people like you who believe in each man according to individual abilities. Your letter has opened a new area of thinking as far as the Republicans and Southern Democrats working together are concerned. It needs much more research. Still, I cannot get it out of my mind that a weak Democrat as president with Southerners heading up the top committees would be far worse than a Republican president who would at least be willing to express himself on this matter of civil rights regardless of the coalition.

I like what you have pointed out and assure you I will give your thoughts a great deal of my time. I don't know what I can do as an individual, but I am at least going to be active.

My best to Mrs. Bowles and the family. I hope everyone is well. Rae sends her regards and wishes you the best also.

Cordially yours,
Jackie Robinson

CHESTER BOWLES TO ROBINSON

Bowles's partisan analysis includes a swipe at progressives who would support New York governor Nelson Rockefeller. While Bowles admired the moderate Republican, he felt that the Republican Party would never back Rockefeller for the presidency. In spite of Bowles's warning, Robinson would devote most of his political attention and energy to Rockefeller following the 1960 presidential election.

August 31, 1959

Dear Jackie:

Many thanks for your fine letter. It is impossible for you or me to know what goes on in any man's mind. However, I think you know how strongly I feel on all questions involving human dignity, and while I cannot explain every move or statement that Jack Kennedy has made over the years, I am convinced by my conversations with him that he feels as strongly on these issues as I do.

The next time you are in Washington, I hope you will have a talk with him. I know he will be glad to see you, and a visit will give you a chance to pose the blunt questions you would like to ask and to judge his answers and attitudes for yourself.

I have just completed an analysis of the House vote on key questions, with the Democrats broken down by sections—the North, the border states (Maryland, Kentucky, Missouri and Oklahoma), and the eleven states of the old Confederate South. The questions analyzed are on the votes on the Landrum-Griffin bill (which was the labor bill supported by the Manufacturers Association and the Dixiecrats); the extensive housing and slum clearance bill passed by the House in May (since then it has been watered down because of the President's veto); the vote on H.R. 3 (a bill to gravely weaken the Supreme Court) and the foreign aid bill. . . .

The analysis shows that Democratic members of the House from the North have been vigorously and consistently liberal. In the border states they have been so-so, leaning to the liberal side. In the eleven Confederate states, their votes have been almost identical with those of the Republicans.

I believe that the evidence shows that the Republican Party is a totally dead-end street for anyone who believes in liberal principles. Nelson Rockefeller is a decent person, and a liberal one. But the Republican Old Guard would destroy him as they have destroyed every other liberal Republican leader since Lincoln.

Teddy Roosevelt, after struggling with the situation, gave up in disgust and left the Republican Party.

Wendell Willkie was repudiated and humiliated by the Republican Party leaders before he died. Ike, with all his prestige and his huge popularity, has become a captive of the most backward elements of the Republican Party. Rockefeller, with all his good instincts, would not last as long as Ike because he could not equal Ike's personal prestige.

What we must do is to put a liberal Democrat in the White House. Having done that we must then *demand* a change of rules in both the House and the Senate which will give the majority in the Democratic Party a chance to express itself and eliminate the dominant power of the Dixiecrat minority which teams up with Republicans to block civil rights and other liberal measures.

Let me add, Jackie, that if dedicated people with your great persuasiveness will join us and exert your influence *within* the Democratic Party, there is a far greater hope that we can get the kind of action on economic, civil rights and foreign policy questions that the American people want and which the world expects from us.

With my warmest regards,

Sincerely,
Chester Bowles

ROBINSON TO CHESTER BOWLES

October 6, 1959

Dear Chet:

Excuse the delay. I have been a little under the weather since my vacation and am having trouble catching up on my mail.

There can be little doubt that the Negro and other minorities have benefited more under the Democrats, but I wonder whether the candidates in the running would wave the same stick that Roosevelt and Truman waved? I just can't get over the feeling that it is the man that's important even more than the party, and whoever, by his record and deeds, appears to be the right man, I must support wholeheartedly.

I keep hearing about Rockefeller, yet I feel certain he would be dominated by the party because of his lack of experience. I am not at all so sure Nixon would yield. There is something about him that leaves me with the feeling of sincerity. To this date, I don't have the same feeling regarding Kennedy, and many of my friends feel the same. There still hasn't been a satisfactory explanation of Alabama's Governor Patterson's support. This and other things frighten me, and unless we are satisfied, I don't see how we can come out for Kennedy.

It's up to the delegates to select the man we can go for. If it is Kennedy, he must do a little dominating of associates. This does not mean we have closed the door, but it does mean a lot will have to be done. We have waited long enough. Now we must resort to every means to get the right person in the right place.

It's good to be able to correspond with you. I am certain everything will work out well in the end.

With all good wishes.

Sincerely,
Jackie Robinson

GLOSTER CURRENT TO ROBERT CARTER

Gloster Current organized Robinson's work with the Freedom Fund campaigns and frequently traveled with him to NAACP speaking engagements. Here he recounts an incident of discrimination to Robert Carter, general counsel of the NAACP.

October 28, 1959

I want to give you information concerning the Greenville incident in the Municipal Airport, Sunday, October 25.

As you know, I was in Greenville attending sessions of the South Carolina State Conference. . . .

On Sunday morning a group of us went to the airport to meet Jackie Robinson, who was a passenger on Eastern Airlines Flight 581 out of New York, scheduled to arrive in Greenville at 11:08 a.m. We arrived at the airport about 10:45 a.m. Among those present were: Attorney Smith of Greenville, Rev. H. P. Sharper of Sumter and Billie Fleming of Manning. We took seats in the main waiting room and shortly after being seated, we were faced with the manager who came over and told the group that we could not occupy seats in that area; that we had to go into the "colored lounge." This is a room which has been specially set aside, off the main entrance of the airport, for Negroes. It contains seats, telephones and lavatory facilities.

We refused to leave the area, although we did arise from our seats and became engaged in conversation with the manager.

The manager's name is Mr. O. L. Andrews. He stated that if we attempted to re-seat ourselves, we would be arrested. To emphasize this, he called Officer No. 87, whose name, I learned later, was Woodall. He told the officer to arrest us if we attempted to sit down.

Several members of the group remonstrated with the manager and told him we had a right to be there; that the airport is federally subsidized; that Mr. Robinson was an interstate passenger and the facilities were rightfully ours to use without discrimination. We made no further protest of the situation at that time and left when the plane was taxiing to the gate. We did not subject Mr. Robinson that morning to the humiliation of the discriminatory treatment indicated by the manager.

Both Mr. Jackie Robinson and myself were passengers on Flight Eastern Airlines 558 scheduled to depart Greenville Sunday, October 25, at 5:20 p.m. We arrived at the airport approximately 5:00 p.m. and in the company of a large group of citizens from Greenville, checked in. Thereafter, Rev. and Mrs. Hall and I took seats in the main area which is reserved for whites, and Mr. Robinson was standing behind me autographing baseballs and talking to admirers.

Once again, the manager walked over to us and told Rev. and Mrs. Hall and myself and also Mr. Robinson that we could not sit there. Another officer accompanied him whom he pointed to and said to arrest us if we persisted in sitting there. Both Mr. Robinson and I pointed out to the manager that we had a lawful right to remain there; that we were interstate passengers and in my own case I said that I had no objection to going to jail. However, no effort was made to arrest either of us. Other than to express our disagreement, we did not attempt to prolong the discussion. We remained standing in that area which was forbidden to colored passengers by the manager.

Another officer went to the telephone, as also happened in the morning, and apparently made a report to someone.

I supply this information in the interest of whatever protest or action is deemed advisable. I am certain that Mr. Robinson will be glad, also, to supply information.

ROBINSON TO CHESTER BOWLES

Unsurprisingly, Bowles's book, The Coming Political Breakthrough *(Harper and Brothers, 1959), predicted a victory for liberal Democrats in the 1960 elections.*

November 12, 1959

Dear Chet:

Thank you very much for sending me a copy of your book. I am positive it will help me during this period of indecision. I cannot help but be a little confused with all that has begun to happen.

I have received an inquiry about doing some public relations work for one of the Republican candidates, but I must wait for awhile so I can see what happens with the Democrats.

I think you know pretty much how I feel, and nothing has occurred to change my thinking. 1960, in my opinion, will be the most important election for the Negro; it perhaps will be so for all Americans. That's why I am so concerned about who is nominated and what his past history is. I am little interested in what one says between now and next November.

Any chances for Chet Bowles? I would have no doubt in my mind about whom I would vote for then. Of course, whomever you stump for will have its effect on me, but I don't know to what extent.

My best to you and Mrs. Bowles. For whatever my voice is worth it will be an active one.

Sincerely yours,
Jackie Robinson

CHESTER BOWLES TO ROBINSON

December 3, 1959

Dear Jackie:

I returned from Europe a few days ago and found your letter of November 12th. I wholly agree with you that the 1960 election will be vitally important. Indeed, I have a feeling it could well turn out to be the most important election of this century.

We are facing some enormous problems, and we are getting almost no leadership from our national government in coping with them. This applies to foreign affairs, our slow rate of economic growth and civil rights.

One of the most disheartening points about the latter situation, in my opinion, is the failure of the Administration to face the issue as a moral question and attempt to rally the strong moral convictions of the American people. I feel that another place it has failed dismally is in its refusal to settle most of these questions by its power of executive order.

As you know, the desegregation of the armed forces was achieved not by legislation but by President Truman's executive order. The Republican Administration has the same power to handle some of these problems especially in public housing through the Federal Housing Administration and other public housing agencies.

It also has the power to eliminate segregation in airports and other terminal facilities built with the help of federal funds and also in universities of the South which receive federal assistance. Yet in all these fields it has done almost nothing.

Steb and I often think of the very pleasant evening we had with you and your wife here in Essex and hope we may see you soon again.

With warmest regards,

Sincerely,
Chester Bowles

ROBINSON TO ABRAHAM RIBICOFF

A devoted golfer, Robinson attacked discrimination on golf courses and in golfing organizations throughout the 1950s and 1960s. Connecticut governor Abraham Ribicoff replied to the following letter just a few days later, noting that he was greatly disturbed at Robinson's news and promised to make a full inquiry after receiving additional details about the case.

December 7, 1959

My dear Governor Ribicoff:

Something quite disturbing was brought to my attention the other day, and knowing of your interest in golf and of your desire for justice, I felt you should be made aware of this act of discrimination.

A friend of mine applied for a State Handicap in golf, and it was made plain that he was turned down because he is a Negro. It's hard to believe a state like ours, whose Governor is from a minority group and has demonstrated his democratic principles, would tolerate such an undemocratic action.

Prejudice has no place in any activity here in America. We are all aware of the fact that it exists, but I hope as the Chief Executive of Connecticut and an avid golf enthusiast you feel as I do that this attitude should not be allowed to exist.

Sincerely yours,
Jackie Robinson

Marshall, head of the NAACP Legal Defense and Educational Fund, had counseled Robinson to delay acting on a complaint about the Greenville Airport incident of October 25. Marshall's reason was that his office was devoting attention to a case against the airport that was already in the appeal stage. Robinson did not welcome the counsel, and below is Marshall's pointed reply.

December 11, 1959

Dear Jackie:

I gather from your letter of December 9th that there could be misunderstanding between us concerning the Greenville case. The present suit of *Henry v. Greenville Airport Commission, et al.*, now pending in the United States Circuit Court of Appeals for the Fourth Circuit, is set for argument in that court on January 15, 1960. In that case, the action is on behalf of the plaintiff Richard B. Henry and "on behalf of all other Negroes similarly situated." The prayer for relief in that case is for an "interlocutory and permanent injunction restraining defendants from making any distinction based upon color in regard to service at the Greenville Municipal Airport." Whichever way this case is decided will determine once and for all the legal or unconstitutional status of the segregation pattern at the Greenville Airport. Of course, I think it would generally be understood that this practice will be declared unconstitutional. Any other case seeking the same relief will be controlled by this case.

With the above in mind, I cannot see how you, I, or anyone else can be "letting the people in Greenville down" by not filing another case on the same subject matter involving the same airport. Again, and for the same reasons, I cannot understand how "the people of Greenville will feel we have forgotten them."

I am sure that your sole aim is to see that justice is done for our people in Greenville as well as in other areas and it still appears to me that the present case, with the money and time already invested in it, will get the Negroes in Greenville just as much as any new case could get them at a later date; bearing in mind that a new case would have to first go through the District Court and then to the Court of Appeals. Assuming the new case could be filed within a week, it could not get to the Court of Appeals earlier than May or June.

It is also quite possible that another case might not even get heard until after the present case is decided because the local district court judge might very well say that the present case is on appeal and he will await the judgment of the Court of Appeals on that case before hearing any other case involving the same subject matter and the same defendants.

As the staff person responsible for the support of litigation involving these problems, I still say that I should not take on an additional case involving the exact same problem, in the exact same airport of a case we are now interested in.

If there is anything not clear in this letter, please let me know.

Sincerely,
Thurgood Marshall

5

SELLING NIXON

· 1960 ·

ROBINSON TO RAY ROBINSON

Ray Robinson, the editor of Coronet *magazine, criticized Jackie Robinson's politics in a personal letter that prompted the following reply. By the end of December 1959, Jackie had publicized his growing support for Nixon, rebuking partisan detractors along the way. In his December 30 column, for example, Jackie had sketched a number of reasons for admiring Nixon: his international stature, his anticommunist credentials, his willingness to tour Africa, and his recognition that U.S. racism was an easy target for communists seeking to advance their interests. "And if it should come to a choice between a weak and indecisive Democratic nominee and Vice President Nixon," Robinson concluded, "I, for one, would enthusiastically support Nixon." Jackie also suggests here that he might be swayed to support Adlai Stevenson, the Democratic candidate for president in the 1952 and 1956 elections, although nothing ever came of this possibility.*

January 4, 1960

Dear Ray:

I, too, must confess I am disturbed by your letter. I agree wholeheartedly with you about the civil rights record of the Eisenhower administration, but don't include me in those who concede Nixon will run on this record. I feel very definitely that his civil rights platform will be his own and one with teeth. Frankly, Ray, I prefer Nixon over any of your Democratic candidates other than Senator Humphrey and repeat my statement that I will enthusiastically support Mr. Nixon if a Kennedy, a Johnson, and unless Mr. Stevenson reverts to his 1952 campaign, a Stevenson is the Democratic nominee. I feel as strongly in favor of Nixon's principles, ethics and intellectual honesty as you are against. Would you have me support a Kennedy who met with one of the worst segregationists in private, and then this man, the Governor of Alabama, comes out with strong support of Senator Kennedy or a Stevenson who wooed the voters in California one way and Southerners another? I have my reasons for my belief in Mr. Nixon and am sorry you feel I should not have them.

Mr. Nixon, like Senator Humphrey, has said the things I, as a Negro, have been hoping to hear. Call him an opportunist if you will. At least he is on record regarding his feelings. That's a great deal more than some of the other candidates can claim.

I don't feel at all that I am being misled. As in the past, I must do and say what I believe. Each of us is entitled to our beliefs and can oppose opinions. Still I must stand on what I believe to be right, not what others think.

Sincerely,
Jackie Robinson

RICHARD NIXON TO ROBINSON

January 16, 1960

Dear Jackie:

I have just had an opportunity to read your column from the December 30 issue of the *New York Post*, and I want you to know how much I enjoyed your comments.

While you disclaimed any pretensions toward being a political expert, it seems to me that you handled this subject with the same agility which you always show on the baseball diamond. Your kind words in my behalf were, of course, especially gratifying for me.

I shall be looking forward to your column as the political situation develops and will hope to have a chance for a talk with you before too long. In the meantime, this note brings to you my very best wishes.

Sincerely,
Richard Nixon

ROBINSON TO RICHARD NIXON

Robinson registers his discontent with Eisenhower's race record—the same issue he addressed in his January 20 column. "I submit that Negroes have been patient for nigh onto a hundred years, and now our patience is rapidly wearing thin," Robinson stated. "In this, the last year of President Eisenhower's stay in the White House, is it too much to hope that he will finally take the reigns firmly in his hands and give the nation some aggressive direction in the field of civil rights?"

January 29, 1960

My dear Mr. Nixon:

Thank you for your letter of the 16th. It was nice of you to write regarding my column. I am certain you know what a favorable column on Richard Nixon does in the *New York Post*. I haven't had so much mail since I left baseball.

Mr. Nixon, I have been and am making a pretty thorough investigation on what individual candidates probably would do regarding civil rights. I feel confident of the personal position you would take but am very concerned about the Republican party itself. The question of why only thirty Republicans in the House of Representatives signed a discharge petition to bring a civil rights bill out of the Rules Committee and to the floor compared to 146 Democrats has many people wondering. My critics keep reminding me that you have pledged to continue the Eisenhower administrative policy. They ask, does this include his civil rights policy too? I am reminded that this means patience. Whenever the President is asked about civil rights, he asks the Negro to be patient. We have been the most patient of any group and cannot afford another four years of waiting. All over the world freedom is the cry of oppressed people. How long can one expect the American Negro to be patient?

If one really believes the principles of our democracy and in our constitution, a strong statement can only better qualify him for the position of leadership. It is true as you said back in, I believe, 1953, "Every act of discrimination is like handing a gun to the Communists. Advocating patience or remaining silent gives courage and determination to die-hard segregationists." Firmness now could lead us to the goals we have set for ourselves.

Again my thanks for your letter. Best wishes for continued success.

Sincerely yours,
Jackie Robinson

HUBERT HUMPHREY TO ROBINSON

Frank Reeves, an attorney prominent in the NAACP and the Democratic Party, talked with Robinson in early February about supporting Humphrey for the presidency. Shortly after telling Reeves that he would campaign for Humphrey, but only if William Black (the president of Chock Full O' Nuts) agreed to it, Robinson used his February 22 column to praise the candidate. "From the very first," he stated, "Humphrey has made it all too plain that his position is one of vigorous action and to assure every American of equal civil rights." Robinson also criticized Kennedy, once again, for his association with segregationist politicians. "With the fires of freedom sweeping the uncommitted, colored peoples of the world today," Robinson concluded, "no man deserves the Presidency of the United States who feels he must make a deal with racists in order to get it."

The conflict between Robinson and Kennedy deepened a few weeks later, when Robinson appeared at a Humphrey rally in Milwaukee. A reporter covering the trip told Robinson of Robert Kennedy's claim that the Humphrey team had paid for his appearance. Robinson fumed at the suggestion and delivered a blistering reply in his March 16 column: "I want right here to emphasize what I told that reporter. Whoever originated such a story is a liar." Robinson added that he "still would like to know more about the reasons behind Kennedy's position as the fair-haired boy of the Southern segregationists."

February 16, 1960

Dear Jackie:

Our mutual friend, Frank Reeves, has told me of his recent visit with you. I am honored with your willingness to work with us and pleased with your approval of my work.

I do hope Mr. Black will permit your participation in our Wisconsin primary campaign. I have written him the enclosed letter, and shall await his response with trust and optimism.

Thank you so much for your friendship and your interest. You might be interested in our most recent campaign literature, which is enclosed.

My good wishes to you personally, and have a happy vacation.

Sincerely yours,
Hubert H. Humphrey

Former president Harry Truman opposed the sit-ins then occurring in the South, and during a visit to Cornell University on April 18 he would state that he would not be surprised to learn that they had been engineered by communists. Truman also disavowed the student demonstrators for "shutting up a man's place of business." In his March 25 column Robinson criticized "Truman's patronizing gradualism" and showed support for the demonstrators by including the following letter from Patricia Stephens, a student involved in the Tallahassee sit-in. Robinson's decision to publish this letter reflected his emerging support for the Congress of Racial Equality (CORE). In June 1959 James Robinson, a cofounder of CORE, had invited Jackie to become a board member, and Jackie obliged without hesitation.

March 25, 1960

The following letter came to my attention yesterday. It is from a Negro college girl, one of eight Fla. A&M students who chose jail rather than pay fines after their arrest while peacefully requesting service at a Woolworth's lunch counter in Tallahassee. The letter is addressed to James Robinson, executive secretary of CORE, one of the organizations supporting the student movement in the South.

County Jail
Tallahassee, Florida
March 20, 1960

Dear Jim,

How are things in New York? I hope the weather is a little warmer now.

Our trial was Thursday and there were eight charges against us. Most of them were added after we were released on bond. Except for the original charges—disturbing the peace, inciting to riot and disturbing the tranquility of the community—I am at a loss as to what the other charges were. Six of them were dropped by the judge after he had a conference with his boys.

On the second count we were given a 60-day sentence or a $300 fine. On the eighth count we were given a mandatory 30-day sentence which was suspended. However, we were placed on probation for one year or for as long as we are students at Fla. A&M. We may well serve those 30 days because we do not plan to discontinue our fight.

There are eight of us in jail, seven A&M students and one high school student. We are in what you call a "bull-rack" with four cells in it. There is running water in only two of the cells. Breakfast (if you can call it that) is served every morning at 6:30. Another meal is served at 12:30 and I am still trying to get up enough courage to eat it. In the evening we are served sweetbreads and watery coffee.

We are all so very happy that we are able to do this to help our city, state and nation. We strongly believe that Martin Luther King was right when he said, "We've got to fill the jails in order to win our equal right."

. . . Well, I've got to dress for our visitors (we have two ministers visit us every day). Write when you can. Tell everyone hello for us.

Yours truly,
Pat (Patricia Stephens)

P.S. My parents were here last night to get us out but we persuaded them to let us stay. Priscilla (my sister) is supposed to be on a special diet and Mother was worried about her.

ROSE MARY WOODS TO RICHARD NIXON

Fred Lowey, a prominent New York Republican, telephoned Rose Mary Woods, Nixon's secretary, on March 30 to report on Robinson's interest in the Nixon campaign, and the following is a memorandum on the conversation. By this point it was clear that Humphrey would not win the Democratic nomination for president.

March 30, 1960

Fred Lowey called and wanted to talk to you. I told him you were completely tied up and he left the following message.

He would very much like to talk with you for one minute in the next couple of days in connection with the following: He had lunch yesterday with Jackie Robinson. He stressed, of course, he did not need to tell you how important Jackie was as far as the Negro vote was concerned. He feels that with the slightest persuasion Robinson could be swung around and would come on the Nixon band wagon. To use his terms, "Robinson is more or less considered sort of a God up here."

I asked him what Robinson specifically said and Lowey said the story is he is first of all interested in Humphrey but he feels Humphrey doesn't have a chance and his second choice would be you. Fred Lowey thinks it is very important that you get together with Robinson so that he can get to know you better. I told him that you had talked with him and that you have had correspondence with him in the past.

At any rate, Lowey thinks this should be super hush-hush, and again repeated that he would like to talk with you in the next couple of days.

I would imagine you want one of the fellows in the office or Len Hall to make any follow up with Lowey.

RICHARD NIXON TO ROBERT FINCH

Nixon's memorandum to Robert Finch, the manager of his presidential campaign, follows up on Woods's March 30 note and foresees difficulties between Robinson and James Wechsler, the editor of the New York Post, *over the political direction of his column.*

April 10, 1960

I think Fred Lowey has a point with regard to seeing Jackie Robinson.

I would suggest that next time we are in New York that we arrange to have him drop in for a visit. Of course, we must remember that he is now employed as a columnist for the *New York Post* and that he will be under great pressure from his editor Wechsler to take whatever nominee the Democrats select. As a matter of fact I think a letter from me to him at this point might be in order.

RICHARD NIXON TO ROBINSON

Because Nixon knew that Robinson had started his column a year earlier, the beginning of the following letter is a bit confusing. Less puzzling is Nixon's pleasure with the April 11 commentary in Time *magazine. "Jackie has been chock full o' zeal and sometimes chock full o' nonsense,"* Time *declared. "Sometimes he dismays even the* Post, *as when he declared that he might be compelled to support Richard Nixon for President if the Democrats failed to nominate a staunch civil rights advocate."*

April 13, 1960

Dear Jackie:

This is just a note to wish you well as you undertake your assignment as a columnist for the *New York Post*. Incidentally, *Time* magazine gave you an unusually friendly send off. As you know, they can put the needle in very effectively when they find themselves in substantial disagreement with the individual about whom they may be writing.

If your duties should happen to bring you to Washington at any time in the next few weeks, I would certainly welcome the opportunity to have a talk with you. There have been several recent developments in the civil rights field, including the legislation which has just been passed by the Senate, on which I would like to get your views. I am sure Bill Rogers would join us in the event you could come for lunch on a day which might fit into your schedule as well as ours.

With every good wish,

Sincerely,
Richard Nixon

JAMES ROBINSON TO ROBINSON

The following is an excerpt of a letter written by the executive secretary of CORE after Jackie helped to raise public awareness about the student sit-ins.

April 22, 1960

Dear Mr. Robinson:

. . . You will be glad to know that the students in Tallahassee are scheduled to be released from jail on May 6th.

Herritt Spaulding, whom you met here in New York, has been arrested once again, but this time the case was rapidly quashed. He was over at the white institution, Florida State, one evening early in April and after meeting with several people there began to walk back to his own campus. One of the white students accompanied him. The police car came along the street, spotted a Negro and white student together, and arrested them both for "night prowling." A local Tallahassee attorney raised Cain about the arrest and the whole thing was dropped.

We certainly very much appreciate your coming to the pledge signing this week. We feel that the pledge campaign is vital in building up the boycott of Woolworth to the point where they will seriously consider making changes in most of their outlets in the South. We also appreciate, of course, the publicity that has been given to the actions in Tallahassee in your column in the *New York Post*.

This elicited one letter to Pat from Yokohama, Japan, from Mr. Thomas McGregory, an American who is taking a trip around the world. He says, "In my travels about the world, I've been approached many times by foreigners, asking about the Negro situation in the United States. They all seem very much concerned. I tried to explain, but it's very hard to explain something to a person who has never been familiar with the American way of life. During the course of the trip I am going to show your letter to all the people who approach me concerning the American Negro. I know there will be many. In the meantime, you and your sister have all my best wishes. And I pray to God that some day this will all be over. For the good of all mankind."

Sincerely yours,
James R. Robinson

ROBINSON TO RICHARD NIXON

On April 24 a race riot followed a wade-in staged by forty to fifty African Americans at the all-white Biloxi Beach in Mississippi. After whites attacked the protestors, riots spread into the city, resulting in gunfire that wounded eight blacks and two whites. In the following telegram Robinson draws a connection between the Biloxi riots and state-sanctioned violence in South Africa. Robinson used his newspaper column on several occasions to transmit accounts of violence in South Africa that he received from George Houser, a founding member of CORE and executive director of the American Committee on Africa (ACOA), an early watchdog group organized to fight apartheid.

April 25, 1960

Biloxi, Mississippi should be a warning the Negro is in an inflammable state. Perhaps when we meet we should discuss this also. Let's not have a South African situation.

Jackie Robinson

ROBINSON TO MARTIN LUTHER KING, JR.

At a student rally in Raleigh on April 15, James Lawson, recently expelled from Vanderbilt University for organizing sit-ins, publicly criticized the NAACP for being too conservative and bourgeois in its focus on lawsuits and fund-raising. Lawson was not a staff member of SCLC at the time, but King seemed on the verge of hiring him. Roy Wilkins sent King a letter complaining about Lawson and warning about the dangers of a split between SCLC and the NAACP. Robinson, by now a board member of the NAACP, echoes Wilkins's concerns and informs King that his pending perjury trial in Montgomery had given rise to unauthorized fund-raising groups. The latter point was of special interest to Robinson because he was an organizing member of the Committee to Defend Martin Luther King, Jr., which formed in early March to subsidize King's legal costs and finance SCLC's efforts to register a million new African American voters in the South.

May 5, 1960

Dear Martin:

First, let me say how much I respect and appreciate all the good you are doing. You have gained the confidence of people the world over, and for that reason I am concerned about the committees that have sprung up to raise money for your defense in the coming farce trial in Alabama.

I am also quite disturbed because of reports I have been receiving that people who claim to represent the Southern Christian Leadership

Conference are saying the N.A.A.C.P. has outlived its usefulness. Let's not be a party to the old game of divide and conquer. The N.A.A.C.P., as any group, has its faults, but the good the organization has done cannot be measured. Talk like this sets our cause back.

I know you would not be party to any individual or group that would use your misfortune for their own selfish interest. We must be wary of groups who may be doing so.

Please let me know what groups you have authorized to solicit funds in your behalf and what you know about individuals who are knocking the N.A.A.C.P. in promoting the Southern Christian Leadership Conference.

I hope you know I am not questioning the need. It's only that I am concerned.

Sincerely yours,
Jackie Robinson

ROBINSON TO ROY WILKINS

Albert Brewer, secretary and treasurer of the Northern California Citizenship Council of the United Auto Workers, had asked Wilkins whether Robinson was authorized to claim that the NAACP opposed Kennedy's candidacy. Robinson's pointed reply refers to Alabama state senator Samuel Englehardt, chair of Alabama's Democratic Executive Committee. Englehardt had accompanied Governor John Patterson to the June 1959 meeting with Kennedy.

May 10, 1960

Dear Roy:

I have never spoken for the N.A.A.C.P. in regard to Kennedy. I am certain you know I have never attempted to do so. As an individual, I will continue to oppose him as long as he is willing to accept Governor Patterson's (of Alabama) support and will entertain the head of the White Citizens Council.

I wish Brewer would get his facts before writing such nonsense.

Sincerely yours,
Jackie Robinson

ROSE MARY WOODS TO RICHARD NIXON

On May 10 Robinson met with Nixon, Attorney General William Rogers, and Secretary of Labor James Mitchell. The margins of the following note include this comment: "rmw called Jackie Robinson & told him RN said 'fine.'"

May 10, 1960

Shortly after you left last night Secretary Mitchell called—said that he took Jackie Robinson back to the airport after lunch today and Jackie said he would like to use—if it is agreeable with the Vice President—the fact that he was down here and talked to the Vice President, the Attorney General and the Secretary. He wants to say that he is more convinced than ever of his support of Nixon after your conversation this noon. OK?????????

ROBINSON TO RICHARD NIXON

Robinson respected James Mitchell, then considered a strong candidate to become Nixon's running mate, because of the secretary of labor's leading role in the Eisenhower administration's opposition to Governor Orval Faubus during the Little Rock crisis of 1957. By contrast Robinson held little respect for the Republican leaders in Congress, Senator Everett Dirksen of Illinois and Representative Charles Halleck of Indiana. Robinson considered both men to be obstructionists to civil rights legislation.

May 11, 1960

My dear Mr. Nixon:

Thank you very much for having me to lunch Tuesday. I was honored to have the opportunity to talk with you, Mr. Rogers and Secretary Mitchell. I have for a long time respected Secretary Mitchell and meeting Mr. Rogers was a real pleasure.

I came away with the feeling what Mr. Rogers had to say went far beyond politics, and I was among three gentlemen whom I felt were sincere and could be trusted. As things stand today, I heartily endorse your candidacy and hope you understand my being so outspoken. It sometimes gets me into difficulty, but at least I walk away knowing my position is clear.

I mentioned also the attitude some people have toward you. While I don't think it is a difficult thing to overcome, I feel you must not hesitate in making your own position as clear to others as it was made to me. There is no question in my mind that you have grown as much as any man in public life and have all the necessary qualifications for leadership. Still, people wonder what control you will have over Dirksen and Halleck and how you can erase the image left by Eisenhower as far as Civil Rights is concerned.

If you wait much longer, it will be hard to convince people that your interest isn't motivated by politics. You must come up with things you did prior to 1955. Go back as far as possible because I am certain Kennedy has sent to others, as he did to me, your record prior to 1950. I, too, need answers to negative questions people constantly put to me. Believe me, it's most difficult to answer people who seem to have documentary evidence of what you said or did. When you withhold positive things, an image isn't easy to erase, but it can be done if you display a warmth or as much sincerity as you can regarding the Negroes status. Laws, as you said, are fine, but the moral issues will do the trick. I repeat what I said at the luncheon. It will not require a great deal more to get the kind of support I feel we can give if you move now. Many of my friends have expressed an interest, but the great majority say I don't feel I can go along at the present time.

Thanks again.

Sincerely yours,
Jackie Robinson

JOHN KENNEDY TO ROBINSON

The New York Post *ran this letter in the June 3 issue. Robinson responded point by point in his column on the same day, concluding that "it is quite clear to me by now that Sen. Kennedy—or any other candidate—cannot expect any self-respecting Negro to support him with the image of Patterson, Englehardt and their ilk sitting across his breakfast table. When and if Kennedy firmly and vigorously repudiates the actions and policies of this crowd, I will be happy to reeval-*

uate my position. But as long as he continues to play politics at the expense of 18,000,000 Negro Americans, then I repeat: Sen. Kennedy is not fit to be President of the U.S."

May 25, 1960

Dear Mr. Robinson:

The column which appeared in the May 16th issue of the *New York Post* has been called to my attention. I respect your right to support Senator Humphrey or any other candidate for public office. However, I should like to take this opportunity to clarify any misunderstanding you may have about my position on questions you raise.

In a prior letter I enclosed a copy of my civil rights record. I assume, therefore, that you are familiar with it. I can only add to that record my votes in connection with the 1960 Civil Rights Bill. You will find that I supported federal registrars or enrollment officers rather than referees, that I supported the strengthening of the bill in every area, and that I voted and spoke in favor of invoking cloture.

You refer in your letter, however, to my "alliances" with Governor Patterson of Alabama and Sam Englehardt of Alabama. There are no such alliances. I have never made any commitment to them. I have never entered into any agreement concerning civil rights. My views are matters of public record. Although it is true that I once had breakfast with them it is equally true that a few days later I had lunch with Mr. Thurgood Marshall. No implications can be drawn from either of these meetings other than my own public statements.

You also refer to "carefully guarded token statements" on the sit-ins. I assume you are aware of the unequivocal position I have taken from the very beginning that these are traditional American expressions, and of my disagreement with the position taken by our former President, Harry Truman.

You also refer to my "peculiar failure to appear" at Wisconsin rallies in Negro areas. I assume you refer to the scheduled rally on March 23, in Milwaukee. That rally took place the night the vote was scheduled upon the Javits-Clark amendment to the Civil Rights Bill. As you know, this was probably the most critical vote on the bill. Upon its outcome depended effective protection of the right to vote. I felt it would be incongruous to go to Milwaukee to make a speech on civil rights while neglecting the opportunity to vote upon a most important civil rights measure. I found it necessary, therefore, to arrange to deliver my talk by telephone from my office in the Senate Office Building. I believe that most of the civil rights supporters appreciated my dilemma and agreed with my decision.

Finally, you refer to my "questionable" voting record on the 1957 Civil Rights Bill. I assume you are referring to my vote on the jury trial amendment, for on every key vote connected with that bill—including the controversial Title III—I supported strong protections for civil rights. My vote on the jury trial amendment was based on the advice and counsel I received from Professor Freund and Professor Mark de-Wolfe Howe whose standing in the field of civil liberties and civil rights is unquestioned. The question presented was basically a civil liberties question for it involved the right to trial by jury in criminal cases. As a matter of fact, I know of no instance in which this provision has handicapped the enforcement of the Civil Rights Act of 1957.

I hope this clarification will give some assistance to you.

With every good wish,

Sincerely,
John F. Kennedy

RICHARD NIXON TO ROBINSON

In his May 23 column Robinson listed favorable "impressions" that he had formed in his May 10 meeting with Nixon—including the vice president's awareness of "the need for using the influence and prestige of the Presidency to advance equal rights and human dignity"; his alliances with Rogers and Mitchell, who "have long been chafing under the conservative, go-slow policies of the present occupant of the White House"; and his own eagerness to "disengage himself from the restraint of supporting Eisenhower policies with which he may not be in full accord." Robinson then published the following letter in his June 10 column, and in spite of what he had reported privately to Nixon, he added this note to the end of his column: "Contrary to some published reports, this corner thus far is still uncommitted to any candidate for the Presidency, now that Sen. Humphrey has withdrawn."

June 3, 1960

Dear Jackie:

I thought you might like to know that I have received many favorable comments, both personally and through correspondence, on your column in the *New York Post* which followed our recent luncheon.

In reading your article, and reflecting upon our conversation, I think we agree that henceforth no political party or special interest group can take the American Negro vote for granted. The growing assurance and political sophistication of this group now goes far beyond economic gain; they want and are entitled to the basic freedoms and opportunities to which you referred in your column. Lip service and demagoguery in the field of civil rights will, I trust, have less effect in the November election than in any previous one in our nation's history.

As I attempted to indicate to you at lunch, I have consistently taken what has been called a strong position on civil rights, not only for the clear-cut moral considerations involved, but for other reasons which reach beyond our nation's borders.

The first reason relates to our leadership of the Free World. Obviously, unless we show consistent, direct action in strengthening our moral posture in this field, we will suffer in the eyes of the emerging nations and the uncommitted peoples. Beyond this, however, our present struggle with the forces of atheistic Communism is an economic as well as an ideological battle. To deny ourselves the full talent and energies of 17 million Negro Americans in this struggle would be stupidity of the greatest magnitude.

A summary of my votes, rulings and positions I have taken in the civil rights field is enclosed, as you requested at the luncheon.

I look forward to the get together in Washington which we discussed on the phone. Don Hughes will call your office and arrange a mutually convenient date for the three of us.

With every good wish,

Sincerely,
Richard Nixon

ROBINSON TO RICHARD NIXON

Robinson lobbies Nixon on behalf of Airlift Africa 1960. This international program brought together a number of Robinson's causes: political independence in Africa, self-help solutions to political problems, the education of dispossessed youth, and civil rights for all.

June 9, 1960

Dear Mr. Vice President:

It was good to hear from you again and gratifying to know that we share a common interest in the struggle for civil rights for all American citizens. As you wrote, the question of race relations is no longer an American problem solely, but in harsh reality, a vital world problem as well. This is so not only because the Communists exploit our deficiencies, and not only because most of the people in the world are non-white, but also (and more importantly in my view) because of the moral leadership expected of the United States government and its people.

In this connection, I have been privileged to be associated with the African American Students Foundation, Inc., which in September 1959 brought to the United States 84 African students from Kenya to take up four year courses of study in 41 colleges and universities in the United States and Canada. The scholarships were primarily obtained through the efforts of our friend and colleague, The Hon. Tom Mboya of Kenya, during his tour here last year. The Foundation took responsibility for the execution of the program, as well as providing all transportation and many supplementary expenses. AIRLIFT AFRICA 1959 brought the largest number of African students ever brought here at one time under any program, including the official exchange program of the United States government. I am attaching herewith a list of the students and the institutions which they are attending.

The airlift of these students received considerable publicity; in fact, the Voice of America and the various U.S.I.A. offices so well publicized this event that we have ever since received literally thousands of requests from students throughout Africa for the same opportunity. This has both created a problem for us and given us an opportunity to be of service.

We have consulted with the outstanding African leaders in each of the countries of East and Central Africa where our program is concentrated—this area because it is still non-self-governing and the need for higher education the greatest. These leaders are Tom Mboya of Kenya, Julius Nyerere of Tanganyika, Abu Mayanja of Uganda, Dr. Hastings Banda of Nyasaland, Joshua Nkomo of Southern Rhodesia and Kenneth Kaunda of Northern Rhodesia. Each of them is the outstanding African nationalist leader in his own country; all of them are committed to democracy and are friends of the United States in particular. By happy coincidence, each of them has visited the United States within the past twelve-month period and has toured many of our leading colleges and universities.

These leaders have each individually, and together, decided to actively associate themselves with this program, and all have agreed to join our Board of Directors. To this end we have laid plans for AIRLIFT AFRICA 1960. Through the efforts of the Foundation, we have obtained firm scholarship offers from over 200 class number one American institutions of higher learning for African students from these six countries. We estimate there are about 250 scholarships offered worth, in the aggregate, over one million dollars. In addition, prior to coming to the United States, the students themselves, in cooperation with their leaders and the African public, will raise in excess of one hundred thousand dollars for pocket money and incidental expenses. (Last year the 84 students from Kenya brought with them about fifty thousand dollars—an amazing instance of self-help from an impoverished country.)

We propose that these students be brought here in three chartered airplanes in September of this year, to duplicate on a much larger scale last year's airlift. The problem that I wish specifically to raise with you is that because the Foundation's resources are so limited and we do not have the ability to provide the planes, can some transport be found for these students among the agencies of the United States Government? The African leaders have suggested an airlift of the U.S. Air Force planes to dramatize this airlift before the world. In my view, it might also be useful to dramatize this peaceful application of the use of our armed forces. If this is not possible, perhaps some funds can be found under the President's recently announced special aid program for Africa amounting to twenty million dollars "to be instituted for the improvement of education and training in Africa, south of the Sahara."

In any event, we think you will agree it is important in view of the unique opportunity afforded these students that some way be found to get them here so they will be able to take up these scholarships so generously offered. This September is a particularly propitious time because in the fall the Soviet Union will open a "University of Friendship of People" in Moscow for the free education of 4,000 African, Asian and Latin American students. Also, in September, Mr. Khrushchev is scheduled to make his first trip to Africa.

I would appreciate hearing from you on this to see if something can be worked out to bring these students here. I would be very happy to come to Washington, together with some of those associated with me on this program, to discuss details or answer specific questions.

Yours sincerely,
Jackie Robinson

RICHARD NIXON TO ROBINSON

Robinson stated in his June 10 column that he could "see no reason why Nixon should not be considered as seriously as anyone else. And when his actual record and position on the issues of the day are given due consideration, I predict that many of Nixon's critics will find themselves taking a second look before making up their minds." Nixon replies with gratitude and mentions meeting Dorothy Schiff, owner of the New York Post.

June 14, 1960

Dear Jackie:

This is just a note to tell you that I thought your column of June 10 in the *New York Post* hit the nail right on the head. I particularly liked your comment to the effect that—"For since Nixon's reply yesterday that he has spelled out his position more often and in greater detail than the other candidates—including Rockefeller—there is bound to be greater attention focused on just what Nixon's record is, rather than the many charges against him often based upon less than full information."

Incidentally, at the luncheon for Prince Philip at the Waldorf on June 10, Dorothy Schiff spoke to me very warmly about you and your column. She indicated that while some of those on the editorial board at the *Post* were somewhat distressed that your line was not the same as theirs with regard to me, she thought it was healthy and constructive for you to indicate an independent viewpoint in the paper she publishes.

I shall be looking forward to seeing you in Washington.

Sincerely,
Richard Nixon

ADAM CLAYTON POWELL, JR. TO ROBINSON

Adam Clayton Powell, Jr. criticizes Nixon's vote against legislation designed to establish a Fair Employment Practices Commission (FEPC) with full enforcement powers—a move favored by Powell because of its promise of increasing industrial training and skilled jobs for African Americans. The McConnell substitute bill, proposed by Representative Samuel McConnell, a Pennsylvania Republican, effectively stripped enforcement powers from the FEPC.

June 15, 1960

Dear Jackie:

I came across your column concerning Nixon and especially his letter to you. I am sending to you the Nixon voting record from the time he started in the Congress in 1947 and of course it is partisan coming from the Democratic National Committee, but at the same time, it is accurate.

There is one omission on March 7th, 1951. Nixon voted to kill the anti-lynching amendment to the Selective Service Act of 1951. This amendment would have provided federal protection for all members of the Armed Forces. There is no doubt that Nixon has grown, but at the same time, it is totally wrong of him to say that his record has been consistently good, because it has not.

I knew Nixon from the very first day I arrived in Congress because at that time, I was Chairman of the FEPC Committee of Congress with full power to pick my Committee. I picked Nixon as a freshman member of Congress to serve on my five men Committee. He voted against FEPC in the Subcommittee; he voted against FEPC in the full Committee; he voted against FEPC on the Floor and then voted to substitute the toothless McConnell-substitute bill. This is not hearsay; this is what I know.

This letter is not for publication and I would like a confidential reply from you after you have perused the enclosed memorandum.

With every good wish.

Sincerely,
Adam C. Powell

MARTIN LUTHER KING, JR. TO ROBINSON

June 19, 1960

My dear Friend Jackie:

This is to acknowledge receipt of your letter of May 5. First, I must apologize for being so tardy in my reply. Actually, the southern student movement, the court case in Montgomery, Alabama, and other pressing responsibilities have kept me out of my office almost consistently for the last two months. Therefore, I have been thrown almost hopelessly behind in my correspondence. Even when I am in a desperate attempt to play a game of catch up, something else emerges to hold me back. I am sure that you can understand this with all of your busy responsibilities.

I am deeply grateful to you for calling my attention to some maladjustments and unfortunate situations that have developed around fund raising for my defense. Frankly, I did not know about these things, and I would want to investigate them immediately. I would certainly not be a party to anything that would damage fund raising for all organizations in the future.

The only organization raising money for my defense is the Defense Committee which was formed in the home of Harry Belafonte the week after I was indicted in Alabama. As you know, this committee was set up to raise funds for a threefold purpose, namely, my defense, the student movement, and the voter registration drive of the Southern Christian Leadership Conference. Therefore, the committee had the joint name of "Committee to Defend Martin Luther King and the Struggle for Freedom in the South." The committee took on this threefold responsibility because of a strong appeal that I made the night of the forming of the committee. I tried to make it palpably clear that it was not enough to defend me because in the long run of history it does not matter whether Martin Luther King spends ten years in jail, but it does matter whether the student movement continues, and it does matter whether the Negro is able to get the ballot in the South. I made it clear that I would not be so selfish as to be concerned merely about my defense and not be concerned about the great creative causes that were taking place in the South. And so I said to them that it would not be enough to defend me and then let the organization die which is a projection of me and my personality. I also made the suggestion because I knew that I would be out of circulation for a while, and that I could not raise as much money for the Southern Christian Leadership Conference as I would ordinarily raise. Therefore, to keep things moving, I felt that it was absolutely imperative that funds be raised for this purpose. Fortunately, the persons present agreed with me. They set up the committee and went out to raise money for these three causes. As you know the committee has made appeals through ads in newspapers, direct mail order appeals, mass meetings, and benefit concerts. As far as I have been able to discern, this committee has operated on the highest level of honesty and integrity. There will be a public accounting of all the money that has been raised and spent in the next few days, and I am sure that the public will agree that it has handled the money properly. As you know, there are always those later problems of organizational differences and the fear on the part of some that something new is offering competition. But I hope no one will get this impression. I have said both publicly and privately that before I become a symbol of division in the Negro community I would retire from the civil rights struggle because I think the cause is too great and too important for a few individuals to halt things by engaging in minor ego battles.

Now to say just a word concerning the second question that you raised with reference to SCLC leaders making derogatory statements concerning the NAACP. I have always stressed the need for great cooperation between SCLC and the NAACP. I have made it clear in all of our board meetings and conference meetings that the NAACP is our chief civil rights organization, and that it has done more to achieve the civil rights of Negroes than any other organization. It, therefore, justifiably deserves our support and respect, and I have constantly said that any Negro who fails to give the NAACP this backing is nothing less than an ingrate. I have always felt that the SCLC could serve as a real supplement for the work of the NAACP, and not a substitute. In areas where the NAACP cannot operate the SCLC can. Also, with the number of ministerial leaders involved in SCLC it has an opportunity to get to the masses in order to mobilize mass action, and assist the NAACP in implementing its great program. So I have never seen any conflict between the two organizations. I only see the possibility of the greatest harmony. If there are those individuals who move under the name of SCLC and say derogatory things about the NAACP I can assure you that they do not speak for me or the organization. They are expressing individual positions which I cannot control. I absolutely agree with you that we cannot afford any division at this time and we cannot afford any conflict. And I can assure you that as long as I am President of SCLC it will not be a party to any development of disunity.

The days ahead are challenging indeed. The future has vast possibilities, and I am convinced that if we will gird our courage and move on in a sense of togetherness and goodwill we will be able to crush the sagging walls of segregation by the battering rams of the forces of justice. In my little way I am trying to help solve this problem. I have no Messiah complex, and I know that we need many leaders to do the job.

And I am convinced that with the leadership of integrity, humility, and dedication to the ideals of freedom and justice we will be able to bring into full realization the principles of our American Democracy. Please be assured that you can count on me to give my ultimate allegiance to the cause. Even if it means pushing myself into the background. I have been so concerned about unity and the ultimate victory that I have refused to fight back or even answer some of the unkind statements that I have been informed that NAACP officials said about me and the Southern Christian Leadership Conference. Frankly, I hear these statements every day, and I have seen efforts on the part of NAACP officials to sabotage our humble efforts. But I have never said anything about it publicly or to the press. I am sure that if criticisms were weighed it would turn out that persons associated with the NAACP have made much more damaging statements about SCLC than persons associated with SCLC have made concerning the NAACP. But I will not allow this to become an issue. The job ahead is too great, and the days are too bright to be bickering in the darkness of jealousy, deadening competition, and internal ego struggles.

I hope that I have in some way answered your very important questions. I am deeply grateful to you for your concern and interest, and always know that I, along with millions of Americans, are deeply indebted to you for your unswerving devotion to the cause of freedom and justice and your willingness at all times to champion the cause of the underdog.

With warm personal regards, I am

Sincerely yours,
Martin L. King, Jr.

ROBINSON TO MARTIN LUTHER KING, JR.

June 29, 1960

Dear Martin:

Thanks for a reassuring letter that really never should have been necessary. Because of a great concern I have of what appears to be a power struggle, I wanted you to know of my concern.

I think you know also I am greatly impressed with what you have done, and I am certain the only way to gain our real freedom is through organizations like the S.C.L.C. and the N.A.A.C.P. working together, and I assure you of my personal support. If people are able to divide the leadership of these two groups, the effectiveness is divided also. We must not allow criticism of any nature towards either organization, that is not deserved, go unannounced. Constructive criticism is good for organizations and individuals, and we should encourage that, but I feel the kind of working agreement you and Roy expressed regarding voting was one of the greatest unifying efforts we have presented. This, I pray, will continue, and if as I have said often, I can be of service, please call.

I respect sincerely your great efforts and hope God gives you strength to continue. You have been a true inspiration.

Sincerely yours,
Jackie Robinson

HUBERT HUMPHREY TO ROBINSON

July 1, 1960

Dear Jackie:

I hope you will forgive me for this unpardonable delay in writing to you following the campaign. I have been so far behind in my correspondence and so deeply involved in the work of the Senate these past few weeks that I simply have not had time to write all the letters I had wanted to. Yes, many letters went out, but the one for you I wanted to give my personal attention and to say just what was on my mind and in my heart.

I shall be ever grateful to you for your faith in me and your valiant and dedicated support. I am sure you realize the love and respect in which you are held by millions of Americans. You are a national hero in the truest sense of the word, and I am one of your fans. I believe in you. I respect you and I cherish your friendship.

I have no bitterness about the campaign. It is always difficult to lose, but sometimes there is a victory in defeat. I am sure that the remaining Democratic candidates are taking a firmer stand on the vital issues of our day. I know that we have educated them in the field of human rights.

What is more, our campaign efforts caused people to think—to think on the big issues and not just about personality and looks.

We are going to win this battle for full equal rights—for meaningful human rights. We are on the victory trail. The breakthrough has been made and the cause of human equality is surging forward. I am happy that I have had a little part in this. I have been mighty fortunate because in this struggle I have found a friend in you. Thanks for the precious gift of your friendship.

That's all for now, except to say that if I have any regret about the campaign it is only this—I will not have the privilege of standing side by side with you on the most important issue of all—human dignity, human rights, and respect for people.

With admiration,

Cordially,
Hubert H. Humphrey

JOHN KENNEDY TO ROBINSON

Shortly before the Democratic National Convention, Democratic leaders stepped up their efforts to enlist Robinson for the Kennedy team. Paul Butler, chair of the Democratic National Committee, invited Robinson to serve on the platform committee to be chaired by Chester Bowles, but Robinson declined. More significant, Bowles opened his Georgetown home on June 29 for a meeting between Robinson and Kennedy—a meeting that Bowles no doubt hoped would result in a shift in Robinson's assessment of Kennedy. Robinson reported on the meeting in his July 6 column, noting that the senator confessed to "limited experience" with African Americans, admitted past mistakes, and asked for additional time to prove himself in the field of civil rights. Robinson concluded: "Sen. Kennedy is an impressive man who makes an impressive point. While I still have reservations about his position, I believe he is sincere in admitting past misunderstandings and expressing his willingness to learn."

July 1, 1960

Dear Jackie:

It was good to see you at Chet Bowles' the other evening. I have long admired your contribution to the world of baseball and good American sportsmanship. Hearing your great personal concern about the denial of civil rights to American citizens by reason of their race or color and your dedication to the achievement of first-class citizenship for all Americans, I believe I understand and appreciate your role in the continuing struggle to fulfill the American promise of equal opportunity for all. I trust that you now understand better my own concern about this problem and my dedication to these same ideals. It is time for us to fulfill the promise of the Declaration of Independence—to make good the guarantee of the Constitution—to make equal opportunity a living reality in all parts of our public life.

I have said this on many occasions in the past and will of course continue to say it. I have called for an end to all discrimination—in voting, in education, in housing, in employment, in the administration of justice, and in public facilities including lunch counters. I have also spoken in favor of the right of peaceful protest, saying that the recent demonstrations have been in the American tradition of people standing up for their rights, even if the new way of standing up for one's rights is to sit down. You may be interested in the enclosed interview in *The Pittsburgh Courier* of June 25, 1960, which goes into detail on some of these points.

But saying these things is not enough. What is required now above all is effective, creative, persuasive Executive leadership. This is not just a matter of law and order. For great moral issues are involved.

You have questioned my talk over sixteen months ago with the Governor of Alabama and some members of his state cabinet. As I told you, any responsible person in my position must be ready to talk with the governor or leading public officials of every state. I suppose I have talked with most of the governors of our states in the last few years. That does not imply my agreement with them or their agreement with me on particular issues. In my one brief meeting with Governor Patterson civil rights was not discussed, but I am sure that he knows that we do not have similar views on this matter.

Needless to say, I have not made and will not make any commitments inconsistent with these essential American principles. As I have said, if anyone expects the next Democratic Administration to betray the cause of human rights, he can look elsewhere for leadership.

I hope to have the support of people of good will in every region in the campaign and in the next Democratic administration. Those who support me have a right to know where I stand on this and other vital matters, and I intend to continue to make my position clear so that all such support is given in the light of that knowledge.

I was happy to have the opportunity to discuss all this with you. With every good wish, I am

Sincerely yours,
John F. Kennedy

BILLIE FLEMING TO ROBINSON

Billie Fleming, president of the Manning branch of the NAACP in Clarendon County, South Carolina, thanks Robinson for pressuring Sealtest, a dairy company, to sell its goods to "our store." The following is the first half of a longer letter in which Fleming invites Robinson to speak at the Manning branch.

July 7, 1960

Dear Jackie:

I wish to take this opportunity to thank you for the telephone calls that you made to Sealtest on behalf of our store here in Manning. I am very happy to tell you that the telephone calls did the job. Sealtest has broken and they are now serving us with their products for our store. I am sure that you will agree that this was a great victory over the White Citizens Councils and those that tried to impede our progress. On behalf of all of us here, I wish to thank you for the part you played in helping us break this barrier. . . .

Yours very truly,
Billie S. Fleming

ROBINSON TO RICHARD NIXON

Joseph Satterthwaite, assistant secretary of state for African affairs, recommended that the State Department not fund the transportation costs that Robinson had addressed in his June 9 letter to Nixon. After receiving the following telegram, however, Nixon again lobbied for funding of the project, and in his August 17 column

Robinson wrote that a Nixon aide had called him with the good news that the State Department had decided to fund the transportation costs for three planeloads of African students. In the meantime, however, Sargent Shriver, John F. Kennedy's brother-in-law, had pledged $400,000 from the Kennedy Foundation—an offer quickly accepted by the African American Students Foundation. Robinson's attempt to increase the stature of Nixon among African American voters—by publicizing his extra efforts to fund the African students—thereby failed, and Kennedy earned public praise for fully funding the airlift project.

July 11, 1960

May I convey my grave disappointment and dissatisfaction with Mr. Satterthwaite's letter of reply of July 7 regarding State Department assistance in transportation of students from East and Central Africa holding scholarships in this country. Am sure you well understand vital need of our African friends to witness concrete demonstration of American interest. This project particularly crucial inasmuch as over one million dollars in scholarships plus supplementary assistance raised by African people themselves, all at no cost to the United States government, will be lost unless transport to America can be arranged. Especially are we concerned with emergency of stable African leadership educated in democracy. This is responsibility not only of private citizens but of federal government. Believe urgent national importance of project AIRLIFT AFRICA 1960 deserves same high priority as when hundreds of Hungarian students flown to America during revolt there. For first time America Negro leaders are demanding program of government support for African education, independence and economic growth before platform committees of both parties. Dr. Martin Luther King, Jr. and A. Philip Randolph will be in Chicago to press for such a program as they are now doing in Los Angeles. A bold State Department role in providing transportation for the 250 students would be inestimable contribution to growth of democracy in Africa as well as tangible evidence of Administration's dedication to civil rights since American Negroes regard such a program as paramount issue. In this year of political consciousness millions will see in the determination of this issue an index of future domestic and international policies. We must not wait until it is too late in these seven African countries as we did in Guinea and now in the Congo. Because of urgency of this matter I request you to meet with me or my representative to clarify your position. Fully aware of your difficult schedule, I nonetheless do not hesitate to raise again this crucial matter for your responses.

Presidential candidate will reveal manner in which overall problem will be met. Under these circumstances I am confident that you will welcome opportunity to use prestige and goodwill of your office to urge State Department or other agency to allocate funds for transportation of students. Hope to have your prompt reply since the seven African leaders and American Negro leaders committed to this program are pressing me for action in this situation. We see no possibility of placing additional financial burdens on friends of the Negro who have already contributed copiously to freedom struggle in the South.

Jackie Robinson

HUGH SCOTT TO ROBINSON

Senator Hugh Scott of Pennsylvania assumes the role of Republican counterpart to Chester Bowles. Scott lobbies Robinson at the time of the Democratic National Convention, paying special attention to problems caused by "Southern Democrat obstructionists"—an issue that became all the more pronounced when Kennedy selected Senator Lyndon Johnson of Texas as his running mate. In his July 15 column Robinson referred to Johnson as a "proven segregationist" and characterized the vice-presidential nomination as "a bid for the appeasement of Southern bigots—just as the Patterson breakfast, the vote with the Southerners to send the 1957 civil rights bill to die with Eastland's committee, and a long list of other Kennedy actions have been." Robinson continued to rant against Kennedy in his July 18 column, calling him "a cold, calculating political machine," and arguing that the Johnson nomination simply confirmed "that Kennedy has no scruples in compromising with Southern bigotry in order to insure Southern votes."

July 12, 1960

Dear Jackie:

With regard to "Airlift Africa," I have taken this up with Jim Bassett and with Bob Finch in the Nixon office and they are both very much in agreement that transportation should be furnished; and Bob Finch has promised me to do everything possible to see whether or not some way can be found to have the United States Government take care of the airlift of the 300 scholarship students. I, personally, think it is a fine idea and I am sure you will shortly be hearing from Bob Finch.

We talked about the Democratic Committee system and statements made by some Democrats that Republicans could not possibly be effective because the chairmanship of the committees is under Southern Democrats. This is not only a phony argument but entirely hypocritical, since it is the majority of the Democrats—that is the Northern Democrats—who support the committee system and have made no effort to change the seniority system at all. And, as a result, a Democratic Congress always has Southern Democrats as chairmen of the major committees who hold their position by seniority.

If the Congress were Republican, not a single Southern Democrat would head any committee in either the House or the Senate. Moreover, even if the Congress remained Democratic with a Republican President, it should be remembered that a great majority of the Republicans—usually better than 90 percent—vote for Civil Rights Bills and similar measures; whereas only 50 percent of the Democrats support them.

Moreover, it is the Republican Members of the Judiciary Committee of the Senate and of the House who have consistently taken the lead in trying to get Civil Rights actions reported out of these Committees. Moreover, the Democrats could, if they wished, secure action on any desired measure in the House by securing a majority of the Members of the House, 218 (the Democrats have 253 Members) on a discharge petition and you could bypass the Rules Committee.

But the Democratic leadership of the House—Rayburn and McCormack—do not favor permitting a majority of the Members to use the discharge petition as a general thing.

The Democratic leadership of the Senate could do the same thing by calling up a bill from the House and taking it off the Calendar before referring it to a committee, thus preventing it from being bottled up, and demanding immediate consideration on the Floor.

Therefore, this whole nonsense about ineffectiveness of Republicans is completely without merit. It is, in fact, the Democrats who have refused to use either the discharge system in the House or the use of a House Bill or a rider on a pending Senate Bill as a means of getting out worthwhile legislation.

I never had heard this particular and thoroughly tricky argument until you told me about it, because I did think that everybody knew that it is solely the fault of the Democrats that we have Southern Democrat obstructionists as Committee Chairmen in both Houses of Congress.

You spoke about the desirability of having more accreditation for negro newspapers at the Republican Convention. I believe we discussed the fact that daily papers have less problems here, but that most negro newspapers are weeklies and this operates, in itself, to discriminate against them. Nevertheless the Vice President and I both agree with you that there should be greater accreditation for these negro journalists; and I have referred this to Mr. Gulay, who is in charge of public relations for the National Committee. I am sending copies of this letter to Bob Finch and to Lou Gulay. The Vice President is particularly anxious on this matter, and I would expect that something will be done.

Now, as to Jack Kennedy's voting record, which we also discussed, I am enclosing a copy of some of the major bills which he did not vote on. Perhaps we should call it a non-voting record, since he appeared and voted on only 41 votes out of a total of 170; and did not vote on 129 measures or amendments which represents 76 percent of the Senate's business.

Of course, his record is even worse because he missed many more quorum calls. . . .

I call your attention on the copy to the fact that Kennedy missed 27 out of 36 votes on amendments and on the passage of the Civil Rights Bill during the debate. Actually, his record is a good deal worse than this, because he missed most of the more than 100 calls of the Senate during the Civil Rights debate, which includes quorum calls as well as votes.

As a matter of fact, there were 56 opportunities for him to answer the quorum call or to vote occurring during the night sessions. During all of the time when most of us stayed up practically all night, or slept fitfully on our cots, Jack Kennedy appeared for only 2 out of the 56 votes; did not even speak on the Civil Rights measure; but made a speech that night on foreign affairs, following which, after he had answered 2 roll calls on Civil Rights, he returned home and missed 4 more which occurred that night.

One of the pages in the cloakroom reported that Senator Kennedy had left a message that, after he went home, he did not want to be awakened and brought back to the Senate for any more votes. As you know, Senator Kennedy has, on other occasions, voted against Title III, the injunctive power of the Civil Rights Bill which was introduced and supported by Senator Javits, Senator Keating and myself and many others. . . .

The whole problem with Senator Kennedy has been that he does not take his responsibilities seriously, especially when his own ambition intervenes. . . .

I do hope this answers some of the questions in your mind. It was a grand opportunity for me to get acquainted with you, and I do wish you the best of everything.

Cordially,
Hugh Scott

RICHARD NIXON TO ROBINSON

Following the Republican National Convention, Robinson praised Nixon for committing himself to a pro–civil rights platform and to a racially progressive running mate, UN ambassador Henry Cabot Lodge, Jr., and in early September Robinson requested—and was granted—a leave of absence from Chock Full O' Nuts so that he could campaign full-time for Nixon. The Post *reported in its September 7 issue that "Jackie Robinson is on leave of absence from the* Post *while serving in Vice President Nixon's campaign organization." While stumping for Nixon, Robinson frequently felt that the campaign ignored or dismissed opportunities to reach out to African American voters. He criticized the team, for instance, when it avoided Harlem during a campaign swing through New York. Perhaps his greatest disappointment, however, occurred in October when Nixon refused to telephone Martin Luther King, Jr., who was just beginning to serve a sentence of four months of hard labor at Reidsville State Prison, Georgia. Robinson pleaded with Nixon at that point, but the candidate stated that telephoning the imprisoned civil rights leader would be "grandstanding." By contrast, John Kennedy telephoned Coretta Scott King, and Robert Kennedy intervened with a local judge to secure King's release. In response, Martin Luther King, Sr., the civil rights leader's father, publicly stated that he would vote for John F. Kennedy.*

November 4, 1960

Dear Jackie:

In the last several weeks of the campaign, I have several times come into cities shortly after you have been there. Without exception, there have been a great many compliments on the appearances you have made and there is no question but that you are making an enormous contribution to our common cause.

Having just made my final swing into the South and the Southwest, I am particularly pleased to add to the report I gave you when we chatted last in New York. In almost every southern state in which I have spoken, including South Carolina this week, I have made it clear where I stand on the need for equality under law for all of our citizens. As I told you before, the fact that these remarks have been greeted with applause must be recognized as solid evidence of the progress we are making nationally in the civil rights field.

I am advised that my office in Washington has had a number of inquiries asking why I did not intervene in the Martin Luther King case. I know that some of these inquiries were prompted by the well known fact that I have frequently counseled with Dr. King and have a great respect for him. It is easy for one who is not in the Administration to make what our good friend, Joe Louis, called a "grandstand play" but you and I know that real progress in the civil rights field is best advanced by the day to day, consistent application of the principles which we know are sound.

I, of course, have no way of knowing what the outcome will be on the election. Our people seem confident and I have attempted to state our case accurately and positively. Whatever the result, I do want you to know that your voluntary campaigning on my behalf has meant a great deal to both Pat and myself and she joins me in sending our warmest regards to you.

Sincerely,
Richard Nixon

JAMES WECHSLER TO ROBINSON

In an August 29 letter to Robinson, Dorothy Schiff, owner of the New York Post, *chided Robinson for being dishonest with the newspaper's readers, especially because he had failed to report his knowledge that the Kennedy Foundation had bested Nixon in sponsoring the African students bound for the United States. And here James Wechsler, editor of the* New York Post, *explains his reasons for not resuming Robinson's column following the 1960 presidential election. Wechsler was a strong advocate of Robinson's civil rights work, but as a professional editor, he was also disappointed with the quality of the column. Like Schiff, Wechsler felt that Robinson's pro-Nixon sentiments had led to unfair reporting during the 1960 campaign. The editor also believed that William Branch's writing did not clearly reflect Robinson's personality.*

November 8, 1960

Dear Jackie:

This letter is being written on Election Day, some hours before any returns are in. I make the point simply to emphasize that it is in no way influenced by the outcome, whatever that may prove to be.

Obviously, the question of a resumption of your column now confronts us. After a great deal of reflection, it is our considered decision that we do not want to resume it. This was neither an easy nor pleasant decision and, as one who worked closely with you on the project, I feel especially unhappy about the failure of the effort. But I cannot in good conscience urge an extension of it.

I would be less than frank if I denied that the incidents surrounding your enlistment on the Nixon team were irrelevant to this decision. Obviously, it is important that a newspaper have complete confidence in its columnists, whether it agrees with them or not, and the fact that the first news of your decision came to the paper via a query from the *Times* to the publisher's office was a painful development. Reviewing your handling of the story of the African student loan, we cannot escape the feeling that partisanship played a larger role than journalism in your handling of it. I have never felt that newspaper writers should be non-combatants in political affairs but, when they do become involved, it seems to me especially important that what they write be factually unassailable.

I suppose I should also add that your sudden appearance in the *Citizen-Call*, again without any advance discussion with us, aggravated the distress we felt about the earlier episodes.

However, above and beyond all these considerations is a larger one for which you are in no way to blame. We have always had the feeling here that it is unwise to have a "ghosted" column. In a sense we violated that rule in your case. I do not mean to suggest that you were not a full participant in the preparation of the column or that it reflected any ideas other than your own. But it is also true, in my judgment, that your personality never came through precisely because your views and attitudes were filtered through another writer. You know that there were times in our relationship when I did express some uneasiness about the tone of the column; what we were really getting, it seems to me, was your general outlook and Bill Branch's rhetoric. Again, I do not want to disparage Bill whose writing talents may be very great.

As I said at the outset, this is not an easy letter to write. My personal association with you has been extremely pleasant and I should like to think that, whatever feelings you may have about this decision, we are friends. I think I have deeply appreciated the passion of your feelings on the civil rights issue, and I hope you know the intensity of my convictions in that area. But the simple truth is that the column project did not work, and I think it is better for all of us to face that fact than to evade it. Best regards.

Sincerely,
Jimmy Wechsler

ROBINSON TO NELSON ROCKEFELLER

"And speaking of Rockefeller," Robinson had stated in his July 29 column, "I really must take my hat off to the governor." Robinson was pleased with the New York governor's leadership at the Republican National Convention in passing a civil rights platform that pledged support for school desegregation, voting rights, desegregation in federally financed housing, and the creation of the Commission on Equal Job Opportunity.

November 15, 1960

My dear Governor Rockefeller:

It was good seeing you at the Marian Anderson luncheon, and I was most happy to know of your efforts to get President Eisenhower and Mr. Nixon to do something in the King case and in Negro areas. It should be obvious now that unless there is something unusual, the South is not going Republican regardless of the candidate and his effort.

While I don't believe your situation is anything like Mr. Nixon's, may I suggest careful consideration by you immediately in Negro areas. Your family name is magic, but the lopsided Kennedy victory in New York City should be given careful study.

Please do not think me presumptuous because of this letter, but I can't help but feel that an effort must be made now if we are to make progress in breaking into what appears to be a solid bloc among the Negro for the Democrats.

I would like, at some time, to sit down with your representative and discuss possible ways of making gains.

Sincerely,
Jackie Robinson

ROBINSON TO ALBERT HERMANN

Albert Hermann, campaign director of the Republican National Committee, thanked Robinson in a November 14 letter "for the magnificent contribution which you have made to our cause." Robinson's reply, transcribed here from handwriting in the margins of Hermann's letter, includes an offer to help the Republicans reach out to African American voters. Hermann thanked Robinson again in a November 23 letter, adding, "Personally, it is my judgment that you could be a 'Messiah' for the Republican Party in the days ahead!"

November 18, 1960

Dear Ab,

Thanks for all you have done. I was terribly disappointed over the election and feel we are at a great loss. I can only hope that Kennedy will prove to be a good president but know we can't hope for that when we look at his past performances.

I cannot help but feel we must work for a two party system as far as the Negro is concerned. There has been a lack of interest as far as the Negro and the Republican Party is concerned, and also the party and the Negro. There are a great number of young aggressive Negroes who feel as I do and I believe we could do a good job if we were given help. Clay and I, along with a great number of young fellows in the cities we visited, would with cooperation make real progress. It would be foolish to wait because there is much to be done.

If you think the idea a sound one let's get together at a time mutually convenient and talk about it. My work with Clay and others in your party has been very rewarding. I feel although we lost the election a great deal was learned and we won't make the same mistakes again. It's pretty obvious to me the biggest mistake was the effort in the South and only a token effort in the Negro area. The southern Dems are too well organized and the Negro is pretty fed up with it, but felt Mr. Nixon's silence in the King situation was too much. Please let me know if you feel we should work now.

Robinson's December 8 letter to Humphrey apparently laid out his concerns about the new Kennedy administration.

December 21, 1960

Dear Jackie:

I was so pleased to receive your letter of December 8. I trust that now you are feeling a little bit better about the cabinet of the new administration. With men like Arthur Goldberg, Governor Freeman, Congressman Udall, and some others, this cabinet will at least have a liberal flavor.

I had a long talk with President-elect Kennedy about two weeks ago. He intends to take forceful and effective action in the field of Civil Rights. Much of this will be done by executive action, but he also intends to submit a strong legislative program for the end of this session of Congress.

May I assure you that your trust in me will not be violated or misplaced. I will keep my word on not only the Civil Rights issue but on all others. My respect for you is sincere and great. Under no circumstances would I ever try to deceive you or in any way knowingly fail to keep my commitments.

Again, my everlasting thanks to you for your friendship, faith, and confidence. It has been a unique privilege in my life to have known you and worked with you. Thanks for all that you have done in my behalf. But more importantly, thanks for what you are doing for America—for people—for this world. My greetings to your charming wife.

As ever, your friend.

Sincerely,
Hubert H. Humphrey

P.S. When you are in Washington be sure to call on me. I want to see you anytime you are in the city.

6

WRONG ABOUT KENNEDY?

· 1961 ·

ROBINSON TO RICHARD NIXON

On the night of January 17, when Eisenhower delivered his famous farewell address warning against the dangers of the military-industrial complex, Nixon hosted a dinner for his closest supporters, including Jackie Robinson. Although not an enthusiastic Nixon supporter, Rachel accompanied her husband to the dinner.

January 18, 1961

My dear Mr. Nixon:

Last night's dinner was one of the highlights of my life. What happened there convinced me more than ever that I supported the right man.

My wife and I will be forever grateful to you for what you stand for and what you have meant to our country. You demonstrated again last night, as far as I am concerned, the kind of man I would like to see as our President. I hope I am wrong in my appraisal of President-elect Kennedy but cannot help but feel our country is the loser, not you.

You said for me not to be discouraged. May I say I was so encouraged by the affair and of the sincerity of all your friends that I feel confident the future is very bright, for I feel you will be back stronger than ever and our country will continue its great growth. It has been an honor and privilege to have known and worked for you. I hope to be able to do so again.

Please express our sincere appreciation to Mrs. Nixon for the invitation. It was a warm and wonderful affair, one that will be long remembered by Rachel and me.

Sincerely yours,
Jackie Robinson

RICHARD NIXON TO ROBINSON

January 19, 1961

Dear Jackie:

Before my term of office as Vice President comes to a close, I want to take this opportunity to tell you how much I appreciated your support in the campaign.

Losing the election was naturally a disappointment from a personal standpoint, but I shall always be proud of the fact that I was privileged to have your friendship and support. I only regret that my efforts could not have been just that extra bit more effective which would have brought victory for those who worked so hard for our cause.

As soon as I have made a final decision with regard to my plans for the future, I shall take the liberty of letting you know where I will be and what I will be doing. I hope we can continue to keep in touch with each other, and I would particularly appreciate it if you will write me whenever you have any suggestions as to how we can better further the cause for which we worked in this campaign.

In the meantime, I want to take this opportunity to extend my very best wishes for the New Year.

Sincerely,
Richard Nixon

ROBINSON TO JOHN KENNEDY

After the campaign, Kennedy hinted at future pro–civil rights actions by offering Louis Martin, editor of the Chicago Daily Defender, *the position of deputy chair at the Democratic National Committee, and on February 8 the new president appointed Harris Wofford as the White House staff member in charge of civil rights issues—a position that had not been filled since 1958.*

February 9, 1961

My dear Mr. President:

I believe I now understand and appreciate better your role in the continuing struggle to fulfill the American promise of equal opportunity for all.

While I am very happy over your obviously fine start as our President, my concern over Civil Rights and my vigorous opposition to your election is one of sincerity. The direction you seem to be going indicates America is in for great leadership, and I will be most happy if my fears continue to be proven wrong. We are naturally keeping a wondering eye on what will happen, and while any opposition or criticism may not be the most popular thing when you are leading so well, you must know that as an individual I am interested because what you do or do not do in the next 4 years could have a serious effect upon my children's future.

In your letter to me of July 1, 1960, you indicated you would use the influence of the White House in cases where moral issues are involved. You have reiterated your stand, and we are very happy. Still, we are going to use whatever voice we have to awaken our people. With the new emerging African nations, Negro Americans must assert themselves more, not for what we can get as individuals, but for the good of the Negro masses.

I thank you for what you have done so far, but it is not how much has been done but how much more there is to do. I would like to be patient, Mr. President, but patience has caused us years in our struggle for human dignity. I will continue to hope and pray for your aggressive leadership but will not refuse to criticize if the feeling persists that Civil Rights is not on the agenda for months to come.

May God give you strength and the energy to accomplish your most difficult task.

Respectfully yours,
Jackie Robinson

ROBINSON TO RICHARD NIXON

Robinson sent Nixon twenty-four pounds of Chock Full O' Nuts coffee and inadvertently stuck him with storage and delivery charges totaling almost ten dollars.

March 3, 1961

Dear Mr. Nixon:

The "Right Hand of Lincoln" plaque is one I will cherish for years to come. It was an honor to have received it and a pleasure to have been able to work for you.

While we lost, I have no doubt that I supported the best man. For the sake of the country, I hope President Kennedy's program brings us all the things I felt you would have given us.

My wife and I have discussed often the dinner you gave. The esteem in which you are held adds greatly to our admiration for you and Mrs. Nixon. We can only hope the best happens in the future.

Under separate cover, I am sending you some of our coffee. It's not on the market in California. Because I feel you are deserving of the best, I would like for you to have the best coffee (smile).

Again, our thanks.

Sincerely yours,
Jackie Robinson

HUBERT HUMPHREY TO ROBINSON

April 20, 1961

Dear Jackie:

Just a note to say how much I appreciated receiving your letter. I am glad to know that you are encouraged over the work that this Administration has been doing. Your kind remarks are very much appreciated. I only hope I continue to merit your support. Be assured I will strive with that end in mind. These are exciting days down here. Being Majority Whip is quite a responsibility. It keeps me hopping but it is a very satisfying experience. I conveyed your good wishes to Muriel and the children. Say hello to your good wife.

Best wishes.

Sincerely yours,
Hubert H. Humphrey

ROBINSON TO ROBERT KENNEDY

This is a May 11 article written by Peter Lisagor, Washington bureau chief of the Chicago Daily News. *Lisagor reports on a letter that Robinson sent on*

May 8, just after the attorney general had delivered a major civil rights speech at the University of Georgia. Robert Kennedy had pledged that when confronted with civil rights violations, "We will not stand by and be aloof. We will move."

May 11, 1961

Jackie Robinson, the former baseball star who campaigned for Republican presidential candidate Richard Nixon, has changed his mind about the Kennedy boys.

He has written a letter of thanks to Atty. Gen. Robert F. Kennedy for his speech at the University of Georgia on May 6, in which he pledged strict enforcement of civil rights laws.

Robinson wrote that he had "grave doubts about your sincerity" before the election.

"I find it a pleasure to be proven wrong," he said. "May you continue to give your demonstrated leadership, which is so necessary at this time."

Robinson called Kennedy's speech "most encouraging" and said that the Attorney General's attitude "tends to increase our prestige in the world."

The Negro business executive, personnel director of a New York restaurant chain, disclosed in a telephone interview that he had sent the letter. A spokesman in the Attorney General's office later acknowledged receipt of it.

Robinson said in the interview that he "was not a Republican," but supported Nixon because of his civil rights position.

He said he had been concerned by Democratic candidate Kennedy's remark "to my face" that he "didn't know the Negro." Since he became President, Robinson added, Kennedy has shown that he is in fact aware of Negro problems and rights.

"They've said so many wonderful things," he added, "but we've been hearing that for a long time. Now we're waiting to see if there is going to be a follow through."

A spokesman at the Justice Department said that the Attorney General's speech at Athens, Ga., had brought a "fair amount" of letters and telegrams, most of them complimentary. A few were bitterly critical and even derogatory, he added.

One response from Louisiana likened Kennedy to Pontius Pilate. Another compared the speech to Lincoln's Gettysburg Address. A New York high school teacher said that every student should read it and asked for 40 copies for her class.

The Rev. Martin Luther King, Jr. said that the Attorney General, like no other in history, "has probed the deep meaning of the struggle of democracy to perfect itself."

A Southerner said that while he didn't agree with everything the Attorney General said, it was better that he said it in Georgia than in New York, Detroit, or some other Northern city.

ROBINSON TO CAROLINE WALLERSTEIN

In a prior letter, Caroline Wallerstein suggested that Robinson was becoming an advocate of the Kennedys, but here Robinson criticizes the president for not setting forth civil rights legislation, especially in response to the May 14 beatings of Freedom Riders just outside Anniston, Alabama. On that day a mob of white segregationists attacked an interracial group of thirteen activists who were riding a bus throughout the South to test implementation of a Supreme Court decision that allowed for the desegregation of buses on interstate roads.

May 16, 1961

Dear Caroline,

Not so fast . . . I have not by any means "seen the light." I just feel when anyone does the right thing it must be recognized. I must admit I have been surprised at the statement the administration has made but am still waiting for action. It's so easy to say we will do certain things. The things that count are how we follow up our words. Pres. Kennedy has given moral leadership but runs when someone suggests he support legislative action. He says none is needed at this time. I submit the beatings the CORE members took in Alabama are proof enough how much legislation is needed. You must know my only interest is the elimination of discrimination. If I honestly felt Kennedy would do more than Nixon I would have supported him. I had grave doubts. Some have been eliminated but until he takes a firm stand on legislative action one must wonder.

. . .

I personally have been thrilled at what has been happening to me. My work at "Chock" is coming along real well. Our stock is acting just right and everyone seems happy. We should be expanding rapidly soon, which should make Chock that much better.

Well, I imagine baseball is taking about all the leisure time you have. I can't get worked up at all over the game. I believe it's primarily because I feel the people connected with the game are such little people. It's bad to say all, and I know there are some very good people connected; however, a bad experience spoils it all.

Don't give up on us. We think of you often and hope when you are in you will call. We will do likewise. Regards to Dave. I hope everything continues to go well.

Love,
Jack

ROBINSON TO ROBERT KENNEDY

Just days before Robinson wrote this letter to the attorney general, President Kennedy had arranged for the Alabama National Guard, the Alabama State Police, the FBI, and the U.S. Border Patrol to provide protection for the Freedom Riders as they traveled by bus through Alabama.

May 25, 1961

My dear Mr. Attorney General:

Many thanks to you for your very kind answer to my letter of May 8th. While I did not anticipate that my previous letter would get the attention it received, I am pleased that my present position is known to all who read it.

You are doing a capital job, and we applaud you.

Because I have no personal ax to grind, I can express my true feelings. I feel that until more Negroes are willing to sacrifice ease and comfort, we will continue to suffer. You can depend upon my expressing my views. I do not pretend to be an expert, but my views will be voiced.

As you know, I had complete confidence in your predecessor. However, your few months in office have been a real source of inspiration. I can only hope that you are allowed to continue your drive for equality among Americans. There can be no denying that your definite action is responsible for worldwide approval. Everywhere, at home and abroad, your department, under your dynamic leadership, shows that it means business.

You have earned our respect. We are proud of the job you are doing. With kindest personal regards I am

Yours most sincerely,
Jackie Robinson

ROBINSON TO RICHARD NIXON

The May 25 issue of Jet *reported on Nixon's recent statement that the Republican Party was "just stupid" in its dealings with African American voters and that the party should stop acting like "an exclusive social club." Nixon had called for the recruitment of African American candidates for the 1962 elections and added that "the difficulty with Republicans is that they have been too far apart from Negroes as individuals."*

May 25, 1961

Dear Mr. Nixon:

May I say how pleased I was to read your statement in *Jet Magazine* last week.

I am afraid that unless some concrete action is taken right away, winning back some of the Negro vote will be a difficult if not an impossible task. Events that are happening in the South today are a disgrace to our country. A firm stand could help.

I am pleased the coffee arrived.

May I say that I have no regrets about my support during the campaign. I did so because I believed. I thought we ran a poor campaign, but nevertheless I feel I supported the right man. No amount of criticism will change that feeling.

Continued good luck.

Sincerely,
Jackie Robinson

ROBINSON TO JAMES EASTLAND

Senator James Eastland of Mississippi, an avowed segregationist and chair of the Senate Judiciary Committee, claimed that the Freedom Riders were part of the communist movement in the United States.

June 1, 1961

Sir:

Your recent attempt to smear the work of the Freedom Riders by using the tactics of shouting "Communist" is ridiculous and despicable.

Long before the Communist Party was given any recognition in this country, Negroes were stirred up. I submit we will be stirred up long after the Party has been dissolved unless prejudice and discrimination has dissolved also. Why leave the impression with Communist Nations that the Party has any influence in the Negro community? We have demonstrated our faith in America, and we will win our rights without the Communist.

Why should you make it more difficult to win the new, emerging Nations by resorting to such untruths?

Your individual prejudices are of no concern to us, but being a representative and spokesman for one of the highest bodies in the land does concern us. Why not use your influence at least to the point of being an honest Senator?

It is statements like yours that give courage and inspiration to the mobs in the South and the loss of American prestige abroad.

Very truly yours,
Jackie Robinson

ROBERT KENNEDY TO ROBINSON

June 2, 1961

Dear Jackie,

Thank you for your letter.

Once again, I appreciate the sentiments you express. It is going to be a long struggle but I am certain we will make a great deal of progress.

If you are ever in Washington, I hope you will stop in to say hello.

Sincerely,
Robert F. Kennedy

RICHARD NIXON TO ROBINSON

June 5, 1961

Dear Jackie:

It was thoughtful of you to write as you did on May 25. I agree with your analysis of trends among Negro voters and I hope that I can give some constructive leadership to Republicans on this issue in the months ahead.

May I tell you again how much we are enjoying the coffee. We have a percolator right in our office and I usually end up having half a dozen cups of coffee a day! This particularly comes in handy since I seldom go out to lunch and usually have a sandwich at my desk with coffee.

Pat joins me in sending our best wishes to you and Mrs. Robinson.

Sincerely,
Dick Nixon

HUBERT HUMPHREY TO ROBINSON

June 19, 1961

Dear Jackie:

Just a note in reply to your recent letter expressing the hope that the President will take a most firm stand on civil rights here at home.

I am convinced, Jackie, that the President will do everything in his power along these lines. He is vitally concerned about freedom, not only abroad, but also here in the United States. What he has been doing and what his brother, the Attorney General, has been doing seems to me a living proof of their devotion to civil rights and civil liberties for all of our citizens. I am convinced that you are going to be very pleased at the President's record in the White House. I see him every week at our legislative breakfasts and I can assure you that he is doing his very best to live up to the Democratic Party's platform commitments in the area of civil rights.

Best wishes.

Sincerely yours,
Hubert H. Humphrey

ROBINSON TO EVERETT HUTCHINSON

As the Freedom Riders continued their campaign, Robinson pressures Everett Hutchinson, chair of the Interstate Commerce Commission, to ban racial segregation and discrimination on all interstate buses.

June 21, 1961

Dear Sir:

The Attorney General's continued plea that a cooling off period take place between the Freedom Riders and some Southern states makes it mandatory, it seems to me, that you issue the proper directive in removing segregation and discrimination from bus transportation.

We are in a constant struggle for the support of the free world. It is our actions that will count, not words. A proper decision from your Commission would prove very effective in combating Communism.

We urge you to take immediate action.

Very truly yours,
Jackie Robinson

JOHN KENNEDY TO ROBINSON

In August Robinson attended a State Department meeting about improving the recruitment of African Americans, and at that point he appeared "in high spirits about the Administration," according to a September 5 memo drafted by Harris Wofford. The following is President Kennedy's reply to a positive letter that Robinson sent just after his trip to Washington. Though short, this letter, coupled with Robinson's appearance at the State Department meeting, suggests a change in his relationship with Kennedy.

September 6, 1961

Dear Mr. Robinson:

Thank you very much for your letter.

The discussion with the citizens group, of which you were a member, was most helpful to us in developing further steps in insuring equal employment in the Foreign Service.

I am most appreciative to you for having given us your time and cooperation in this most important work.

With kind regards, I am

Sincerely,
John F. Kennedy

RICHARD NIXON TO ROBINSON

Ever the politician, Nixon stays in touch.

November 8, 1961

Dear Jackie:

As I looked at my desk calendar this morning, it seemed hardly possible that a year had gone by since our campaign of 1960 came to a close.

I would not want this day to pass without taking the opportunity to tell you again how deeply grateful I am for all that you did for our cause. No candidate for the Presidency could have had a more dedicated and loyal group of supporters.

Pat joins me in sending our best wishes.

Sincerely,
Dick Nixon

ROBINSON TO NELSON ROCKEFELLER

In two prior letters Robinson offered to help shore up African American votes for Rockefeller's 1962 gubernatorial campaign. Robinson offers his assistance yet again and commends Rockefeller's November 1961 appointment of George Fowler to the State Commission Against Discrimination.

December 7, 1961

My dear Governor Rockefeller:

Because of my growing admiration for you I sincerely hope I can be of assistance. Of all the men I have met in the political field, you offer the greatest potential for the things that will make America the country we all want it to be. It is a big job, but with your leadership and a determined effort to erase the image the Republican Party has among the Negro, it is not an impossible one. The appointment of George Fowler is a step in the right direction, but investigation shows that much more is needed.

I repeat, I hope I can be of service. You are our biggest asset.

Respectfully,
Jackie Robinson

ROBINSON TO RICHARD NIXON

In a November 1961 speech to southern Republican leaders in Atlanta, Senator Barry Goldwater of Arizona stated, "We're not going to get the Negro vote as a bloc in 1964 and 1968, so we ought to go hunting where the ducks are." Robinson criticizes this approach and advises Nixon to seek the African American vote in his 1962 gubernatorial campaign in California.

December 8, 1961

Dear Mr. Nixon:

Your letter of November 8th was a welcomed surprise. I appreciate your thoughtfulness in sending it.

I do not want to belabor a point, Mr. Nixon, but I feel it is a shame that dedicated men lose out because of the image the Republican Party has. The statement by Senator Goldwater, a few days ago in Atlanta, will be Republican policy until someone other than Goldwater vigorously denies that the Republican Party is not interested in the Negro vote. Goldwater, if he is able to be the spokesman for the Party, will cause the Negro to support the Democratic Party even more. I have been doing some research to find reasons for the overwhelming Negro vote for the Democrats. It all adds to the apathy toward the Negro by the Party. Generally speaking, the Negro vote is the balance of power. Unless a concerted drive is started now, 1962 doesn't look too promising. It is difficult to defend against a record that is there for all to see.

In working for you during the Presidential election, I came to trust and respect you. I was disappointed your advisors felt it wise to practically ignore the Negro and am positive this cost the election. The growing Negro population in California cannot be ignored during your drive for the top spot there.

Yours is a most difficult task in the Negro area. The picture your opposition has painted makes your job that much more difficult but not an impossible one. This is not only true of you as an individual but also as a member of the Republican Party. Most Negroes feel that the Republican Party is not interested in their problem and only a good public relation effort can change that image.

I hope, Mr. Nixon, that you understand that I am writing in this manner because I sincerely believe men of your ability and integrity should get better support in all areas. Until this is done, the chances of equal opportunity are lessened.

Again, many thanks for your nice letter.

Sincerely,
Jackie Robinson

7

FROM THE HALL OF FAME TO HALLOWED ASHES

· 1962 ·

BILL WHITE TO ROBINSON

On January 15 Robinson invited a host of celebrities—including Willie Mays, Sarah Vaughan, Hank Aaron, Diahann Carroll, Bill Russell, Della Reese, and Curt Flood—to join him for an NAACP rally in Jackson, Mississippi, where Medgar Evers was the local field secretary. Bill White, first baseman for the St. Louis Cardinals and recipient of the Gold Glove Award, sends his reply.

January 20, 1962

Dear Jackie:

It would be almost impossible for me to go to Jackson, Mississippi on the 25th of February. I think that this will be the case with most of us ballplayers since we will be either in camp by then or on the way.

In my case, I'll be on the way with my family since I certainly want to take advantage of the unsegregated housing the Cardinals have provided for the first time this year. I talked to you about this last year in Miami and, with the publicity given by Joe Reichler and the AP wire service, we have made progress.

If it is possible to move the date back a little in February, I would gladly attend. And if I get my contract straightened out in time to go South, I'll fly in from St. Petersburg, Florida.

Thank you for inviting me, for I consider this a moral obligation to my people and will attend if at all possible.

Sincerely,
Bill White

RICHARD NIXON TO ROBINSON

Robinson was elected to the Baseball Hall of Fame in his first year of eligibility.

January 29, 1962

Dear Jackie:

There are days when I feel a special pride simply in being an American—and Tuesday, January 23, 1962 was certainly one of them.

I can hardly match your elation and sense of accomplishment on this really memorable occasion, but I can at least share some of your feelings. And I can truly say that never was an honor more richly deserved and that no man could enter the Hall of Fame with better credentials.

Also, I want to thank you for your recent letter and for your usual candor in spotlighting a problem that will cost the Republican Party dearly unless and until it is solved. For my own part, both from the standpoint of keeping faith with my convictions and of facing political reality, I can assure you that I do not intend to ignore the American Negro community in my campaign for Governor.

Again, my sincere tribute on your election to Cooperstown—although I'm not sure who is to be congratulated more, you or the Hall of Fame itself.

With kindest personal regards,

Sincerely,
Dick Nixon

ROBINSON TO RICHARD NIXON

February 8, 1962

My dear Mr. Nixon:

Your letter of January 29th was of special importance to me. It will long be cherished.

Your letters always reaffirm the high regard I hold for you. People have questioned me about my constant support, even today when President Kennedy is doing "a good job." My reaction is the same now as it was during the campaign. In my humble opinion, you were the best candidate in 1960. As I said in Hartford, Connecticut last week, in response to a question by a reporter who wanted to know the significance of my being at a Democratic meeting when I supported you in the election, it was not political, because if the election was tomorrow, I would still support you. I say this because of my sincere belief that you would have lived up to all the things I believed about you, and I am firmly convinced that the best thing that can happen to us as American Negroes is a big Negro vote for you in California and for Governor Rockefeller in New York.

I have no doubt, if you are elected, that you both will improve greatly our drive for equal opportunity. I hope you win. We need men like you in public office.

My regards to Mrs. Nixon.

Sincerely,
Jackie Robinson

ROY WILKINS TO ROBINSON

Early 1962 saw Robinson making several public appearances for the NAACP, including the rally in Jackson, Mississippi, that attracted more than four thousand activists.

March 23, 1962

Dear Jack Robinson:

You have done so much for the NAACP that I find it difficult to discover fresh ways of saying "thank you."

We are deeply grateful for your suggestion of inviting the prominent persons in the athletic world to be present at the NAACP state rally in Jackson, Mississippi upon the occasion of the regional meeting. We have written letters of appreciation to those who inspired the Negro population of Mississippi by their presence. Needless to say, as popular as each of them is and as gratifying as their appearance was, your own presence offered the supreme satisfaction in the hearts of our people.

In a thousand ways they have shown their great pride in not only your accomplishments in major league baseball, but in your philosophy and action as a citizen. We here who feel privileged to regard you as a member of "the family" nevertheless are also inspired by you and indebted to you for the sacrifices you have made in behalf of the cause.

Sincerely,
Roy Wilkins

ROBINSON TO PAUL ZUBER

With the help of the writer Alfred Duckett, Robinson began offering a weekly column to the New York Amsterdam News *in January 1962. Robinson used his April 21 column to deliver a political threat to Paul Zuber, the lead attorney in a 1961 case against the segregated school system maintained by the New Rochelle Board of Education in Westchester County, New York. Zuber had announced that he was quitting the Republican Party and considering a run as an independent against Representative Adam Clayton Powell, Jr. While no fan of Powell, Robinson also rebukes Zuber for publicly criticizing the NAACP, Roy Wilkins, the State Commission on Human Rights, and Governor Rockefeller. The "Harlem Nine," noted below, refers to the nine African American pupils (and their parents) who opposed the inferior education of neighborhood schools in Harlem. The pupils and their parents filed suit against New York City and requested transfer of the students to integrated schools outside of Harlem.*

April 21, 1962

Dear Paul (Attorney Zuber): For some time now we have watched your career with a great deal of interest. A few years back, when you figured so prominently in the cause of the "Harlem Nine," you were helping to put the spotlight on the fact that there is discrimination in New York City; not the same kind of bold discrimination which exists in the South, but discrimination brought about because of residential segregation in the East.

From the Harlem Nine case, you went on to become associated with similar situations throughout the Northern part of our country and in the Midwest. Your efforts have earned you a great deal of publicity in the national press, especially after the famed New Rochelle case.

Like we say, we were very much interested. We felt that perhaps here was a young man who knew how to delicately and skillfully apply the needle which is necessary to correct some of the evils of our Northern society. We were happy to see the results which were being attained and the credit you were receiving for your work.

In recent weeks, however, we have been amazed and disappointed. You have been using your sharp needle to attack the National Association for the Advancement of Colored People and its leaders.

Knowing the tremendous role which has been played over the years by the NAACP legal forces, under Thurgood Marshall, it seems to us that you are not only making a tragic mistake, but also committing a terrible injustice in your public attacks on the organization and its techniques.

Not too many people know, as we do, how close the decision was in the New Rochelle matter. Not too many people know that had not Thurgood Marshall entered into the picture, this important triumph might not have been achieved.

Have you forgotten so soon the trips Roy Wilkins made to New Rochelle and the speeches he made in support of the case? Have you forgotten the part played in the victory by the New Rochelle NAACP?

There were a number of people, close to the New Rochelle situation, who were concerned about the way the case was being handled before Judge Marshall was brought in. They were aware that the decision at stake was one of the important decisions of our era. We are aware, Paul, that you are credited with the success in New Rochelle.

Deep down in your heart, we are sure you admit that this success was by no means solely yours; that it was insured and accelerated by some of the very people you are now attacking.

It seems to us that you personally owe a great deal to the legal forces of the NAACP for stepping into a mess and untangling it. We are certain that no one begrudges you the generous publicity you have received. In our opinion, you can prove a most effective fighter in the cause of equality. Don't spoil it by forcing some of us to tell the whole New Rochelle story.

It is amusing—but bitterly so—to hear you denouncing New York State's Commission on Human Rights. Obviously, you haven't done your homework on this one. If you had, you might realize that the Commission is doing a pretty fine job. Three new offices have been established by the Commission and are located in key spots—125th Street in Manhattan and in Brooklyn and Queens.

This enables so many more people who have been discriminated against to make complaints. I wonder if you realize that under the administration of Governor Rockefeller, who you also attacked, a measure has been enacted prohibiting racial and religious discrimination by employers, labor unions or employment agencies in operation of apprenticeship programs; or that the State Commission for Human Rights (formerly known as the State Commission Against Discrimination) has been reorganized, providing for addition of two new members and expansion of the powers of the chairman.

A measure has been passed outlawing racially restrictive covenants in mortgages, leases, deeds or transfers of property.

These are only a selected few of the progressive steps which have been taken under the Rockefeller Administration. Yet you, Paul, give no credit for them.

You seem to give little or no credit to the atmosphere created by the NAACP over the long years which has enabled you to accomplish some of the things you have accomplished. The NAACP fought when it was unpopular to fight. It also fought in the danger areas of America where a man could lose his life trying to win a case.

Instead of crying out against the NAACP, Roy Wilkins, the State Commission on Human Rights and Governor Rockefeller—all of whom are working for the same cause which you espouse—why not attack the bigots, Paul? Don't dull the needle of your effectiveness by making irresponsible charges, jumping into situations unprepared, and sacrificing principle for publicity.

ROBINSON TO JOHN KENNEDY

Kennedy successfully negotiated a rollback in steel prices in April, just after industry leaders had raised the price of steel by over six dollars per ton. On May 5, Robinson published this open letter in his Amsterdam News *column.*

May 5, 1962

Dear President Kennedy:

All over the world, the headlines reported that you had shown your muscle and won an important victory.

You had won the battle, as they put it, against the barons of steel.

There are many people who think you looked heroic in this battle. There are others who claim that you abused the office of the Presidency and took upon yourself extraordinary powers which have struck fear in the hearts of big business.

We, ourselves, will not go into the subject of whether we feel you were right or wrong.

One thing is sure. You were definite. You were strong in your stand and you displayed a flash of anger and spunk which many people admired.

To make a long story short—you got angry.

When it was all over and you were declared the winner, you had no apologies for getting angry. You said you did it in the best interests of the nation.

We believe you believe that—and if you believe it, whether you were right or wrong, we have respect for you for standing up for your beliefs.

Mr. President, we wonder if you believe something else.

We wonder if you believe that it is in the best interests of the country, or in the best interests of our democracy, or in the best interests of world peace for a city like Augusta, Georgia to become an armed camp because of racial tensions between white and colored citizens there.

CHIEF'S STATEMENT

We wonder if you believe that it is in the best interests of all which the free world holds dear for the police chief of this city to announce that he feels his force can keep trouble down but that he isn't quite sure there won't be horrible bloodshed.

We hold no brief for what happened in Augusta, Georgia where a white youth was killed after race feeling rose high because Negro citizens were publicly demonstrating for jobs better than porter or janitor jobs.

We do not believe in violence as a solution to the problems of the Negro in this country.

TALK NOT ENOUGH

But, with all due respect to the wonderful preachments of Dr. Martin Luther King, we do not believe that the Negro is going to continue to turn the other cheek when his children are denied schooling, his family is denied bread and butter, when he is denied the right to vote, to strike for advancement, to live where his desire urges him and his pocketbook entitles him.

Mr. President, don't you believe that the explosive situation in the South and the sneaky, covered up prejudice in the North are as damaging to the public interest, to democracy and to world peace as a $6 raise in steel prices?

You have said you believe it. You said it in your campaign speeches.

But talk isn't enough, Mr. President. Talk is important, especially from the White House. But it isn't enough.

ANGRY AGAIN

Without meaning to be impertinent, Mr. President, we have a suggestion. Why don't you wander off from all those advisors and FBI men; wander off somewhere where you can sit down, all alone—and think about the high cost of race prejudice—just as you thought about the threatened high cost of steel.

You know what, Mr. President? We believe that if you do that, you will get angry again. And wouldn't it be good for you to go down in history, not only as the President who won the battle against the steel barons but also as the President who won the battle against the bigots in this country who are working harder to destroy it from within than any foreign power is working to destroy it from without?

Why, Mr. President, why don't you get angry again?

MARTIN LUTHER KING, JR. TO ROBINSON

The SCLC hosted a tribute dinner for Robinson at the Waldorf-Astoria in New York City to honor his pending induction into the Baseball Hall of Fame. In this letter King thanks Robinson for agreeing to pledge the dinner's proceeds to SCLC—a decision that irritated Roy Wilkins, who nevertheless agreed to be an honorary chair of the dinner.

May 14, 1962

Dear Jackie:

I did not want too much time to pass before saying to you personally how grateful we are for your enthusiasm in allowing the Hall of Fame Dinner at the Waldorf to be a total benefit for our voter registration drive in the South. You cannot imagine how great a boost this will give our work.

You would be interested to know that in cooperation with local groups in the State of Georgia, we have registered 25,000 new Negro voters since the first of the year. We have been able to do this through our Citizenship Training Center in south Georgia, our Voter Registration Clinics held in the rural and urban centers, and supplying professional staff in organizing 20 intensive drives throughout the State.

I have been following your column in the *Amsterdam News*. The "Zuber" series has been interesting. Your remarks at Raleigh were most pertinent.

Let me formally congratulate you again for your selection to Baseball's *Hall of Fame*. You have made every Negro in America proud through your baseball prowess and your inflexible demand for equal opportunity for all.

Very truly yours,
Martin Luther King, Jr.

RALPH ABERNATHY TO ROBINSON

Ralph David Abernathy, King's best friend and the second most powerful person in the SCLC, thanks Robinson for his article on Kennedy and for his appearance as the keynote speaker at an SCLC event in Montgomery.

June 7, 1962

Dear Jackie,

With great interest and appreciation I read your recent column on President Kennedy and the steel price increase. I just want you to know that I thought it was one of the finest articles which I have ever read. I have always been proud of you and your stand for freedom but in that article you spoke like a prophet, a scholar and a great American, having authority and power. Please keep up the good work.

Again, may I thank you for coming to the rescue of the people in Montgomery and delivering that masterful address for us. If ever I can be of service to you, do not hesitate to call upon me.

With sincere wishes for your continued success from all of us here at SCLC, I remain

Sincerely yours,
Ralph D. Abernathy

ROBINSON TO WILLIAM BLACK

In his July 14 column Robinson defended the right of Frank Schiffman, the owner of the Apollo Theater in Harlem, to lease a neighborhood property to Sol Singer for the purpose of opening a new steakhouse. Robinson's column was especially critical of anti-Semitic remarks chanted at the Apollo by picketers organized by Lewis Michaux, the Harlem bookstore owner and activist. Angered by Robinson's defense of Schiffman, Michaux's supporters then began to picket the Chock Full O' Nuts coffee shop in Harlem. Robinson received praise for his stance from major civil rights leaders, including Roy Wilkins, Whitney Young, and Ralph Bunche. His stance also earned threatening letters from anonymous writers.

July 16, 1962

Dear Mr. Black:

I am sure that you are aware of the picketing outside our 125th Street store. I do not believe that we are going to be hurt badly as far as business is concerned. I wondered if you wanted me to do anything specifically.

I shall talk with Attorney General Lefkowitz tomorrow asking, on a personal basis, his advice.

As of this moment, the only picketing we had was done last Saturday. Knowing these people, they may come back.

Is there anything you would want me to do about this? I am sure you know that I personally will never retract my statement because, regardless of what these people threaten, I feel that they are wrong and someone should speak out against them.

Cordially,
Jackie Robinson

ROY WILKINS TO ROBINSON

Wilkins wires Robinson about the Michaux controversy.

July 16, 1962

When I returned from Atlanta where our national convention reported on the fight against racism and bigotry I found that you had been attacked by so-called African nationalists for your condemnation of their use of racism and anti-Semitism in a dispute in 125th Street. National Association for Advancement of Colored People supports you one hundred percent. Our convention resolutions declared, "We abhor racism of any kind" and "Because we oppose any form of bigotry we oppose and condemn anti-Semitism." The personalities involved on 125th Street and the dispute itself are secondary. The main point that must be insisted upon is that in their fight for equality and opportunity, Negroes cannot use the slimy tool of anti-Semitism or indulge in racism, the very tactics against which we cry out when they are employed against us. Black dictatorship and religious persecution are as vicious and despicable as white dictatorship and religious persecution. The basic battle will not be won by noisemakers and name-callers and race baiters but by men and women mature emotionally as well as physically. We are lost if we adopt Klan methods in the name of exalting Black people. We join you in your straight statement that this is a matter of principle from which there can be no retreat.

Roy Wilkins

"HATE WHITE" MOVEMENT TO ROBINSON

July 18, 1962

Jackie Robinson,

You have banished yourself from the Black Race. You are no longer one of us. You are a man without a race. The proud Black Race has ceased to recognize you as one of us. Uncle Toms do not belong in our ranks. We can never destroy the white race with rattlesnakes like you.

We are glad you have shown your true colors in time. Colors that indicate that you are a traitor to our causes—the cause that compels the Black Man to destroy the white races in order to make this world a better place to live in. So goodbye Jackie, this means exist, for you and all other white folks' niggers. To us a good white man is a dead white man. Good riddance to all "Uncle Toms" and all white men.

The "Hate White"
Movement

ROBINSON TO ROY WILKINS

Nation of Islam minister Malcolm X, the premier representative of black nationalism in the United States, was scheduled to join Michaux at a Harlem rally in response to the Robinson and Schiffman controversy, but Michaux and Robinson settled their differences before the rally could take place.

July 20, 1962

Dear Roy:

While it appears the tension has eased on 125th Street, I want to express my thanks to you for your most encouraging stand.

We were not concerned about a loss in business, but the principle involved here was most important. Your immediate response and decisive stand was the tonic needed to bring about this understanding. It is my sincere belief that leaders like yourself, in standing up for right, even where members of our own race are involved, increases your stature and role as responsible representatives of your organization. While I am sending this letter to all of the people who responded, I could not be more personal.

I hope somehow all of us can get together and perhaps bring about a better understanding among all the groups. Now that an area of agreement has been reached, it might be wise if a meeting could be arranged to air all our grievances. I would appreciate your voice on this.

Again, many thanks. I needed your support. I am certain you know how much it meant personally.

Sincerely yours,
Jackie Robinson

ROBINSON TO BRANCH RICKEY

Branch Rickey traveled to Cooperstown for Jackie Robinson's induction into the Baseball Hall of Fame.

July 24, 1962

Dear Mr. Rickey:

When I said at Cooperstown I felt inadequate, I meant it. I wanted so very much to have you at my side on the platform. I regret I did not follow my feelings rather than the advice I received.

Mr. Rickey, you know how proud I was that you came to Cooperstown. If you had been unable to make it, the day would not have been complete. I owe much to you, not because you brought me into baseball as the first—but because your life has been such an inspiration to me. I am a better man for having had the rich years of association with you.

May God give you the strength to carry on. America needs more Mr. Rickeys—and personally—I need the assurance of a man I respect, admire and love.

Give my regards to Mrs. Rickey. Thank your family for everything. The last four days were important because you were so much a part of all that happened.

Very sincerely yours,
Jackie Robinson

ROBINSON TO WALTER O'MALLEY

Robinson and O'Malley had not spoken with each other at least since early 1957, when Robinson retired in the wake of his trade from the Dodgers to the New York Giants. The meeting that Robinson proposes here did not take place.

July 25, 1962

Dear Mr. O'Malley:

Sunday night, as I had dinner with my family at the Otesaga Hotel in Cooperstown, I had the opportunity of chatting with Mrs. O'Malley briefly. We talked about things I am sure she does not remember, but I really wanted to talk with her about you and I.

I couldn't help but feel sad by the fact that the next day I was entering the Hall of Fame and I did not have any real ties with the game. I thought back to my days at Ebbets Field, and kept wondering how our relationship had deteriorated. Being stubborn, and believing that it all stemmed from my relationship with Mr. Rickey, I made no attempt to find the cause. I assure you, Rae has on many occasions discussed this, and she too feels we should at least talk over our problems. Of course, there is the possibility that we are at an impasse, and nothing can be done. I feel, however, I must make this attempt to let you know I sincerely regret we have not tried to find the cause for this breach.

I will be in Los Angeles on Friday. If you feel you have about fifteen minutes, I'll drop by. I shall call your office when I arrive.

Sincerely yours,
Jackie Robinson

NELSON ROCKEFELLER TO ROBINSON

Invited by Martin Luther King, Jr., Robinson traveled to Albany, Georgia, on August 26 to speak at a rally for a group of tired activists. The ill-fated Albany Movement attacked all kinds of segregation throughout the city, and King would grow to regret the movement's lack of clear, specific objectives. After delivering his speech, Robinson went to Sasser, a small community just outside Albany, where he stood atop the ashes of Mount Olive Baptist Church, which had been one of three black churches scorched because of its efforts to register African American voters. King asked Robinson to chair a national campaign that would raise funds to rebuild the churches, and Robinson used his September 22 column to appeal for money. "The Negro people," he stated, "must rebuild [the churches] to let the Klans and the Citizens Councils and the world know that we will not be frightened and will not allow our leaders to be intimidated." As the following letter shows, Nelson Rockefeller quickly bolstered the fund—a move that gave Robinson yet another reason to stump for the New York governor.

September 19, 1962

Dear Jackie:

As a Baptist layman and as an American deeply concerned that all my fellow Americans shall be assured the right to worship and the right to vote, I count it a high privilege to make a contribution to the rebuilding of the Baptist churches recently destroyed by fire in Georgia, apparently because they were involved in the current drive for the registration of Negroes to vote.

I therefore have asked my office to deliver to you securities having an approximate value at the time of $10,000 payable to the Mount Olive Building Fund, understanding that this is a sum sufficient to rebuild one of the churches but that the money shall be used at the discretion of the Rev. Martin Luther King and the pastors of the churches involved toward the rebuilding of all the churches should that seem more desirable.

I am delighted that you have accepted the important responsibility of raising funds to rebuild these churches and I am confident that all who share our mutual belief in the brotherhood of man under the Fatherhood of God will see to it that this campaign is quickly consummated.

With best wishes and personal regards,

Sincerely,
Nelson A. Rockefeller

RALPH ABERNATHY TO ROBINSON

October 5, 1962

Dear Jackie:

We have received in our office a total of $1,113.00 for the burned churches. We have acknowledged and receipted each contribution and herewith forward a check to you to cover that amount.

Again, may I thank you for the great service you are rendering humanity and the stimulating and challenging address which you delivered at our convention last week. It was a real joy to see you again, and indeed a privilege to have you honor us with your presence and moving message. Truly, there is only one Jackie Robinson and we are thankful to God for him.

I remain

Sincerely,
Ralph D. Abernathy

ROBINSON TO RALPH ABERNATHY

It took Robinson nearly two years to raise the fifty thousand dollars required for rebuilding the burned churches.

October 8, 1962

Dear Ralph:

Many thanks for your inspiring message. It bolsters a sagging spirit to know how you feel. Actually, despite some protest, I feel that it is an obligation and an honor to do all I can. Witnessing the role all of you are playing makes it even more mandatory that we continue to work.

From all indications we will start soon to rebuild. With your contribution and what appears to be a good effort in Stamford, Connecticut and perhaps in Boston, we should start to build in a month or so. It might be wise to check the Atlanta paper to see if their contribution will be used to rebuild the churches. If they have a rough thousand, and we raise about $10,000 in Stamford and Boston, we should have enough to do a good job. Please let me know about the Atlanta paper.

Again, my thanks.

Cordially,
Jackie Robinson

L. K. JACKSON TO ROBINSON

In the 1940s the Reverend L. K. Jackson, a Baptist minister who referred to himself as "The Servant of the Lord's Servant," organized boycotts of stores and banks in Gary, Indiana, that would not hire African Americans. His actions were significantly successful. Many people got decent jobs, which was a first for the city. Jackson's letter targets the Dixiecrat politicians, a faction of the Democratic Party at that time, who denounced all efforts to establish racial integration.

October 8, 1962

My dear Mr. Robinson:

In keeping with my promise to you last week, please find enclosed our check for $100.00, made payable to the Mt. Olive Baptist Building Fund.

I am so intensely impressed with your sincerity and dedication to worthwhile causes that anything and everything I can do to encourage you in these worthwhile ventures, I am willing and ready to do so.

I read your column in the *Journal & Guide* last week and was deeply impressed with what you had to say about Mr. Rockefeller and the Negro vote.

It is super-colossally tragic about the great majority of Negroes. They have been so completely victimized by the relief, welfare and hand-out programs of the Democratic Party and have been so completely "brainwashed" with false propaganda that the Democratic Party is the "little folk's" friend that they cannot see and do not care to know that so far as Negroes are concerned, the Southern political demagogues control the Democrats' attitude toward the Negro. Big, high-powered, educated Negroes all over America do not give a "tinkers year before last Almanac" about what happens to 20,000,000 of us as long as they can get a little job and a personal handout for themselves. They do not realize that the only reason why Mr. Kennedy has not issued the Executive Order he so faithfully promised to issue and has not given more statesman-like leadership to the awful conditions that are going throughout the South, is that he is afraid to infuriate the political demagogues of the South against his program.

These high-powered, intellectual "Uncle Toms and Aunt Sallies" can find some excuse for everything that Mr. Kennedy does not do and at the same time attempt to sweep under the rug all of the barbarity and inhumanity to humanity that is being carried on by Governor Ross Barnett, General Edwin J. Walker and the political termites of Albany, Georgia.

I am with the NAACP's Civil Rights Program 100%, but it is the most difficult thing that I have ever tried to understand, how Roy Wilkins can spend everything we can raise for him fighting against the Ku Klux Klan, White Citizens Council, John Birch Society and such political termites as Governor Marvin Griffin of Georgia, Governor Ross Barnett of Mississippi, and when election time comes, indirectly and in a backhanded way, throws all of the support he can to that element by voting the Democratic ticket.

Enclosed is a letter which I have written President Kennedy. Please read it over carefully and give me your reaction to same.

I am

Yours very truly,
L. K. Jackson
"The Servant of the Lord's
Servant"

ROBINSON TO MARTIN LUTHER KING, JR.

In an earlier letter King thanked Robinson for delivering the keynote speech at the Freedom Dinner for the sixth annual convention of the SCLC, and in this note Robinson seeks King's advice about Rockefeller's 1962 gubernatorial race.

October 9, 1962

Dear Martin:

I am sure you know that no thanks is needed. I am happy to be able to accept my share of the responsibility. I consider my participation a privilege. If I have helped, I am only repaying a debt.

Since my somewhat brief active association I have come to understand what your beliefs are, and you certainly deserve much credit for your work.

I cannot help but wonder in what way we can help Rockefeller get a bigger plurality. If he does, I believe that we will see changes made in the Kennedy administration. Do you have any suggestions? Can you participate in anything like this either by being here or by an honest appraisal of the Governor? I know that you cannot endorse a candidate, but I think we need a big vote and need any help we can get.

Please let me know.

Cordially,
Jackie Robinson

ROBINSON TO ROBERT KENNEDY

Shortly before sending this letter, Robinson criticized President Kennedy for demonstrating a lack of leadership in efforts to help James Meredith integrate the University of Mississippi. Meredith's attempt to matriculate resulted in campus rioting, and Kennedy eventually sent U.S. Army troops to help quell the situation. "In my opinion," Robinson stated, "Mr. Kennedy sent in the troops only because there was nothing else he could do after he allowed the south to get away with defying the government." While criticizing the president, Robinson also seemed to acquit Robert Kennedy, who blamed himself for allowing Meredith's campaign to deteriorate into violence, and in the following letter Robinson praises the attorney general for delivering yet another progressive speech on civil rights. Kennedy told the American Jewish Congress on October 28 that the crisis with the Soviet Union over Cuba was inextricably linked to the domestic fight against intolerance and discrimination. "We will not win this struggle just by confronting the enemy," Kennedy stated. "What we do at home in the final analysis is just as important. Thus we must accelerate our efforts to banish religious prejudice, racial discrimination and any intolerance which denies to any American the rights guaranteed them by the Declaration of Independence and the Constitution. That is what this crisis is all about."

October 30, 1962

My dear Mr. Kennedy:

I read the speech which you made before the American Jewish Congress, and I was very pleased. Your understanding and continued action to secure the rights for all people is of great importance to our democratic way of life.

You are fast becoming the symbol of law and order and wear the office of the Attorney General with added stature.

I hope you will accept the gratitude of one who is proud of your devotion to the principles on which this Country was founded.

Sincerely yours,
Jackie Robinson

ROBINSON TO RICHARD NIXON

Robinson encourages Nixon to remain in politics in spite of his loss in the 1962 gubernatorial race in California. Following the defeat, Nixon announced that he was holding his last press conference. "You won't have Nixon to kick around anymore, because, gentlemen, this is my last press conference," he stated.

November 12, 1962

Dear Dick:

It is difficult to write a letter such as this, but I shall do the best I can.

The only regret I have in supporting you twice is that I was unfortunate not to have been able to help more than I did. I am sorry also that most Negroes were unwilling to believe the promises you made. I personally was, and still am, convinced that you were the best candidate for the presidency in 1960 and a man we need very much in Government Service.

I am concerned because you have said that you have had your last press conference. I hope that you will reconsider, Dick, because it is the great men people attack. You are good for politics; good for America. As one who has great confidence in you and who sincerely appreciates the opportunity of having known you and worked for you, I urge you to remain active. There is so much to be done and there are too few qualified people to do the job now. Your loss would be an added blow to our efforts.

Do not let your critics cause you to give up your career. Each of us came into this world for a purpose. I believe that yours is service to our country.

Cordially,
Jackie Robinson

ROBERT KENNEDY TO ROBINSON

November 13, 1962

Dear Jackie:

Thanks very much for your letter of October 30—I appreciated your comments very much.

There is no question in my mind that the progress which was made in the last 22 months will be sustained and accelerated in the next two years. It is good to know that we have the support of men like yourself who are making such a positive contribution to the advancement of civil rights and human liberties.

Sincerely,
Robert F. Kennedy

On November 20 President Kennedy signed an executive order that criminalized racial discrimination in federal housing. Robinson praised the president's "resolute action" in his December 1 column, but here he criticizes Kennedy, albeit implicitly, for not taking a vocal stance against Senator Allen Ellender of Louisiana, an avowed segregationist, for making racist comments during a November trip to Africa. "The average African," Ellender had stated, "is incapable of leadership except through the assistance of Europeans."

December 29, 1962

IF I WERE PRESIDENT

It's only one man's opinion, but there are two steps which I believe should be taken for the good of the country and in the interests of world peace.

If, by some tremendous miracle, I could become President of the United States for a few hours, I would do these two things.

I would sit down and write a personal letter to the chief of state of every African Government. The letter would go something like this:

"Dear Mr. Chief of State:

"As you are aware, there has been a great deal of publicity given to the fact that a United States Senator—Allen J. Ellender of Louisiana—has made statements which reflect his views that the African people are not ready for self-government.

"Senator Ellender, unfortunately, has been making so-called 'fact-finding trips' for the Senate Appropriations Committee to inspect United States foreign operations abroad.

"I use the word 'unfortunately' because, while it is the prerogative of the Senate of this nation to designate its members for such assignments, I consider the Senator from Louisiana a disastrous choice for the task of conducting an objective investigation in Africa or Asia.

"Anyone, knowing the stand that Senator Ellender has taken with regard to people of color within his own nation, could have accurately predicted what his conclusions would be—even before he set out on his journey.

"As you are well aware, the Western powers have been bending every effort to persuade the people of the world that our way of life is superior to Communism.

"It is true that the State Department has already announced that Senator Ellender's observations do not reflect official policy.

A DREAM

"However, due to the fact that we who preach democracy must practice it more vigorously, if we are to be believed by the people of the world whose skins are dark, I thought that I should express to you my personal regrets concerning Senator Ellender's ill-chosen statements and my personal conviction that freedom is a thing for which man is innately 'ready' by virtue of birth."

The second thing I would do would be to call in my press secretary (I might even be a little cunning and call in my dark-skinned press secretary, Andy Hatcher) and tell him to get the press boys together so I could personally read them the text of my letter.

I know that many Senators—Northern as well as Southern—would be angry with me.

I know that many of the people—Northern and Southern—would be upset.

I know I would catch the devil getting some of my legislative proposals through—which might make it harder for me to get reelected.

But I would take the position that there are times when it is more important to be a President than to be a politician.

"But, Jackie," I imagine someone is saying over my shoulder. "You are not the President and it isn't likely that you will be anytime soon."

Gosh, I can dream, can't I?

8

BACK OUR BROTHERS—
EXCEPT ADAM AND MALCOLM

· 1963 ·

ROBINSON TO ADAM CLAYTON POWELL, JR.

Robinson uses an open letter to criticize Powell for allegedly calling upon African Americans, during a mid-March rally in Harlem, to boycott major civil rights organizations that they did not control. While he later denied that he had called for a boycott, Powell continued to insist that African Americans should assume primary leadership positions in civil rights organizations. "We must seize control of these organizations," he stated at the end of March. "We must put into policy control those persons who represent the black masses." Robinson's rebuttal here refers to Arthur Spingarn, president of the NAACP from 1940 to 1966; Marion Meyer Spingarn, a social worker and ardent NAACP supporter; and the philanthropist Kivie Kaplan, who would succeed Arthur Spingarn and serve as president of the NAACP from 1966 to 1975. The Amsterdam News *did not publish a reply from Powell.*

March 30, 1963

AN OPEN LETTER TO A FRIEND

Most columnists who write open letters to public personalities don't really want an answer. Let me state at the beginning that I would appreciate an answer from the person to whom I am directing this open letter and, if this is forthcoming, I will carry every line in this space regardless of what it says.

Most people who use the word "friend" use it loosely. I don't. But when I believe that the friend is in the wrong, I feel I have the right to tell him so and if the wrong I think he committed was a public act or utterance, then I feel I have the right to tell him so publicly.

This letter is for you—Adam Clayton Powell, Jr.

I write it because it is my sincere belief that you have grievously set back the cause of the Negro, let your race down and failed miserably in the role which our people justly expect you to play as an important national leader of the Negro in this nation.

I refer to your vicious attacks upon the National Association for the Advancement of Colored People, your intemperate and ill-advised suggestion that the Negro people boycott the NAACP because of the participation in its affairs of white people and your rallying call to the Negro people to support Malcolm X and the Black Muslims.

You know, Adam, that the NAACP, whatever shortcomings it may have, has been and still is the greatest organization working in behalf of all those principles of freedom and human dignity for the black man in America which was ever put together in this nation.

You also know that people like the Spingarns and Kivie Kaplan have done a dedicated job and organized more moral and financial support for this cause than any ten Negroes including yourself.

You know also, in spite of the fact that you and I share deep respect for Minister Malcolm X as an individual, that the way pointed by the Black Muslims is not the true way to the solution of the Negro problem. For you are aware—and you have preached for many years—that the answer for the Negro is to be found, not in segregation or in separation, but by his insistence upon moving into his rightful place, the same place as that of any other American within our society.

I can only conclude, Adam, that this latest tantrum of yours stems from the fact that you are infuriated because Roy Wilkins and the Board of the NAACP did not rush to your defense in your recent battle with your fellow Congressmen. You set up the usual crybaby yell that you were being persecuted because you are a black man when it was pretty obvious that you had placed yourself in a vulnerable position to be condemned by many people with many different motives. The Negro people are growing up, Adam, and I do not believe they are sympathetic any longer to the business of supporting anything anyone does, wrong or right, simply because he belongs to the race.

Whatever you may believe, Adam, I write this letter more in sadness than in anger. I, like many others, have been troubled by what has seemed to be your growing insensitivity to the cause of our people and your seemingly increasing disregard for your responsibilities to the job you have been sent to Washington to do.

Like many others I have hesitated to say this because you have done a magnificent job in years gone by and because I did not want to give ammunition to those enemies of yours who have been the enemies of the Negro people.

The people who were your enemies and ours, the segregationists, are probably thinking very highly of you right now although they probably have contempt even for an enemy who would desert his own cause. At any rate you have played right into their hands. They want nothing better than to hurt the NAACP and you have volunteered to give that aim a tremendous boost.

Recently on the campus of Howard University, I received a tongue lashing from a student who demanded to know how I could balance my beliefs and personal principles with my consistent defense of "a demagogue like Adam Powell." I replied that I, too, felt you had been derelict in your duties on many occasions but that I did not wish to help our common enemy.

As I close this letter, Adam, I must confess with a deep sense of sadness that I no longer know who your enemies really are.

LETTERS TO THE EDITOR OF THE *NEW YORK AMSTERDAM NEWS*

Robinson's open letter to Powell provoked numerous letters to the editor in the April 6 issue, and most of them reflected growing tensions between integrationists like Robinson and separatists like Malcolm X.

One writer suggested that Robinson was alienated from the black masses: "If Jackie is really interested in the man in the street who catches hell daily, the disinherited Black mass, he should stop grinning at 'Charlie' for a few hours and seek the masses out. Speak to us from Harlem Square, Jackie! Make your position plain, baby; we want to see you when you talk."

Another writer claimed to notice a striking difference between the latter years of Robinson's baseball career and his recent defense of leading whites in the NAACP: "Towards the end of your baseball career you stirred up quite a number of white people as a result of your aggressiveness and your tendency to assert your rights as an individual. Of course, by acting thusly you as a Negro were not playing the role that white American society naturally expected of you as a Negro. Judging by your remarks in your effort to get Adam Powell to see the error of his ways, you are departing from your Negro militancy which has been so prevalent in your weekly column in the Amsterdam News."

Still another writer drew a parallel between Robinson's "deep sense of sadness" and seemingly benevolent white oppression. "Were not your actions and words the 'method' so often used by white men? 'Stab them in the back, but do it gentle and be sorry.'"

Robinson responded especially to the many critics who called for black unity, stating in his April 20 column that "if 'sticking together' means you continue to blindly endorse a man simply because he is black—or green—or white—when you truly feel he has been wrong, you can have that kind of sticking together. One of the most precious assets a man has is his right to speak the truth as he sees it."

ROBINSON TO RICHARD NIXON

Just a year earlier Robinson told Nixon, "We need men like you in public office," but in this open letter, published in his May 4 column, Robinson foreshadows a public split with Nixon over their opposing stances on civil rights and Barry Goldwater, who would be the Republican nominee for president in 1964. Unsurprisingly, Robinson also continues to criticize President Kennedy. At the beginning of the year he denounced the president for delivering a State of the Union address that "completely ignored the entire area of civil rights legislation."

May 4, 1963

Dear Dick:

On my desk at Chock Full O' Nuts there is a beautiful bronze memento inscribed "from Pat and Dick." You will recall that you and your charming wife gave me this gift after I had taken a leave of absence to campaign for you when you ran for the Presidency in 1960.

When the political battle was over and the returns were in, you will recall that Robert Kennedy attributed his brother's election to the fact that he had won heavy Negro support in large cities. The Republican National Committee post-scripted that had you made a bold play for the Negro vote, you might have won. You yourself have admitted this.

I am not one of those people who regrets having been with the loser. I supported you on principle. I am neither a Republican nor a Democrat. I vote for people who I believe in, regardless of their party affiliations. I fought for you because I believed you to be sincere on the racial question and because I believed Senator Kennedy to be insincere.

Personally, I would again oppose Mr. Kennedy in a political campaign.

I have to say sorrowfully, however, that there is a strong question in my mind as to whether I would again support you or a candidate with your blessing.

I say this because I am deeply disturbed about a United Press International dispatch which quotes you as saying that you believe civil rights will not be the prime 1964 political issue in the South. I know that you have said you will not be a candidate but that you intend to exert some influence over party policy, platform and choice of candidate.

If quoted correctly, you are counseling the 1964 frontrunner to take it easy on civil rights and to attempt to carry the South on a platform of economic conservatism. If quoted correctly, you reveal that you have learned nothing from your experience in the last Presidential campaign.

BARRY GOLDWATER

Evidently you are not persuaded, as many others are, that no man will become President of the United States in this day and time, who does not have the confidence of the Negro voter and the millions of decent Americans who believe in our democracy.

This is a lesson of which your fellow Republican, Senator Barry Goldwater, is not aware. The Senator seems to think that he or someone else who embraces his philosophy can win the Presidency on a platform of conservatism and writing off the Negro vote in the North. He has been quoted as saying that when someone questions him about integration, he counter-questions with: "Where are you from?"

I think the Negro knows where Mr. Goldwater is from. I don't mean where he lives. I mean that he is strictly from hunger on the race issue. I believe Barry Goldwater, or anyone who thinks as he does, would be trounced handsomely if his party made the fatal error of giving him the baton to carry in 1964. Let's set the record straight.

I have no illusions about my ability to sway masses of people politically. I have no pretensions to leadership. Yet, I would exert every ounce of whatever influence I might have in order to help defeat Goldwater or anyone of his ilk.

ROCKEFELLER

I have great faith in Governor Nelson Rockefeller. I find it hard to believe that he would compromise what I know to be his strong principle on the issue of human rights in order to wrest from Mr. Goldwater the mantle of favor with the extreme rightists and conservatives.

But, if it should happen that Mr. Rockefeller allowed advisers to steer him away from the unequivocal championship, which he has been consistently giving to civil rights, I would not only withdraw my personal support from but I would also oppose him vigorously. Mr. Rockefeller knows this because I have told him so and I think he respects my conviction on the matter.

I hope that you were misunderstood and that if you were not, you will revise your thinking. I invite you to answer this open letter in this column.

ROBINSON TO JOHN KENNEDY

In early May over one thousand African American children and teenagers joined the SCLC campaign to desegregate Birmingham. Marching from the Sixteenth Street Baptist Church and through city streets, most of the youths ended up in police paddy wagons and jail cells. Here Robinson wires President Kennedy in response to Police Commissioner Eugene "Bull" Connor's decision to unleash dogs and turn fire hoses on schoolchildren who joined the demonstrations, marches, and rallies. The criticism that appears in this telegram resurfaced in Robinson's May 18 column. "The fact is that the problems created by the tense Birmingham, Alabama situation lie smack on the doorsteps of the White House," Robinson stated. "Lie down with dogs and you are due to arise with fleas."

May 7, 1963

Dear Mr. Kennedy:

In the past, I have been generally critical of your civil rights policy. Despite some fine appointments and a few executive orders, the civil rights platform—which was a major stepping stone for you in your quest for the presidency—has collapsed. It is my sincere belief that your personal intentions are honorable. However, the pace at which our country is moving toward total equality for all peoples is miserably slow. As is being demonstrated in Birmingham, Alabama, moderation and gradualism, as far as civil rights are concerned, are antique words, to say the least. The revolution that is taking place in this country cannot be squelched by police dogs or high power hoses.

The hypocrisy of the atrocities that are allowed to occur in the South are disgusting enough from a social and moral point of view. Even more hypocritical, however, is the image of the United States that is being transmitted to the other countries of the world. A May 5 *New York Times* report, datelined Accra, Ghana, reads in part: "America's greatness is meaningless so long as racial discrimination continues . . . We know of the predicament of 18,000,000 third class citizens of the United States, denied the fundamental rights of man, and forced to live in and endure the horrors of segregation." How can those newly formed governments of Africa possibly be expected to emulate our way of life, and adhere to those basic principles of democracy that we speak loudly and freely about, when the federal government allows such unmentionables to exist in Alabama. I could not possibly conceive that the federal government would stop short of an all-out effort to end the tension that now exists. I must state bluntly that there will be grave doubts as to the sincerity of your administration, unless you face this issue in the forthright manner with which you handled the steel industry and the Cuban situation. I submit that you do have the power to cut off federal expenditures within a state which has become a police state and to declare martial law for the purpose of guaranteeing the safety of American citizens.

The eyes of the world are on America and Americans of both races are looking to you.

Jackie Robinson

ROBINSON TO THE EDITOR OF THE NEW YORK *DAILY NEWS*

Robinson and Floyd Patterson, the former world heavyweight boxing champion, traveled to Birmingham at King's invitation and took part in movement activities. At a mass rally there, Robinson delivered a speech criticizing President Kennedy for failing to send U.S. troops to protect the civil rights demonstrators.

Although praised by civil rights leaders for making the trip, Robinson and Patterson were also subjected to the same criticism that King had endured for many years: the charge that communities in the South had been tranquil until "outside agitators" began to stir up resentment among local African Americans. The New York Daily News *joined many newspapers in the South in charging Robinson and Patterson with increasing racial tensions in Birmingham.*

May 23, 1963

Sir:

I could not care less that the *News* agrees with the Alabama Editor who advises President Kennedy that everything would be peachy in Birmingham if "outsiders" like myself and Floyd Patterson stayed away from the scene.

Based on your past attitudes, it was consistent that you took this stand, although I notice you did not go so far as to include the name of Dr. King, who was also labeled an "outsider" by the Southern editor. It just so happened that the Negro people of Birmingham invited Outsider King in to help them. It also happened that Outsider King invited Outsider Patterson and Outsider Robinson to come to Birmingham.

Whenever and wherever in the South the leaders believe I can help just the tiniest bit, I intend to go. I assess the dictates of my own conscience as infinitely more important than the approval of your newspaper.

Very truly yours,
Jackie Robinson

LEE WHITE TO ROBINSON

Lee White, assistant special counsel to President Kennedy, replies to Robinson's concerns about Birmingham, addressing his letter also to Noel Marder, a white publisher from Yonkers, New York, who had traveled to Birmingham to strategize with King and other SCLC leaders. The Kennedy administration helped to negotiate the release of the jailed young marchers, as well as their return to schools without further legal recriminations.

May 27, 1963

Dear Messrs Marder and Robinson:

In response to your telegram to the President regarding the Birmingham school children, I am sure you know that Judge Tuttle of the Court of Appeals has opposed the decision of the District Court and that the children have returned to school.

You may also be interested in knowing that the Justice Department intervened in the case and presented an amicus curiae brief supporting the reversal of the lower court.

Sincerely,
Lee C. White

ROBINSON TO JOHN KENNEDY

This column, drafted on June 12, includes the text of a telegram that Robinson sent Kennedy following his televised June 11 speech on civil rights. The telegram is remarkable for its praise of Kennedy and for its virtual endorsement of his reelection. No doubt pleased with the evolution of his relationship with Robinson, Kennedy sent a brief thank-you note on June 22, the day this column was published.

June 12, 1963

As an American citizen, I am deeply proud of our President. In my opinion, the address which Mr. Kennedy made to the American people on the color question is one of the finest declarations ever issued in the cause of human rights.

As consistent readers of this column know, I have been highly critical of this Administration and its handling of the civil rights issue.

I must state now that I believe the President has come through with statesmanship, with courage, with wisdom and absolute sincerity.

Speaking as one person, I can honestly say that Mr. Kennedy has now done everything I hoped he would do.

I expressed that sentiment in a telegram which I sent to The White House—a telegram in which I said to Mr. Kennedy:

"Thank you for emerging as the most forthright President we have ever had and for providing us with the inspired leadership that we so desperately needed. I am more proud than ever of my American heritage."

This column believes that Mr. Kennedy's message to the nation is a document which every American ought to study thoughtfully.

I liked the way he called upon each of us to "examine his conscience." I liked the way he pointed out that racial injustice is contrary to the principles upon which America was founded and observed that "the rights of every man are diminished when the rights of one man are threatened."

The President, in this message, did eloquently what many of us felt he ought to do for some time. He addressed himself to the "moral issues involved in the denial of rights to every human."

The moral issue involved, Mr. Kennedy stated, "is as old as the Scriptures and as clear as the American Constitution."

He expressed his concern for the kind of image we present on the international scene. He added how much more important it is to stop and realize what we are saying to each other, through our conduct and treatment of fellow humans.

"Are we saying," the President asked, "that this is the land of the free except for the Negroes; that we have no second-class citizens except Negroes; that we have no class system or caste system, no ghettoes, no master race, except with respect to Negroes?

"Now the time has come," Mr. Kennedy continued, "for the nation to fulfill its promise."

Well, President Kennedy has fulfilled his promise. He was not only speaking, however. He had acted that same day, throwing the weight of the Government behind the two Negro students who Governor Wallace attempted to ban from Alabama State University. He pledged even more significant action through proposal of sweeping civil rights reforms to Congress.

Mr. Kennedy's address was not the speech of a politician. It was the pronouncement of a statesman. Yet, I agree with my wife, who said to me, "Tonight, Mr. Kennedy was reelected."

P.S. Word comes to me as this column is written that Medgar Evers, the courageous NAACP official, has been brutally murdered in Mississippi. I knew this dedicated man and I know that he was aware of the dangers he faced. I pray that Negro people all over the nation will help to make this tragic death have positive meaning. If we will dedicate ourselves more earnestly to the fight, it might mean that Medgar Evers did not die in vain.

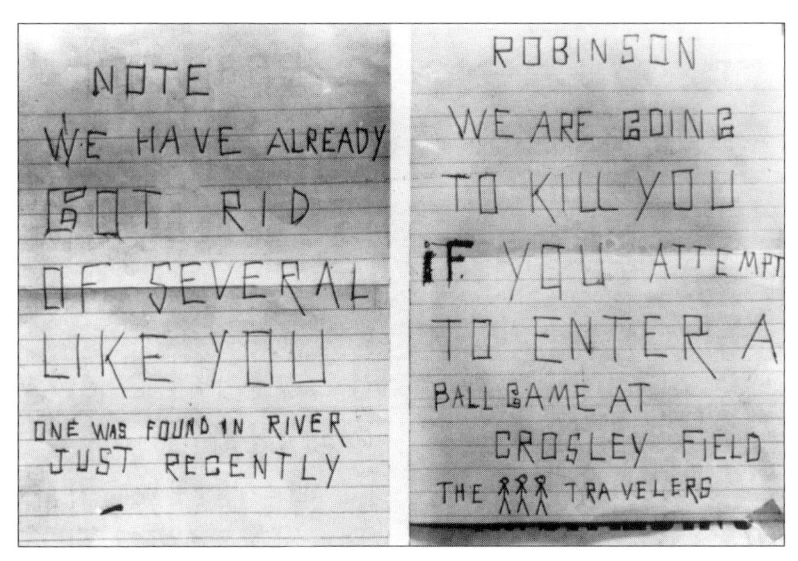

NOTE
WE HAVE ALREADY
GOT RID
OF SEVERAL
LIKE YOU
ONE WAS FOUND IN RIVER
JUST RECENTLY

ROBINSON
WE ARE GOING
TO KILL YOU
IF YOU ATTEMPT
TO ENTER A
BALL GAME AT
CROSLEY FIELD
THE TRAVELERS

Robinson received this death threat on May 20, 1951, when the Brooklyn Dodgers were visiting the Cincinnati Reds. Anonymous threats against his life—first from white racists and later from black militants—appeared in Robinson's mailbox throughout his professional life. *(National Baseball Hall of Fame Library, Cooperstown, New York)*

By the end of his life, Robinson would regret making this appearance before the House Un-American Activities Committee on July 18, 1949, when he criticized Paul Robeson for allegedly claiming that African Americans would not fight in a war against the Soviet Union. *(AP Photos/William J. Smith)*

Robinson sitting at his desk at Chock Full O' Nuts on January 7, 1957, shortly after agreeing to become vice president of personnel. He considered his business career as advancing the cause of African Americans in commerce and industry, and many of his civil rights letters appear on Chock's green-lettered stationery. *(AP Photos/Jack Harris)*

The White House
Washington

WA012 NL PD 1957 AUG 13 AM 6 31

STAMFORD CONN AUG 12

FRED MORROW

THE WHITE HOUSE

AM OPPOSED TO CIVIL RIGHTS BILL IN ITS PRESENT FORM HAVE BEEN IN TOUCH WITH A NUMBER OF MY FRIENDS WE DISAGREE THAT HALF LOAF BETTER THAN ONE HAVE WAITED THIS LONG FOR BILL WITH MEANING CAN WAIT A LITTLE LONGER UNLESS HOUSE AMENDS BILL HOPE THE PRESIDENT WILL VETO IT WE SINCERELY APPRECIATE THE MANY TRUE AMERICANS WHO INSIST ON EQUAL RIGHTS FOR ALL

JACKIE ROBINSON.

Robinson frequently wrote letters and telegrams about legislative issues, and here he wires Fred Morrow, one of the few African Americans employed in the Eisenhower White House, about the 1957 civil rights bill. *(National Archives and Records Administration)*

Telephone
MUrray Hill 2-0500

425 LEXINGTON AVENUE
New York 17, N. Y.

THE WHITE HOUSE
MAY 14 11 36 AM '58
RECEIVED

May 13, 1958

The President
The White House
Washington, D. C.

My dear Mr. President:

I was sitting in the audience at the Summit Meeting of Negro Leaders yesterday when you said we must have patience. On hearing you say this, I felt like standing up and saying, "Oh no! Not again."

I respectfully remind you sir, that we have been the most patient of all people. When you said we must have self-respect, I wondered how we could have self-respect and remain patient considering the treatment accorded us through the years.

17 million Negroes cannot do as you suggest and wait for the hearts of men to change. We want to enjoy now the rights that we feel we are entitled to as Americans. This we cannot do unless we pursue aggressively goals which all other Americans achieved over 150 years ago.

As the chief executive of our nation, I respectfully suggest that you unwittingly crush the spirit of freedom in Negroes by constantly urging forbearance and give hope to those pro-segregation leaders like Governor Faubus who would take from us even those freedoms we now enjoy. Your own experience with Governor Faubus is proof enough that forbearance and not eventual integration is the goal the pro-segregation leaders seek.

In my view, an unequivocal statement backed up by action such as you demonstrated you could take last fall in deal-

MAY 26 1958

The President   Page 2   May 13, 1958

ing with Governor Faubus if it became necessary, would let it be known that America is determined to provide -- in the near future -- for Negroes -- the freedoms we are entitled to under the constitution.

Respectfully yours,

Jackie Robinson

Jackie Robinson

JR:cc

Robinson had been a supporter of President Dwight Eisenhower, but when the president called upon African Americans to exercise "patience" in 1958 Robinson shifted his loyalty to Vice President Richard Nixon. *(National Archives and Records Administration)*

As general manager of the Brooklyn Dodgers, Branch Rickey had signed Robinson to his first major league contract. The two would remain close friends throughout their post-baseball years, and Rickey would encourage Robinson to campaign for Nixon and, later, for Nelson Rockefeller. *(AP/Wide World Photos)*

Robinson campaigned full-time for Nixon during the 1960 presidential race, and he would later state that Nixon lost the race because his campaign team, and the Republican Party at large, had ignored African American voters. *(AP/Wide World Photos)*

Telephone
MUrray Hill 2-0500

jkc Robinson

THE WHITE HOUSE
FEB 13 4 52 PM '61
RECEIVED

Chock full o' Nuts
425 LEXINGTON AVENUE
New York 17, N.Y.

February 9, 1961

The President
The White House

My dear Mr. President:

I believe I now understand and appreciate better your role in the continuing struggle to fulfill the American promise of equal opportunity for all.

While I am very happy over your obviously fine start as our President, my concern over Civil Rights and my vigorous opposition to your election is one of sincerity. The direction you seem to be going indicates America is in for great leadership, and I will be most happy if my fears continue to be proven wrong. We are naturally keeping a wondering eye on what will happen, and while any opposition or criticism may not be the most popular thing when you are leading so well, you must know that as an individual I am interested because what you do or do not do in the next 4 years could have a serious effect upon my children's future.

In your letter to me of July 1, 1960, you indicated you would use the influence of the White House in cases where moral issues are involved. You have reiterated your stand, and we are very happy. Still, we are going to use whatever voice we have to awaken our people. With the new emerging African nations, Negro Americans must assert themselves more, not for what we can get as individuals, but for the good of the Negro masses.

I thank you for what you have done so far, but it is not how much has been done but how much more there is to do. I would like to be patient Mr. President, but patience has caused us years in our struggle for human dignity. I will continue to hope and pray for your aggressive leadership but will not refuse to criticise if the feeling persist that Civil Rights is not on the agenda for months to come.

Telephone
MUrray Hill 2-0500

Chock full o' Nuts
425 LEXINGTON AVENUE
New York 17, N.Y.

The President Page 2 February 9, 1961

May God give you strength and the energy to accomplish your most difficult task.

Respectfuuly yours,

Jackie Robinson

Jackie Robinson

JR:cbc

Robinson traded barbs with John and Robert Kennedy during the 1960 presidential election, often accusing them of courting Southern segregationists, and, although he extends a short olive branch in this letter, he would remain a critic of the Kennedys. *(National Archives and Records Administration)*

Boxing champion Floyd Patterson, far left, and Robinson talk with Martin Luther King, Jr., and Ralph David Abernathy at a civil rights rally in Birmingham, Alabama, in May 1963. Robinson frequently invited celebrity athletes to help raise money for the movement. *(AP/Wide World Photos)*

Robinson played a leading role in several civil rights groups, and here he joins the Congress of Racial Equality (CORE) at a demonstration in Brooklyn, New York, in August 1963, to protest publicly financed projects that did not hire sufficient numbers of blacks. *(AP/Wide World Photos)*

Robinson was devoted to advancing civil rights through economic opportunities, and in August 1963 he attended the March on Washington for Jobs and Freedom with his family, including his son David. *(National Archives and Records Administration)*

Robinson stood against the tide at the 1964 Republican National Convention, depicting nominee Barry Goldwater as a "bigot" and an "advocate of white supremacy." He would never apologize for these remarks, but Robinson would begin a cordial relationship with Goldwater in 1967. *(© Bettmann/CORBIS)*

Robinson had long admired New York governor Nelson Rockefeller's progressive race politics, and the governor hired him as a special assistant for community affairs in 1966. In 1972, however, Robinson would become disillusioned with Rockefeller, claiming that the governor had deserted his progressivism in an effort to appeal to Republican conservatives. *(© Bettmann/CORBIS)*

Robinson endorsed Vice President Hubert Humphrey in the 1968 presidential race during an event held at Freedom National Bank in Harlem, where Robinson served as founding chairman of the board. *(© Bettmann/CORBIS)*

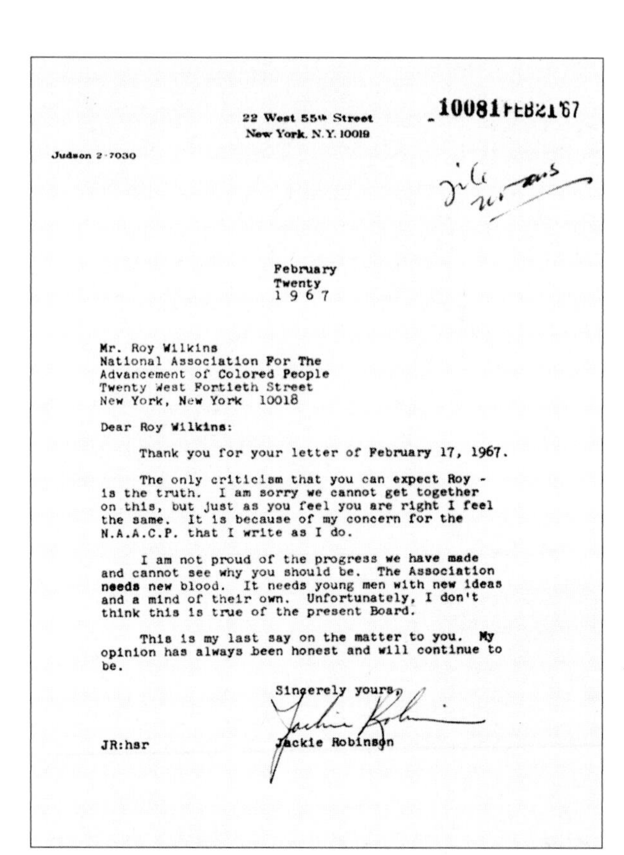

22 West 55th Street
New York, N.Y. 10019

Judson 2-7030

10081 FEB21 '67

file

February
Twenty
1 9 6 7

Mr. Roy Wilkins
National Association For The
Advancement of Colored People
Twenty West Fortieth Street
New York, New York 10018

Dear Roy Wilkins:

Thank you for your letter of February 17, 1967.

The only criticism that you can expect Roy - is the truth. I am sorry we cannot get together on this, but just as you feel you are right I feel the same. It is because of my concern for the N.A.A.C.P. that I write as I do.

I am not proud of the progress we have made and cannot see why you should be. The Association needs new blood. It needs young men with new ideas and a mind of their own. Unfortunately, I don't think this is true of the present Board.

This is my last say on the matter to you. My opinion has always been honest and will continue to be.

Sincerely yours,

Jackie Robinson

JR:hsr

Robinson had publicly criticized Roy Wilkins, executive director of the NAACP, for allegedly squelching dissent and alienating the "black masses." Robinson would later praise Wilkins's opposition to young black militants who questioned the value of racial integration. *(Library of Congress/photograph by Michael G. Long)*

In his last public appearance, Robinson throws out the first pitch of the second game of the 1972 World Series in Cincinnati on October 15, 1972. He did not agree to appear at the game until Baseball Commissioner Bowie Kuhn convinced him that Major League Baseball was taking steps to hire African Americans for management positions. *(AP/Wide World Photos)*

ROBINSON TO JOHN KENNEDY

In the following telegram, most likely coauthored by Alfred Duckett, Robinson pleads for federal protection of Martin Luther King, Jr. at the funeral of Medgar Evers, who was gunned down by Byron De La Beckwith in Jackson, Mississippi, on June 12.

June 15, 1963

It might seem fantastic to imagine that even in the state of Mississippi anyone would seek to do injury to a nonviolent leader like Dr. Martin King as he goes there this morning on a mission of sorrow. Yet it was fantastic but true that some depraved assassin gunned down another man of nonviolence, the late Medgar Evers, whose funeral Dr. King and his associates will be attending today in Jackson. Should harm come to Dr. King to add to the misery which decent Americans of both races experienced with the murder of Mr. Evers, the restraint of many people all over this nation might burst its bonds and bring about a brutal bloody holocaust the like of which this country has not seen. I therefore implore you in the spirit of your recent magnificent appeal for justice to utilize every federal facility to protect a man sorely needed for this era. For to millions Martin King symbolizes the bearing forward of the torch for freedom so savagely wrested from the dying grip of Medgar Evers. America needs and the world cannot afford to lose him to the whims of murderous maniacs.

HUGH MORROW TO NELSON ROCKEFELLER

Hugh Morrow, a special assistant to Rockefeller, asks the governor to consider making, and publicizing, a financial gift that Robinson requested during an "Afternoon of Jazz," a fund-raising event that Rachel and Jackie held at their Connecticut home to benefit civil rights causes. Rockefeller's note at the end of this memorandum reads "No—any suggestions anonymous?"

June 27, 1963

Last Sunday, I attended a jazz festival at Jackie Robinson's home in Connecticut. Late in the day, Reverend Wyatt Walker, Dr. Martin Luther King's executive assistant, flew in from the Midwest to make a speech about his experiences in the South and to make a plea for funds. He said that the Birmingham and other current operations had already tied up some $400,000 in bail money.

Jackie then did a UJA-type fundraising job, calling on people in the interracial audience, and obtained pledges totaling about $7500 for Dr. King's work. Total profits of the day came to $14,400 with these pledges. Afterward, Jackie fixed his beady eye on me—the upshot being that he thinks it sure would be great if you would agree to match the $7500 in pledges. I said I would see what might be done.

Now it appears that *Life* magazine is doing a picture spread on this jazz festival including the money-raising aspect.

If you would go along with this idea, which both Sam Aldrich and I heartily recommend, and have someone phone me Friday so I can let Jackie know, it would appear in *Life* that you had made this additional contribution to Dr. King in connection with the jazz festival (through a representative present on the occasion).

George Hinman commented to me yesterday that he felt we should go very strong in the civil rights field (as of course you are doing at the State level). Sam Aldrich thinks the timing would be perfect. My own opinion is that you are so thoroughly committed anyway in this area that you can't possibly hope to benefit from this sickening game of some Republicans who are trying to make ours the white man's party—that you should above all pursue your own convictions, regardless of political expediency—and it is my conviction that this in the end will prove to be the best politics. The civil rights situation in this country is now so explosive that I honestly feel the Negro vote could swing either way, depending on circumstances existing as of September–October 1964.

I therefore consider it important that you continue to maintain a position with the Negro leaders of dependable and sympathetic friend. I think the Robinson caper, which would immensely please both Jackie and Dr. King, is therefore worthwhile—and I also emphasize that I can get you out of this gracefully should you decide not to take it up.

NELSON ROCKEFELLER TO ROBINSON

Robinson's June 15 column depicted Rockefeller's divorce and remarriage as evidence of political courage. "We call what the Governor has done an indication of the kind of courage which makes him take steps he believes to be right even if he knows they may be unpopular," Robinson stated. *"This kind of courage can make the difference between a President who allows wrongs to exist because he is afraid of losing favor and a true statesman who takes a stand which he believes to be just and fair."*

July 25, 1963

Dear Jackie:

Just a note to let you know how deeply I appreciate the sensitivity and understanding of your column about my marriage and the political future. It is wonderful indeed to have a friend such as you; it is even more gratifying to realize the depth and the human warmth behind your friendship.

With every good wish and personal regards,

Sincerely,
Nelson A. Rockefeller

ROBINSON TO WILLIAM BLACK

While Robinson was on vacation from his personnel work at Chock Full O' Nuts, William Black and two of his executives, including Herb Samuel, fired six employees. Robinson wrote Samuel a critical note, and Black admonished Robinson in turn. Robinson's reply here clearly indicates that he was not afraid to criticize his white employer.

August 14, 1963

Dear Mr. Black:

After giving considerable thought to your note, I felt it had to be answered.

First, let me say I don't agree that my note to Herb was uncalled for. Firings are a part of personnel, and I am justified in insisting that in the future firings have my approval.

I do not see where this has anything to do with my wanting the company to stand still while I am away. I can't believe you really feel this is what I want. It is true, had I been here, I would have done exactly as you did, but where does this affect future hirings?

I don't like getting a notice of a hearing on a discharged employee and not even having an idea the employee was fired, or by chance running across a record of another discharged employee, or being embarrassed when asked why an assistant manager was discharged, embarrassed because I knew nothing of the discharge.

I am sorry you are angry, because I feel strongly about this, and I do as a matter of principle feel strongly about it. I am sorry also that you don't have more faith in me when you question my respect of your judgment. I did not question it. I don't intend to unless of course I feel something is uncalled for.

My note was not intended in any way to refer to the dismissal of the six while I was away. Certainly it was not intended to offend you. I am sorry that it did. I have, in every way, indicated my respect for you because I do respect you, and regardless of the outcome of this, I always will.

I feel that I, too, am entitled to this same respect when I simply insist that as head of personnel I be given the right to pass on all dismissals.

I hope you will accept this as I write it. It has nothing to do with my personal high regard for you, but it certainly has a great deal to do with what I think about myself.

Sincerely yours,
Jackie Robinson

O. L. WELLER TO ROBINSON

The August 10 issue of the Saturday Evening Post *included a Robinson editorial that criticized Nixon for ignoring African American voters in 1960 and warned Republicans that forming a "white man's party" and focusing on economics to the exclusion of civil rights would result in yet another failure at the polls.*

August 17, 1963

Dear Mr. Robinson:

I have just got through reading your article in the 10 August issue of the *Sat Ev Post*. I'm with you. Perhaps not all the way, but I'm with you in the basics.

First let me say (it still seems necessary) that I'm white, 50, have voted Republican (not straight) since 21, am Christian of liberal protestant leanings (if I am to be categorized), and still believe that the American (U.S.) way is still the best way for mankind—if, that is, we can just get sort of brainy and sort of human.

Your article was very well done. If you want to recruit Republicans to the cause—that was the way to do it. It's a sane approach, and I'm for you. But if Goldwater or other dumb damn sons-a-bitches, who are going to play the thing on the basis of political considerations, are going to sabotage mankind—how come we got to stick with the Republican party? What's a party?

In some ways I'm not so nuts about Kennedy. But I'll tell you, he's done more for the progress of this country and for its people than have some of the other administrations that I voted for. And next time, my vote's going to the party that gives best promise of giving people an even break.

You liberal Negroes have been doing a good job. It puts some of us what you call lily-whiters to shame. I'm lily-white by accident, just as you are blackern the aces (looks like in your picture) by accident. We're humans, we're people, we're part of this country—and that makes us Americans. And we as Americans have somehow got to show the rest of the world of human beings that we do believe in freedom and decency and the equal right of every person to strive to be a useful, functioning part of his community.

This letter isn't well written. It isn't a proper response to your darn well-done article. Actually, all it is intended to do is tell you thanks, and to tell you that human considerations should go beyond party lines. I think there are still enough good Republicans and enough enlightened Southerners to vote a well-scratched ticket for whatever man (men) are for us humans.

Best wishes,
O. L. Weller

P.S. My wife says I shouldn't swear. But he is a son of a bitch for my money—and all like him are—so why not call it by name? OLW

ROBINSON TO O. L. WELLER

This is Robinson's handwritten reply, as found in the margins of the Weller letter.

No date [August 1963]

I appreciate your letter very much. We feel strongly about Goldwater and must admit are quite concerned. I feel if he is nominated the Negro must go all out to give the Democrats their greatest support. I am certain there are many more decent Americans who feel as you do and will support the man who will give all Americans the leadership that's necessary. Thanks again for writing.

ROBINSON TO A. PHILIP RANDOLPH

Robinson lobbies A. Philip Randolph, international president of the Brotherhood of Sleeping Car Porters and vice president of the AFL-CIO, regarding the historic August 28 March on Washington for Jobs and Freedom. Following the suggestion in this telegram—which reflected his own undefined status as a celebrity-activist—march organizers granted celebrities a place at the speaker's lectern. Robinson attended the march with Rachel and their three children—Jackie, Jr., Sharon, and David. "I have never been so proud to be a Negro," he later observed. "I have never been so proud to be an American."

August 23, 1963

If rumors I hear from creditable sources are correct the decision has been made that special contingent of celebrities chartering plane for march will not be allowed a single spokesman. All of these personalities are making significant sacrifices to lend their tremendous prestige to our cause. Some are coming from Europe. I hope we will not alienate them by failure to adequately acknowledge their interest in aiding in the securing of significant legislation. If information is correct I appeal to you to reconsider and to allow them to have one spokesman of their selection make a two or three minute statement and read all their names. I am aware that great responsibilities rest on your shoulders and do not seek to add to them. However I firmly believe that failure to follow this procedure would be both unwise and possibly quite harmful to the goals we all seek.

MARTIN LUTHER KING, JR. TO RACHEL ROBINSON

On September 9 Rachel and Jackie, with the assistance of their close friend Marian Logan, hosted another "Afternoon of Jazz." This time the event raised funds for both the SCLC and the NAACP, and both King and Wilkins were in attendance. As influential fund-raisers and social hosts, Rachel and Jackie frequently tried to bring together the diverse branches of the civil rights movement.

October 24, 1963

Dear Rachel:

For quite some time I have longed to write you to express my personal appreciation for what Jackie and you are doing to aid the Southern Christian Leadership Conference. Such moral and financial support is of inestimable value for the continuance of our humble efforts. Without your dollars for freedom, the Conference would be unable to work effectively toward its goal of the full integration of the Negro into all aspects of American life. Your contributions will help our work in Birmingham and all across the South. At present, SCLC has staff members in more than 20 communities seeking through nonviolent direct action and voter registration campaigns to break down the barriers of racial segregation and discrimination.

Without your moral support we would be caught in a dungeon of despair without knowing that many people all over the nation are supporting us in our struggle. By aiding us in this significant way, you are telling the world that the rights of Negroes cannot be trampled in any community without impairing the rights of every other American.

Thank you again for making our financial problems a little less burdensome. The "Afternoon of Jazz" was a delightful experience and if we continue to gain this type of support, this sweltering summer of discontent can be transformed into an invigorating autumn of justice and freedom for all people . . .

With kindest regards and best wishes to Jackie and your lovely children, I am

Sincerely yours,
Martin Luther King, Jr.

RALPH BUNCHE TO ROBINSON

In his November 16 column Robinson defended Bunche, UN undersecretary for special political affairs, from public attacks launched by Adam Clayton Powell, Jr. and Malcolm X. The two militant leaders were disturbed by a speech in which Bunche had described them as embracing "a black form of the racist virus." Bunche details the criticism—his, Powell's, and Malcolm's—in this letter of thanks to Robinson. The letter is remarkable for its description of the tensions between black Muslims and African Americans who felt they had "a stake in this country" and wanted to "cash in on it," as Bunche put it.

November 20, 1963

Dear Jackie:

I am deeply grateful to you for your kind words about me in your column in the *New York Amsterdam News* of 16 November 1963. May I say in return that among the many reasons for my long admiration of you not the least are your courage in standing by your convictions and your intellectual probity. I treasure your friendship.

The attack upon me by Malcolm X and Adam Clayton Powell to which you refer had escaped my notice, but it is not the first by either of them. I claim no immunity from attack but naturally feel that those attacking should be honest and not falsify the record, as was done by Powell and Malcolm X.

I note, for example, that you quote Powell as saying that "we have not heard from Ralph Bunche since we helped fight to get his son into the Forest Hills Tennis Club." I was unaware of Mr. Powell's "help" in this matter. The facts are that when my son's application for a Junior membership in the club was rejected, I reluctantly permitted this to be known publicly solely because to do otherwise would be to protect the discriminatory policy of a club which depended heavily on public and municipal support. The public reaction against the Club's policy was spontaneous and surprisingly strong, and the Club quickly changed presidents and reversed its policy. My son, however, no longer wished to join the Club and did not do so. Incidentally, Jackie, I never sought membership in the Club—my tennis playing days are far behind me.

That was in July 1959. As to Mr. Powell not having heard from me since then, this may be due to the fact that Adam does not speak very often in the deep south as I do and seems to avoid NAACP meetings. Just to give you an idea, I list some of the speeches I have made in the deep south in recent years, all of them dealing frankly with race relations and integration . . .

At the March on Washington, in which Mrs. Bunche and I participated (at which you and I both spoke), we saw you and your family, but we did not see Malcolm X at all, and Adam Powell only briefly when the group of Congressmen put in their short appearance at the Lincoln Memorial.

These events were all well reported in the press, so there is no room for doubt about where I stand or about my constant readiness to express my views on full equality and integration for the American Negro.

I see from your column that Malcolm X intimates that I am not free to say what I believe. My record of fully frank public utterances refutes that canard, of course. What Malcolm X really means is that he does not like to hear what I have to say, and neither does Adam, when, as most recently in Jackson, Miss. I said, ". . . I reject racists and racism, whoever and wherever they are, and whatever their color, as poisonous and vicious, as evidenced by the infamous so-called white citizens councils. I deplore Negroes embracing, as the Black Muslims and Adam Powell have done, a black form of the racist virus. I take my stand firmly and unflinchingly as an American. This is my country; my ancestors and I helped to build it. I say my color has nothing to do with it. I have a stake in this country, and I am determined that I and my children will cash in on it. I am determined to fight therefore for what is mine. I want no one—Malcolm X or anyone else—to tell me to give up this fight because equality is unattainable and to look elsewhere, in some mythical, fanciful state of black men for my salvation. I say that is surrender and escapism and I want none of it."

You may be interested in the enclosed copy of the news story about my recent speech in Jackson which was published in that city's leading newspaper.

What you have written in the column will not in the least endear you to Adam and Malcolm, but knowing you and your strength and fortitude as I do, I can be sure that you will not be losing any sleep about that.

Your friend and admirer, as always.

Sincerely,
Ralph J. Bunche

MALCOLM X TO ROBINSON

The November 16 column also saw Robinson chiding both Powell ("When we have heard from him it has usually been in the form of some grandstand, publicity-conscious barrage of wild promises which the Congressman failed to keep") and Malcolm ("Malcolm owes a great deal more to white people than Dr. Bunche ever will. As Dick Gregory says, white people invented the Muslims and the Negroes didn't even know they existed until the white man put them on his television"). Robinson rebuked Malcolm particularly for not attending the funeral of Medgar Evers. "Malcolm," he wrote, "is very militant on Harlem street corners where militancy is not dangerous." (The ellipses below are found in the letter as it was published in the Amsterdam News.*)*

November 30, 1963

Dear Good Friend, Jackie Roosevelt Robinson:

You became a great baseball player after your White Boss (Mr. Rickey) lifted you to the Major Leagues. You proved that your White Boss had chosen the "right" Negro by getting plenty of hits, stealing plenty of bases, winning many games and bringing much money through the gates and into the pockets of your White Boss.

In those days I was one of your many ardent fans; your speed and shifty base running used to hold me spellbound . . . and, according to the attack you leveled against me and Congressman Powell in your recent column, I must confess that even today you still display the same old "speed," the same "cunning," and "shiftiness" . . . and you are still trying to win "The Big Game" for your White Boss.

Shortly after the White Man lifted you from poverty and obscurity to the Major Leagues, Paul Robeson was condemning America for her injustices against American Negroes. Mr. Robeson questioned the intelligence of Negroes fighting to defend a country that treated them with such open contempt and bestial brutality.

ROBESON'S STAND

Robeson's brilliant stand in behalf of our people left the guilty American whites speechless: they had no defense.

They sought desperately to find another Negro who would be dumb enough to champion their bankrupt "white" cause against Paul Robeson.

It was you who let yourself be used by the whites even in those days against your own kind. You let them sic you on Paul Robeson.

You let them use you to destroy Paul Robeson. You let your White Boss send you before a congressional hearing in Washington, D.C. (the capitol of Segregationville) to dispute and condemn Paul Robeson, because he had these guilty American whites frightened silly.

Your White Boss sent you to Washington to assure all the worried white folks that Negroes were still thankful to the Great White Father for bringing us to America, that Negroes were grateful to America (despite our not being treated as full citizens), and that Negroes would still lay down our lives to defend this white country (though this same white government wasn't ready nor willing to defend Negroes) . . . even in those days, Jackie!

JACKIE'S COLUMN

In this same recent column you also accused me and Dr. Powell of misleading our people. Aren't you the same ex-baseball player who tried to "MISLEAD" Negroes into Nixon's camp during the last presidential election?

Evidently you were the only Negro who voted for Nixon, because according to the polls taken afterward, very few Negroes were dumb enough to follow your "MISLEAD."

Today you confess to our people that you **now** think Nixon would have been the wrong man. Aren't you also confessing that if Negroes had been dumb enough to follow you three years ago that you would have been guilty of MISLEADING them?

You never gave up. You are now trying to lead Negroes into Nelson Rockefeller's political camp. If you admit that you were wrong about Richard Nixon three years ago, how are we to be sure that you've become so politically mature in the meantime to be right in your choice today? Your "shiftiness" is confusing and very misleading.

We hear that you are about to be appointed Boxing Commissioner of New York State by Governor Nelson Rockefeller. Does this have any bearing on your efforts to get Negroes into Rockefeller's camp? Just who are you playing ball for today, good Friend?

Our people followed you on the football field and the baseball field, but we are cautious and doubtful about your shifty position in this political field.

When Mr. Rickey picked you up from obscurity and made you a Big Leaguer, you never let Mr. Rickey down; and since Mr. Black has given you a well-paying position with Chock-Full-O-Nuts, you have never let Mr. Black down . . . and now with Mr. Rockefeller promising to make you the Boxing Commissioner of New York State, we know that you can't afford to let Ole Rocky down.

You have never shown appreciation for the support given you by the Negro masses, but you have a record of being very faithful to your White Benefactors. Perhaps, if Nixon had not been such a relatively poorer man, he too would have fared much better with your support.

Your column also accused me of attacking Dr. Ralph Bunche. This is untrue. I have never **attacked** Ralph Bunche. No Muslim ever **initiates** an attack on anyone. Dr. Bunche had attacked the Muslims in general and me in particular from a college campus in the state of Mississippi, and his venomous poison was carried by all the major networks. My reply to Dr. Bunche's unwarranted attack was made strictly in self-defense (as is this present letter an answer to your unjust attack).

If Dr. Bunche's UN position is supposed to confine him to matters "above and beyond" America's race problems, whenever he does escape the confines of UN protocol, why does he always attack our Muslim religious group? This is the third time he has attacked our religion. Is he anti-Islam?

MISSISSIPPI

Since he was in Mississippi while making his recent speech, he would have shown more intelligence had he directed his full attention toward the whites in that area who are bombing Negro churches and murdering innocent little Negro girls.

Why waste precious time and energy on us? Muslims don't bomb churches. Muslims don't shoot Medgar Evers in the back. Muslims have never lynched anyone.

Dr. Bunche should realize he can't fight an effective battle on two different fronts at the same time. He can't fight the Muslims and at the same time be effective against the lynchers of Negroes.

But Dr. Bunche seems more anxious to discredit and destroy the Muslim religious group than he does the white lynchers of Negroes. Whenever I read the speeches he makes for American consumption, I often wonder if his scriptwriter isn't some anti-Muslim Israeli?

You also quoted the comedian, Dick Gregory, whose scriptwriter has him saying that most Negroes never knew the Muslims existed until the white man put the Muslims on television. I must confess that this is part-true.

The Muslims have been in the Negro Community for a long time, but Negroes such as yourself, who regard yourselves as Negro "leaders," never know what is going on in the Negro Community until the white man tells you.

You stay as far away from the Negro Community as you can get, and you never take an interest in anything in the Negro Community until the white man himself takes an interest in it. You, yourself would never shake my hand until you saw some of your white friends shaking it.

Negro "leaders" never knew Muslims existed until the white man discovered them, and right today most of these same Negro "leaders" know about Muslims only what the white man has told them.

MEDGAR EVERS

Finally, good Friend Jackie: you attacked me for not attending the funeral of Medgar Evers, who was murdered in Mississippi. When I go to a Mississippi funeral it won't be to attend the funeral of a black man!

And you Negro "leaders," whose bread and butter depend on your ability to make your white boss think you have all these Negroes "under control," better be thankful that I wasn't in Mississippi after Medgar Evers was murdered, nor in Birmingham after the murder of those four innocent little Negro girls.

If my integrity or sincerity is to be measured in your eyesight by my attendance at funerals of Negroes who have been murdered by whites, if you should ever meet with such misfortune I promise to attend your funeral, and then perhaps you will be able to see me in a different light?

If you should ever become as militant in behalf of our oppressed people as Medgar Evers was, the same whites whom you now take to be your friends will be the first to put the bullet or the dagger in your back, just as they put it in the back of Medgar Evers . . .

And I sincerely fear, good Friend Jackie, that if the whites do murder you, you are still gullible enough to die thinking they are still your white friends, and that the dagger in your back is only an accident!

Whereas if whites were to murder me for the religious philosophy that I represent and stand for, I would die **KNOWING** that it was at the hands of **OPEN ENEMIES OF TRUTH AND JUSTICE!**

ROBINSON TO MALCOLM X

Robinson criticizes Malcolm's views as "racist" and ridicules his devotion to Elijah Muhammad, leader of the Nation of Islam.

December 14, 1963

Dear Malcolm:

Frankly, your letter to me in the *New York Amsterdam News* is one of the things I shall cherish. Coming from you, an attack is a tribute. I am also honored to have been placed in the distinguished company of Dr. Ralph Bunche, whom you have also attacked.

I am proud of my associations with the men whom you choose to call my "white bosses"—Mr. Branch Rickey, my boss at Chock Full O' Nuts, Mr. William Black, and Governor Nelson Rockefeller. I am also proud that so many others whom you would undoubtedly label as "white bosses," marched with us to Washington and have been and are now working with our leaders to help achieve equality here in America.

I will not dignify your attempted slur against my appearance before the House Un-American Activities Committee some years back. All I can say is that if I were called upon to defend my country today, I would gladly do so. Nor do I hide behind any coat-tails as you do when caught in one of your numerous outlandish statements. Your usual "out" is to duck responsibility by stating: "The Honorable Elijah Muhammad says . . ."

Personally, I reject your racist views. I reject your dream of a separate state. I believe that many Americans, black and white, are committed to fighting for those freedoms for which Medgar Evers, William Moore, the Birmingham children and President John F. Kennedy died.

Those of us who are so committed have no intention of supporting the idea of a separate black state where the Honorable Muhammad can be the ruler and you his immediate successor—and all because you, Malcolm, hate white people. Too many of our young people have gone to jail and too many millions of dollars have been invested in our fight for equality for us to pay serious heed to your advice. Whether you like this country or not is of little concern to me. America is not perfect, by a long shot, but I happen to like it here and will do all I can to help make it the kind of place where my children and theirs can live in dignity.

As for Governor Rockefeller, I sincerely hope that whatever contribution I can make to his campaign for nomination and election will be meaningful. I don't know where you went to school, Malcolm. If you attended virtually any Negro college, I venture to say that a Rockefeller helped make your education possible. Neither do I apologize for my support of Mr. Nixon.

If conditions were the same today as they were in 1960, I would still support him. I do not do things to please "white bosses" or "black agitators" unless they are the things which please me. I respect Governor Rockefeller's leadership of the present and what his family has meant to us in the past. I fully intend to do all I can to aid him.

The fact that I am supporting him does not mean you should. Rest assured, I am not doing so in the hope that you will come aboard.

You say I have never shown my appreciation to the Negro masses. I assume that is why NAACP branches all over the country constantly invite me to address them. I guess this is the reason the NAACP gave me its highest award, the Spingarn Medal, and why Dr. Martin King has consistently invited me to participate in the Southern Freedom Fight and invited me to co-chair with him the drive to raise funds to rebuild the burned churches in Georgia. By the way, Malcolm, I don't remember our receiving your contribution.

Negroes are not fooled by your vicious theories that they are dying for freedom to please the white man. Negroes are fighting for freedom and rejecting your racism because we feel our stake in America is worth fighting for. Whom do you think you are kidding, Malcolm, when you say that Negro leaders ought to be "thankful" that you were not personally present in Birmingham or Mississippi after racial atrocities had been committed there? The inference seems to be that you would have played some dramatic, avenging role. I don't think you would have.

I think you would have done exactly what you did after your own Muslim brothers were shot and killed in Los Angeles. You left it to the law to take its course.

You mouth a big and bitter battle, Malcolm, but it is noticeable that your militancy is mainly expressed in Harlem where it is safe.

I have always contended for your right—as for that of every American—to say and think and believe what you choose. I just happen to believe you are supporting and advocating policies which could not possibly interest the masses. Thank God for our Dr. Bunche, our Roy Wilkins, our Dr. King, and Mr. Randolph. I am also grateful for those people you consider "white bosses."

I am glad that I have been able to come through for the people at whom you sneer. I am glad that Negroes spent so many millions for paid admissions to baseball. I am glad that we have sold an awful lot of Chock Full O' Nuts Coffee. I am hopeful that we will be able to get a great many votes for Governor Rockefeller.

I shall always be happy to associate myself with decent Americans of either race who believe in justice for all. I hate to think of where we would be if we followed your leadership. Strictly in my personal opinion, it is a sick leadership which should rightfully be rejected by the vast majority of Americans.

9

THE CAMPAIGN AGAINST BIGOTRY

· 1964 ·

BRANCH RICKEY TO ROBINSON

Robinson left Chock Full O' Nuts in early 1964, partly because of what he perceived to be his diminishing role at the company, and partly because he agreed to become a deputy national director of Nelson Rockefeller's 1964 presidential campaign. Robinson had touted Rockefeller in his newspaper column at the end of 1963. "The Republican Party," he stated, "would be in a pretty mess if it didn't have one national personality, mentioned as Presidential timbre, who believes forthrightly in the civil rights cause. Naturally, I am talking about Governor Nelson Rockefeller." And in his November 30 column on the assassination of President Kennedy, Robinson added that Goldwater's anti–civil rights stance, coupled with President Johnson's past record on segregation, "is why I believe it is important that the Republican Party line up behind the banner of Nelson Rockefeller." Robinson's decision to campaign for Rockefeller met with little surprise, and in the letter below Rickey applauds Robinson's move and comments on several related political issues. Rickey refers to the period just before Election Day 1960, when Robinson, frustrated by Nixon's refusal to call King, gave thought to abandoning the campaign. After speaking with Rickey, who insisted that Nixon was still a "fine man," Robinson decided to remain with the Nixon team.

February 21, 1964

Dear Robbie:

I have just learned that you are going to do some work for Governor Rockefeller. That pleases me more than I can tell you. He is by far the most able man in either party to be the next President of the United States. His experience, his industry, his forthrightness, and ability place him in a position of unparalleled potential leadership. I have doubt about the probability of his nomination due entirely to the lack of support of Republican women. It has always been my feeling that there should be no conflicting relationship between the private domestic misfortune of any man and his high qualifications for public service. The very reason why sentimental women oppose Nelson Rockefeller really emphasizes the man's exceptional quality for public service. Not one word has been uttered by anybody anywhere, orally or in public print, as far as I know to reflect in the slightest way an immoral act on the part of the Governor. He has moral courage to the nth degree in the way he has handled himself in public office with complete disregard of his domestic unhappiness. I think he has political guts beyond any one man I have ever known. Every voter in America has complete confidence and assurance that his public duty would always control him regardless of any personal discomfiture. I have been in his corner long before his marital trouble and I am stronger for him now than ever before.

I deeply oppose Mr. Goldwater because I believe that down deep in his heart he is in favor of the States handling very much of the Civil Rights issue instead of the Federal Government. He has weakened a bit recently in public statements about it but he cannot change enough to merit a single negro vote anywhere nor the vote of anyone else who believes in the full citizenship of all our minority groups. I hope he is not nominated. And if he is nominated, I don't know how I could vote for him—even against Johnson.

If Nelson Rockefeller were to be nominated, he would beat Lyndon Johnson. Go back and read the newspapers covering the last week preceding and including the Democratic National Convention in 1960 and particularly the last 24 hours. At that time, Johnson became a small potato in my book . . .

It just so happens that I have had several political battles both in Western Pennsylvania and in St. Louis within the last six months and I think I have won most of them. I have proof positive, as you have, that Nelson Rockefeller did not give indifferent support to the candidacy of Dick Nixon. I tried to get a half dozen of our leaders to get in touch with you on Thursday before election . . . The only one who did make the effort was Governor Rockefeller and that incident alone reflected not only the personal integrity of the man but his complete party loyalty. And I wrote a letter to Dick Nixon covering that matter in some detail.

Dick Nixon is not a candidate—really not. He does not want to be nominated unless indeed he has changed his mind more or less recently. His political ambition has not been terminated. It simply embraces delay. If Nelson Rockefeller had been and were now in Dick Nixon's place, he would be a candidate and a very aggressive one regardless of prospects of success.

You see how deeply I feel that no one is so highly qualified to be our

President as the man you have determined to support and therefore you will understand the second sentence in this letter. I am very sure that you will always have a feeling of pride and satisfaction in your identification with Governor Rockefeller's candidacy and I pray for complete success. I really do.

Sincerely yours,
Branch Rickey

ROBINSON TO WALTER THAYER

Walter Thayer, president of the New York Herald Tribune, *had sent Robinson a book, and here Robinson offers not only his thanks but also the bold suggestion that he write a column for Thayer's newspaper. Although pleased with his column for the* Amsterdam News, *Robinson hoped for a wider audience that would include blacks, whites, and all other races. The book referenced below is unidentified, and Robinson did not end up writing a column for the* Herald Tribune.

No date [February 1964]

Dear Mr. Thayer,

During my visit here in Florida I have sensed a growing concern about the future relationship our country will have with colored nations the world over. It has awakened me to the fact that something must be done. We cannot expect people to like us because we are generous with our aid program. We must, and soon, reevaluate our whole structure and come up with answers to solve our problems. There must be more communication between races. The news media must be willing to allow the views of people who will say what should be said, not of those who will say what most people want to hear.

I appreciated the book you sent. It tells such a beautiful story and has been quite effective when guests arrive. I hope more people will get a chance to see it.

I would like someday to discuss the possibility of doing a column for you. *Now is the time* for this kind of action.

Sincerely,
Jackie

ROBINSON TO A. PHILIP RANDOLPH

Robinson attempts to enlist Randolph, widely recognized as the senior statesman of the civil rights movement, to help solve the school integration crisis in New York City. In mid-March Milton Galamison, the pastor of Siloam Presbyterian Church in Brooklyn, had called for parents to keep their children home from schools. This was a call for a second boycott—the first was unsuccessful—and it met with opposition from moderate leaders in the white and black communities. Powell and Malcolm, however, publicly sided with Galamison, and during a Harlem rally on the issue, Malcolm also encouraged blacks to arm themselves for a coming race riot. Robinson's concern in the following letter centers on the fracture of the civil rights movement, the popularity of Malcolm and other black militants, and the rising white backlash.

March 28, 1964

Dear Mr. Randolph:

I address this open letter to you for two reasons.

One, that I deeply respect and honor you as the undisputed senior statesman of the movement for freedom and justice for the Negro and the social catalyst who has traditionally demonstrated the ability to bring together our finest, wisest and most reasonable leaders in times of stress.

My second reason is that I am deeply concerned over what I—and others of my acquaintance—judge to be a vital crisis in the cause of civil rights.

This crisis, we fear, could result in three most dangerous consequences. They are:

1. The alienation from our cause of Americans of good will and sincere conviction about the struggle for equality and justice for our people.
2. The thwarting of passage of meaningful civil rights legislation by the Senate.
3. The eruption of violence in the North, precipitated and prompted by men of prominence who have adopted and projected rash, irresponsible and opportunistic attitudes and uttered reckless and inflammatory statements.

I place in evidence as indicative of a breakdown in racial relations the recent disgraceful Boston stoning of an NAACP float in the St. Patrick's Day Parade.

I place in evidence as threats to passage of civil rights law, the statements of liberal Senators of both parties that there has been a major shift from approval to disapproval in their mail from white constituents, with regard to the pending legislation.

I place in evidence as an example of the expression of demagogic Negro leadership in the recent call of Mr. Malcolm X for Negro people to form gun clubs and to arm themselves with weapons of violence.

Finally, I place in evidence newspaper accounts of recent date which report a new coalition of leadership between Mr. X, Congressman Adam Clayton Powell and the Rev. Milton Galamison. These newspaper accounts indicate that this coalition has decided that the militant but reasonable civil rights organizations—NAACP, Urban League and SCLC—so long faithful in our fight—have somehow become outmoded, useless and rejected by the Negro masses.

Mr. Randolph, we are living in an age when extremism captures the headlines; the extremism of a Faubus or a Wallace or a Malcolm X. This projection wrongly gives the impression, for instance, that a Faubus speaks for all Southern whites and that a Malcolm X expresses the disenchantment of all Negroes. The coverage given Cassius Clay for embracing Black Muslimism dwarfs the attention given a Floyd Patterson for devoting time and energy to help underprivileged youngsters.

I believe the time has come for the glare of publicity to be leveled upon the true hopes and aspirations of the Negro masses as expressed through their responsible and responsive leadership. I believe the time has come for leaders of character and conscience like yourself to come together and to stand together, saying to the world:

"We will not be silent when misguided members of our race seek to give the impression that the Negro, in his fight for integration, would seek to win that fight through separation or segregation or rejection of the white friends who share a common belief in democracy.

"We will not subscribe to appeals to violence, either physical or of the spirit.

"We shall continue, with integrity and nonviolent militancy, to fight for justice and equality.

"We will not permit the years of blood, sweat, anguish and agony invested by men and women of integrity and purpose in the cause of human rights, to be forgotten in a few, fleeting moments or through the unthinking acts of a handful of extremists whose acts seem, at times, to be guided more by considerations of personal publicity than of principle."

The writer was thrilled, during the first boycott, to note the unity which Rev. Galamison was able to achieve with the established civil rights organizations. We were much disturbed with the coalition with which Rev. Galamison worked in the second boycott.

We want still to have faith in Rev. Galamison and we believe his leadership potential is needed. Somehow, the dialog between Rev. Galamison and the genuine civil rights leadership has been lost.

You, Mr. Randolph, are the one single leader of our people who has always been able to reopen the lines of communication among our leaders in the interest of our cause.

I respectfully suggest that you summon together the true and earnest architects of the "Freedom Now" movement for a frank and honest discussion of these issues. Having done so, we suggest that a joint statement be issued; a statement reestablishing in the public mind that we have not abdicated the throne of leadership to be taken over by those who emphasize the negatives; a statement affirming that a black superiority is as immoral as a white superiority; a statement re-pledging and rededicating the Negro people to the unyielding, aggressive, intelligent and courageous fight for liberty and justice for all—upon these shores, throughout this land and within the Judeo-Christian principles of our heritage.

You can do this successfully, Mr. Randolph—in my opinion—alone.

HUBERT HUMPHREY TO ROBINSON

At the same time Malcolm X was calling for Harlem residents to arm themselves, Hubert Humphrey was leading congressional efforts to pass the Civil Rights Act of 1964, and on April 15 he and other pro-civil rights legislators issued a press release stating that "illegal disturbances and demonstrations which lead to violence or injury" would undermine congressional passage of civil rights legislation. "Civil wrongs do not bring civil rights," they warned. In response to the statement, Robinson sent the Minnesota senator a telegram of support, and Humphrey replied in kind.

April 24, 1964

Dear Jackie:

Many thanks for your recent wire. As you can imagine, reactions to my statement regarding the self-defeating nature of violent and irresponsible civil rights demonstrations was mixed. Unfortunately, some people have interpreted my remarks as a weakening of my commitment to the cause of civil rights and equal opportunity. Nothing could be further from the truth.

Your understanding and support means a great deal to me.

Best wishes.

Sincerely,
Hubert H. Humphrey

ROBINSON TO NELSON ROCKEFELLER

By this point Rockefeller had lost his candidacy for the Republican presidential nomination, and Robinson, although working on various business ventures, inquires about future work that would focus on attracting minority voters to the Republican Party. The following text is the second half of Robinson's memorandum to the governor.

July 2, 1964

. . .

There is, however, one pressing problem as to which I would very much appreciate having your views at your earliest convenience. That is with respect to the areas in which you would wish to have me work during the weeks and months ahead. As you may know, I plan to become immersed in several private business ventures commencing the first part of August. However, before I undertake any commitments which might take up all of my time during the months ahead, I would like to have your thinking as to what if anything I can do to be of aid to you. In that regard, I have become convinced of one thing during the past several months, and that is that the Republican Party in the City of New York and in various other portions of the State desperately needs some concentrated activity to attract to its banner and to the banner of its candidates the support and interest of the minorities. I am absolutely convinced that with some concentrated effort we can, under your leadership, attract to the banner of the Republican Party the support of a sizable segment of the Negro, Puerto Rican, Jewish and other minority groups. The minorities are, I find, rapidly becoming convinced that they are being taken for granted by the Democratic Party and whereas certain Republican leaders such as yourself are genuinely interested in helping them, the Democratic Party, by and large, is interested only in their votes and not their problems. However, this will require some considerable effort. The need for this effort will be particularly acute this year in the tragic event that Goldwater becomes our nominee. Should that tragedy occur, I can visualize the possibility of minorities voting en masse against all Republican candidates irrespective of their own views unless some determined effort is made to keep them in the fold. Of course, if I can be of help in this area, I would be delighted to do so. However, I would appreciate hearing from you as to what if anything you would wish to have me do so that I can make my plans accordingly.

BARRY GOLDWATER TO ROBINSON

Barry Goldwater, the Republican nominee for president, complains about being labeled a "bigot" and a "menace to our country." Robinson made these accusations while campaigning for Rockefeller during the presidential primary season, and his July 4 column included the following indictment: "I never could nor never will buy Barry Goldwater. In my opinion, he is a bigot, an advocate of white supremacy and more dangerous than Governor Wallace."

July 25, 1964

Dear Mr. Robinson:

If I were to term you a bigot and a menace to our country you would resent it, I am sure, and resent it mostly because I would make the statement without ever having done you the courtesy of visiting with you to discuss your views. Yet, you have attacked me rather viciously on several occasions without ever having done me the courtesy to call and say—let's sit down and see just where you stand on these various issues.

From the venomous attack leveled at me by some members of the press and even some members of our own Party, I can't rightly blame you for holding these views, but because you occupy a place of prominence in our citizenry, your remarks aren't just the remarks of somebody else. I would deem it a great pleasure to sit down and break bread with you sometime to give me the opportunity to explain my lifelong feeling in the field of civil rights and to give you the chance to interrogate me further on them and other issues. If you are inclined to say yes, let me know, and I am sure we can set up a date to our mutual satisfaction.

Sincerely,
Barry Goldwater

ROBINSON TO BARRY GOLDWATER

With the assistance of the writer Alfred Duckett, Robinson wrote this reply to Goldwater and released both letters to the national media. Robinson refers to Goldwater delegates who booed and jeered Nelson Rockefeller when he denounced political extremism during his brief speech at the 1964 Republican National Convention in San Francisco.

No date [August 1964]

Dear Senator Goldwater:

I am in receipt of yours of July 25th regarding my attitude toward your candidacy and your willingness to meet with me to discuss your convictions on civil rights.

My failure to respond more promptly denotes no lack of respect or appreciation for your invitation. It has always been my view that differences of opinion between reasonable men can be resolved by quiet conference and exchange of honest views. However, my hesitancy in replying has been predicated on a genuine doubt as to whether such a conference as you propose would serve any legitimate purpose.

You say to me that you are interested in breaking bread with me and discussing your views on civil rights. Senator, on pain of appearing facetious, I must relate to you a rather well-known story regarding the noted musician, Louis Armstrong, who was once asked to explain jazz. "If you have to ask," Mr. Armstrong replied, "you wouldn't understand."

If at this late date, I have to ask your views on civil rights, Senator, I doubt if I would understand. I seek no private, privileged information which you are unwilling to give to the electorate. Furthermore, my opposition to you has not been based solely on my concerns as a Negro, but generally, on my fears for the future of this nation if our government were placed in your stewardship. If our national security is endangered, then civil rights becomes a meaningless phrase.

Relating to your proposal that we discuss civil rights, what could you possibly have to say?

Are you going to tell me that you worked for desegregation of eating facilities at local airports, when you were a member of the Phoenix City Council?

Are you going to tell me that you desegregated the Arizona Air National Guard?

Are you going to tell me that you contributed $200 to the Phoenix NAACP to aid school desegregation?

Are you going to tell me that you are a member of the National Urban League?

Are you also going to tell me why the Phoenix and Tucson branches of the NAACP, as you have been quoted, "started attacking me politically," resulting in your resignation?

Are you going to tell me why you have consistently attacked the Constitutionality of the United States Supreme Court edict on schools?

Are you going to tell me why you have constantly taken the position that decency in human rights should be left to the states, in spite of the many obvious and flagrant violations of human dignity which you must be aware have taken place in the deep South?

Are you going to tell me what constituted your genuine motive in voting against the civil rights bill? Did you really believe certain sections to be unconstitutional or did you and do you feel that it presented an opportunity to capitalize on anti–civil rights reaction, North and South?

Are you going to tell me why you have allowed yourself to become a political bedfellow with some of the slimiest elements in the nation, such as the Ku Klux Klan and the John Birch Society? Are you going to explain why you attacked Communism and not Fascism and the brutalities and indignities heaped upon heads of American Negroes? Have you spoken one word of sorrow or commiseration with regard to the three Americans executed in Mississippi by extremists of the Klan ilk whose support your running mate, William Miller, has stated he is willing to accept?

Are you going to tell me why you became so concerned over the injection of civil rights into the campaign when, as Roy Wilkins has observed, you yourself have been guilty of injecting it?

Are you going to tell me the whole story about the withdrawal of Governor Wallace?

Are you going to tell me whether the appointment of John Grenier, of Birmingham, . . . to the Executive Directorship of the National Republican Committee, is a harbinger that people like Wallace might become Cabinet officers under a Goldwater Administration? If a Wallace became Attorney General, for instance, might it not ease your concern about the implementation of laws you consider unconstitutional?

Are you going to expand upon your desire, as quoted in the *New York Times* of August 2, to place "states' rights" judges upon the Supreme Court bench?

What are you going to tell me, Senator Goldwater, which you cannot or do not choose to tell the country—or which you could not have told the Convention which you controlled so rigidly that it booed Nelson Rockefeller, a distinguished fellow Republican, to whom you now extend the peace pipe of unity? Is it unity you seek or uniformity, compromise or conformity, cooperation or complaisance?

What are you going to say about extremism now? You called for it—and the answer came in the thudding feet and the crashing store windows and the Molotov cocktails and the crack of police bullets and the clubbing of heads and the hate and the violence and the fear which electrified Harlem and Rochester and Jersey. I am solidly committed to the peaceful, nonviolent mass action of the Negro people in pursuit of long-overdue justice. But I am just as much opposed to the extremism of Negro rioters and Negro hoodlums as I am to the sheeted Klan, to the sinister Birchers, to the insidious Citizens' Councils.

I am firmly committed also to work, to travel, to speak, to implore to sacrifice to attempt to bring about in November a victory for the way of life we have known and loved. I am working to help strengthen the thrust of Republicans for Johnson, Independents for Johnson and any and every freedom-loving, extremism-defying movement which will help to insure that the farce of San Francisco shall not engulf our nation in a long nightmare of hopelessness and havoc and holocaust.

If, in view of these questions, which I raise in absolute sincerity and conviction, you still think a meeting between us would be fruitful, I am available at your convenience.

I am releasing our exchange of correspondence to the press for Friday morning, August 7 newspapers. By that time, you will have received this letter.

Sincerely yours,
Jackie Robinson

HUBERT HUMPHREY TO ROBINSON

Like millions of others, Humphrey was aware of Robinson's public criticism of Goldwater.

August 5, 1964

Dear Jackie,

This is just a note to say congratulations on the outstanding job you have been doing since the Republican Convention. It is truly a great national tragedy to see the Party which played such an important role in the successful passage of the Civil Rights Bill being captured and kidnapped by those "extremists."

Of course civil rights will be an issue in the presidential campaign. It will be an issue and we will win. Keep up the good work!

Best personal regards.

Sincerely yours,
Hubert H. Humphrey

ROBINSON TO HUBERT HUMPHREY

Although critical of Lyndon Johnson's efforts as Senate majority leader to weaken the Civil Rights Act of 1957, Robinson changed his assessment after Kennedy's assassination. Impressed with Johnson's words (in his first presidential speech to Congress, he stated, "We have talked long enough in this country about civil rights. We have talked for a hundred years or more") and deeds (he negotiated successful passage of the Civil Rights Act of 1964), Robinson offers to campaign for the Johnson-Humphrey ticket in the 1964 presidential race.

August 14, 1964

Dear Senator Humphrey:

I truly appreciated your kind letter of August 5.

I am sure you recognize that principle is important to me. Any man who shifts position as often and as easily as Senator Goldwater does is not the kind of man I would like to see running this country.

It seems to me that I read somewhere that a favorite Senator of mine predicted that we would be in serious trouble if we had a man for President who would have a nervous finger on the nuclear button. I hope that many Americans are as deeply concerned over the threat to our institutions which Goldwater represents as you and I are.

I am further concerned that many Negroes may react to the current situation by staying home from the polls. I hear frequent remarks from Negro people that they cannot possibly vote for Goldwater, but that they feel that the President's past civil rights record is not one to inspire confidence in spite of his recent accomplishments and statements. There is a danger that many Negro people will shrug their shoulders and decide to pass up their duty to vote. This could hurt the President and help the opposition.

My personal feeling is that Mr. Johnson's record before 1960 was not at all a good one but I have said publicly many times, even when campaigning for Governor Rockefeller, that if Mr. Johnson is sincere on civil rights, it will be a wonderful thing because there is no better friend to this cause than a converted Southerner.

We must get word to the Negro electorate that it is better to have someone in office who is working for civil rights as Mr. Johnson is—regardless of the past—than to have someone who is apparently seeking to gain the Presidency through an appeal to anti-Negro reaction.

Getting this message across is not going to be easy. It will be a lot easier, however, if the President has the foresight to select you as his running mate.

I would like to help the Johnson campaign. I am sure I can but, as you are well aware, I could not do it in a halfhearted way. I will be willing to spend time and to travel if you feel I can be of service. Please understand that I am not seeking a political appointment. I simply feel that all of us must do what we can to help save the country.

We will take a leave of absence and work as hard as we can for the ticket, providing our services are desired and that we can be compensated only for the loss we would suffer because of the leave.

Let me know what you think. If you feel we can help, perhaps we can get together and discuss specifics.

Once again, thanks for your words of encouragement. They mean much to me, considering the source.

Sincerely yours,
Jackie Robinson

ROBINSON TO HUBERT HUMPHREY

On August 26 the Democratic National Convention nominated Humphrey as Johnson's running mate, and Robinson wires his congratulations. He was so pleased with the nomination that he helped to chair the group Republicans for Johnson.

August 26, 1964

I am happy for America.

Jackie Robinson

ROBINSON TO NELSON ROCKEFELLER

Although Goldwater supporters had drowned out Rockefeller's speech at the Republican convention, the New York governor nevertheless supported Goldwater's bid for the presidency. Robinson was disappointed with both Rockefeller and another Republican who toured the country campaigning for Goldwater: Richard Nixon. Following Goldwater's defeat, Robinson stated, "As for the Republican Party, it should know by now that racism can no longer win elections in America."

October 7, 1964

Dear Governor Rockefeller:

I see that Barry Goldwater is now, in your opinion, a man of courage and integrity. You know and I know that a Goldwater victory would result in violence and bloodshed. His candidacy reeks with prejudice and bigotry. His remark that this has become a nation ruled by minorities while the majority suffers is not only stupid, but undeserving of support from a man with real courage and integrity.

Perhaps it makes no difference, but I have to let you know that I am truly sorry you have taken this stand, for you know what Barry Goldwater means—not only to the Negro people—but to so many other Americans of goodwill. It seems to me that to support him is to reject the ideals and principles for which the Rockefeller name has always stood. Your doing so is one of the most disappointing things which has ever happened to me.

The picture I have of the Goldwater supporters giving you discourtesy and contempt as you attempted to speak to them at San Francisco is one which will never be erased from my memory. I did not believe it could be erased from yours. I am certain there is more to this than meets the eye, but because of our relationship, I felt I must express my true feelings to you.

Your friend,
Jackie Robinson

MARTIN LUTHER KING, JR. TO ROBINSON

October 7, 1964

Dear Jackie:

Your address at our annual SCLC banquet made it one of the highlights of our convention. I don't know what we would have done through these past years without your ardent support and interest. We certainly count you among our most valuable friends and it pleases me to say that you have continued to give the kind of leadership throughout your career that we are proud to be identified with. This is certainly an important contribution to mankind as a whole and especially to Negro people, who too often must see their heroes of their youth tarnished by selfish compromises and mediocre judgment. May God continue to enable you to maintain the high level of leadership and integrity which has been yours throughout your career.

Enclosed is a small honorarium for your services. While it is not our policy to give honorariums to convention speakers, we feel that you have gone so far beyond the call of duty in continually rendering your services to the cause that we would like for you to accept this as a small token of our appreciation. My regards to your wife and children.

Sincerely yours,
Martin Luther King, Jr.

ROBINSON TO JOHN DEMPSEY

Robinson's daughter, Sharon, was dating a young man from Southfield Village, a federal housing project operated by the Housing Authority of Stamford. In the following letter to Connecticut governor John Dempsey, Robinson expresses concern that Southfield Village Neighborhood Center, directed by Ambalal Rawal, lacked the funding required to instill hope in the poverty-stricken youth of the neighborhood.

October 25, 1964

Dear Gov. Dempsey,

First let me say I enjoyed sharing the dais with you last week. It was a wonderful night for me.

Now let me say I am appalled to learn that Southfield village in Stamford, Connecticut, has a budget of $17,000, which includes salaries and whatever else is needed to meet their expenses. Their Director, Mr. Rawal, is a dedicated public servant who is doing an amazing job despite the handicap of an inadequate budget.

This area needs help. The people in it are of the feeling no one cares. The youngsters see their parents and feel there is no hope. Conditions are bad yet our officials expect miracles on a measly $17,000 budget which must service the needs of 1,400 families.

As Governor of our state, I urge you to investigate conditions at Southfield Village and I am sure you will see the need as I do and help Mr. Rawal do a job. In so doing you will give inspiration to our future citizens who need to know someone cares.

I hope Governor Dempsey you do care and will lend a helping hand. In the long run it will save the state money.

Very truly yours,
Jackie Robinson

ROBINSON TO JOHN DEMPSEY

In his October 29 reply Dempsey stated that he had asked one of his staffers for a report on Southfield Village so that he and his staff could determine the possibility of funding the village more adequately through additional state and federal programs.

November 4, 1964

Dear Governor Dempsey,

We are extremely pleased to get your report on our discussion with Mr. Rawal. An indicated emergency situation required me to express my concern. We feel that Southfield Village is a potential explosive neighborhood. Something has to be done if these youngsters are to grow and develop into useful citizens. I know pretty much the problems that exist. My young daughter dates one of the boys from the village. Your immediate response and interest brings a great deal of gratitude. Speaking of gratitude I must express my pride in being a Connecticut citizen. The smashing defeat of Goldwater indicates that the vast majority of our citizens are interested in growth and development.

Your leadership has been invaluable. My sincere best wishes for your continued dedication and services to all your constituents.

Sincerely,
Jackie Robinson

ROBINSON TO A. PHILIP RANDOLPH

As 1964 came to an end, Robinson pressed his friends, including A. Philip Randolph, to join him in supporting Freedom National Bank in Harlem. An early proposal for the bank had declared that Harlem was suffering from a "serious deficiency of banking facilities" and that Harlem residents were "unrepresented in the formation of policies that prominently affect the economic life of the community." Because of these problems, Robinson and other business-savvy colleagues set out to establish "the first national bank organized by, directed by, and attuned to the needs of the Harlem community." As chair of the new bank, Robinson believed that he could help Harlem residents achieve economic freedom from white institutions that often discriminated against African Americans when offering loans and setting mortgage rates—a point he emphasized in his January 2 column. "We need to fight on the civil rights front, it is true," he observed. "But it is just as important for us to make inroads on an economic level, if we are to solve some of our many problems." Although unremarkable at first glance, the following letter to Randolph provides insight into the direct and persistent style of Robinson's business tactics. Randolph was not able to speak at the dedication, but he promised in his reply on January 8 that he would stop by the bank for a chat.

December 30, 1964

Dear Mr. Randolph:

We were very sorry that you were unable to attend the preview opening of the Freedom National Bank on December 18, 1964. An invitation was sent to your office.

On Monday, January 4, 1965, at 11 a.m., the formal dedication will take place. We would appreciate it very much if you would come and say a few words on this long awaited occasion. Knowing your interest in the progress of our people, I would like to sit down and discuss with you the possibility of getting an account for the Freedom National Bank. May we set up an appointment at your convenience?

My best wishes for a "Happy and Healthy New Year."

Very truly yours,
Jackie Robinson

10

A ROCKEFELLER REPUBLICAN

· 1965–1966 ·

NELSON ROCKEFELLER TO ROBINSON

Rockefeller begins the New Year with a positive letter about Robinson's successful lobbying efforts to direct the governor's attention to the growing drug crisis among teenagers.

January 4, 1965

Dear Jackie:

My message to the 1965 Legislature includes the following paragraph in the section on narcotics:

"There has also been an alarming increase in the consumption by teenagers of habit-forming patent medicines and other substances which have an incidental narcotic effect. To meet this problem, I shall recommend to your honorable bodies legislation to bar the sale of these medicines to children except upon prescription."

You may recall that you brought the patent medicine problem to my attention through Hugh Morrow some time ago, and I thought you'd be interested to know that your report has resulted in this recommendation to the Legislature. Many thanks, once again, for a contribution in the public interest.

With best wishes and personal regards,

Sincerely,
Nelson A. Rockefeller

ROBINSON TO NELSON ROCKEFELLER

Robinson praises Robert Choate, a progressive Republican in Phoenix politics, and implores Rockefeller "to put the party back on the track." In the speech he cites below, Robinson stated, "If the Republican Party is to be strong; if it is to accept and play out magnificently its role as the intelligent loyal opposition; if it is to build among its ruins and repair its image and come thundering back into power—then, I say to you, my friends, that it is not enough to defeat Goldwater. We must, once and for all, defeat Goldwaterism."

February 1, 1965

Dear Governor,

At the urging of Mr. Sam Aldridge and Mr. Hugh Morrow, I accepted the invitation of Robert Choate to address the closing session of the South West Conference on Poverty. Mr. Choate, who seems to be our kind of Republican, indicated that there was a need for a strong statement addressing the progressive goals of the Republican Party. He felt that the Conservative voice and influence are still potent in that area.

I hope that you will be able to find time to read the enclosed copy of my speech. I was deeply gratified at the reception and quite pleasantly surprised at the applause which interrupted the speech about a dozen times. Your ears should have been burning, Governor, for when I referred to you as one of the few men in the Party who had stood by his principle, the approval from the audience was loud and heartening. It is significant that there were quite a number of Democrats present, as well as representatives of the various ethnic groups to which I referred in my speech.

This experience has served to fortify me in my deep belief that the liberal wing of the Republican Party certainly must rally around you to present and execute a vigorous program to put the Party back on the track. We must let minority people in America know that they are wanted and needed in order that the two party system—and therefore the political health of our nation—may be preserved.

Your friend,
Jackie Robinson

ROBINSON TO LYNDON JOHNSON

Although they never formed a friendship, Johnson respected Robinson enough to invite him to a White House dinner honoring Vice President Hubert Humphrey and others on February 2. An uncharacteristic optimism is evident in this letter of appreciation for Johnson's "inspired leadership" in civil rights.

February 4, 1965

My dear Mr. President:

Words cannot express the gratitude my wife and I felt for one of the most enjoyable evenings of our lives.

The warmth and friendliness of your guests was inspiring. My wife is still floating on cloud nine because she had the honor of dancing with the President of the United States, and having a dream come true.

Your inspired leadership more than justifies the confidence we all have in you. May God give you continued good health and wisdom—in my humble opinion, no American in public office has grown as you have. No President could have affected the progress in our drive for human dignity as you have done.

The day is rapidly approaching when all Americans will be judged on the contents of character, rather than skin color. The speed by which we achieve our goals will depend on how you continue the dedicated work you are now involved in.

I am pleased to be able to write this letter of appreciation. You have been a real inspiration. I feel certain, we not only will continue to feel gratified, but through your leadership, we will make even greater progress.

Please give our thanks to Mrs. Johnson as well. She was a most charming hostess.

Sincerely yours,
Jackie Robinson

ROBINSON TO NELSON ROCKEFELLER

In a February 11 letter Rockefeller thanked Robinson for his "generous expressions" about Rockefeller's possible role in the future. Robinson's reply here cites "the 1964 debacle," and, while praising the appointment of Ersa Poston as director of the New York State Office of Economic Opportunity, he encourages Rockefeller to take additional steps to attract African American voters.

February 22, 1965

Dear Governor:

Thanks for your letter of the 11th. I was very pleased to receive it. I was afraid that you were disturbed because of the Tucson speech. As we saw things and as we see them now this is the only way the Party can overcome the 1964 debacle.

I am certain you know me well enough now to understand what motivates me. The sooner there is a strong two party system in New York as well as nationwide the sooner we get our Rights. President Johnson obviously understands the importance of the minority vote. He is making strong strides to cement it. The Republican Party on the other hand keeps saying we can't win this vote, forget it. You can't do this in 1965. The minority vote continues to grow and is becoming more sophisticated. An awareness on the part of the power structure is badly needed. To overcome the image what is needed is the appointment by the Party of someone to an important position who will tell you what you should hear, not what you want to hear. I believe it would do a great deal to strengthen the Party. How can a Party win representing only 27% of the total vote?

I humbly suggest that while the states are the key, the Party must understand that the role of a Governor Rockefeller could be the start to changing the picture. If the national committee would recognize your image in this area, the first step could be made. Like everything else, that first step is so important. Don't make the mistake of appointing a Negro because he is a Negro. The appointment of Ersa Poston was a ten strike; however, it did not get the message to the right place because you have not done as the Democrats have. They take over the Negro news media and reap all the benefit from appointments.

I didn't mean to ramble but feel it's so important. I hope you don't feel I am presumptuous.

Please give our regards to Mrs. Rockefeller. When your hectic schedule eases we hope we can have the visit Mrs. Rockefeller and my wife talked about.

Regards to all. Thanks again for the letter. I appreciate it because of the great respect I hold for you. In my view, I must repeat, at this time you are perhaps the only powerful Republican who can win the minority vote.

Sincerely,
Jackie

ROBINSON TO LYNDON JOHNSON

In the following telegram Robinson pleads with Johnson to take federal action in response to "Bloody Sunday," the March 7 clubbing and gassing of nonviolent marchers by state troopers positioned just beyond the Edmund Pettus Bridge on the outskirts of Selma, Alabama. John Lewis, chairman of the Student Nonviolent Coordinating Committee (SNCC), and Hosea Williams, an SCLC staff member, had led the marchers in a protest for voting rights and a commemoration of the February 26 death of Jimmie Lee Jackson, a young African American activist who was shot while helping to protect his family at a civil rights rally.

March 9, 1965

Important you take immediate action in Alabama. One more day of savage treatment by legalized hatchet men could lead to open warfare by aroused Negroes. America cannot afford this in 1965.

Jackie Robinson

ROBINSON TO HUBERT HUMPHREY

On March 9, six hundred marchers converged on the White House to demand that the president send federal marshals or troops to Selma and to arrest the Alabama officials responsible for Bloody Sunday. The leaders of the march met with Vice President Humphrey, and although they found that he had a "good attitude," they were disappointed with his immediate failure to help meet their demands. Note the form of address in the following letter. Robinson tended to use this when addressing someone whose actions or statements disturbed him.

March 10, 1965

Sir:

I am surprised at the lack of action by the Administration re. Selma, Alabama. The report by the committee that met with you yesterday was, I am certain, inaccurate. I can't believe, as reported, that you have a lack of understanding of the magnitude of the situation in Selma. Your dedication to the principles of our country has been most encouraging. I hope there have not been orders to curtail these interests towards the things that have made our country strong.

The President has been extremely active as far as getting his picture taken with prominent Negroes. This is not enough, Mr. Humphrey; we will not be satisfied because prominent people are invited to discuss problems, but it ends there. We are no longer going to tolerate the treatment by legalized hatchetmen. Another Selma, Alabama, could result in open warfare. These are not idle threats, Sir; they come because of my great concern for our country. We cannot afford in 1965 Black against White. It would help no one.

The administration cannot expect us to give in on every occasion. President Johnson must be more aware of his responsibility in this area.

Please understand I am writing because of my great concern. I hope you too have this concern and will express it to the President, and all those who sincerely believe in the dignity of all men.

Very truly yours,
Jackie Robinson

HUBERT HUMPHREY TO ROBINSON

The Johnson administration responded to Bloody Sunday by sending federal troops to protect the marchers as they finally made their way from Selma to Montgomery, and on March 15 Johnson appeared before a joint session of Congress to propose voting legislation. "But even if we pass this bill," he announced, "the battle will not be over. What happened in Selma is part of a far larger movement which reaches into every section and State of America. It is the effort of American Negroes to secure for themselves the full blessings of American life. Their cause must be our cause too. Because it's not just Negroes, but really it's all of us, who must overcome the crippling legacy of bigotry and injustice. And we shall overcome."

March 29, 1965

Dear Jackie:

Please forgive this somewhat belated reply to your letter expressing concerns about events in Selma, Alabama. As you can imagine, we were simply deluged with mail on this subject, at the same time as we were engaged in a constant effort to work out a practical solution to the problems it presented.

The President's recent actions must surely have convinced you of this government's total commitment to the cause of civil rights and opportunities for all citizens. In providing federal protection for marchers in Alabama, and in recommending to the Congress comprehensive voting legislation, the President has acted with unprecedented vigor and determination to guarantee these fundamental rights.

I appreciate your concern, of course, and I hope you will always feel free to offer your suggestions and advice.

Best wishes.

Sincerely,
Hubert H. Humphrey

ROBINSON TO BRANCH RICKEY

The early months of 1965 saw Robinson devoting much of his business attention to Gibraltar Life Insurance Company, an interracial company he founded with Arthur Logan, a leading Harlem physician, and other business leaders. In this letter Robinson invites Rickey, a longtime proponent of multiracial companies, to play a role in the young company and agrees to Rickey's earlier suggestion that he lend his name to help Japan International Christian University raise funds for the construction of a new gymnasium. Rickey agreed to chair the board of Gibraltar, and in 1966 the company merged with Manhattan-based

Hamilton Life Insurance Co. The business venture was not financially successful for Robinson.

No date
[received April 12, 1965]

Dear Mr. Rickey,

Things have really been happening with me. We did organize a bank. Our charter came through in January and we are doing very well up to now. I am chairman of the board and have been very active, spending most of my mornings there. We are an interracial bank and seem to be making an impact on the community.

My main interest, however, is in our insurance company. We are in our final stages and with a bit of luck should be operating by May 15. It's a life insurance company. We were granted the name Gibraltar Life. Our board is very active with business and professional men on it. We have a great potential. Our only problem is to keep it from getting out of control. The duties are simple and most of the board members will meet only about four times a year. This is probably the greatest opportunity I have had. Our stock will sell for $5 a share, and we expect it to open at a premium because of the promised insurance we have had. It would be a great honor for me if you would consider being a part of the company. I would not expect anything other than to have you listed as a board member. Things have been very rewarding for me, but had it not been for you, nothing would be possible. We are already oversubscribed as far as people wanting stock. Requests are coming in, but due to regulations we cannot even talk about issuing any. As I mentioned, it holds a great potential, and if you would like a few shares, I'll see that you get some on the ground floor. It might be wise to ask your accountant what he feels about a new company (Life) licensed in New York with a potential of about 20,000 in the first month. Of course no stock company is a sure thing, but I sincerely believe our opportunity is unlimited.

I hope everyone is fine. We all are well. Rachel will probably accept an offer to become head of the nursing school at Yale Univ. It's a big responsibility but I know she can handle it. Jackie, Jr. is in the army, and while he does not like it, we feel it's the best thing for him. He did not want to stay in school, and the army was the next best thing. Sharon and David are both hard workers in school. They are doing well.

As for the Int. Univ. of Japan, I'll join if there is no responsibility. As pres. of the United Churchmen and chairman of the board of the bank and soon President of Gibraltar Life, my schedule is not my own. If Dr. Sockman feels my name is of value, I would be honored to serve.

Well, Mr. Rickey, I think that about covers it. Please don't feel you have to accept my offer. I realize what your schedule is but I believe you would want to be a part of an interracial company, and I do think we can make a strong impact.

Give my regards to Mrs. Rickey. I do hope she is well and about. I am sure the children and grandchildren are well. Say hello also.

Even though I don't write much, you are always on our minds. We feel so very close to you and I am sure you know our love and admiration is sincere and dedicated. Please take care of yourself. We know where your heart is. We will take care of the Selma Alabamas and do a job.

Sincerely,
Jackie

P.S. Rae sends her love along with the children.

ROBINSON TO KENNETH KEATING

Robinson had invited former senator Kenneth Keating of New York to join the board of Gibraltar Life, but he declined in an April 16 letter, citing potential conflicts of interest. "On another subject," Keating added, "I have been interested to read about the possibility of your candidacy for mayor. When the press called me, I need hardly say that I jumped at the opportunity to express my high regard for you and my confidence that you would . . . render distinguished service as mayor." Robinson's reply addresses this development and expresses regret that Robert Kennedy defeated Keating in the 1964 senatorial race.

April 27, 1965

Dear Senator:

Thank you for your very nice letter. We are sorry you cannot become associated with us at this time, but we do appreciate your interest. I don't know if you saw the *New York Times* article of the 20th. It gave a good picture of what we are trying to do.

As to the reports about my interest in running for an office, they are premature and without foundation. I am not interested in being a candidate, and only would give consideration to getting involved if I felt the Republican Party really wanted to develop a two party system among minority groups. At this writing, I don't feel there is an interest in doing so.

I felt it was a tragic mistake for Negroes to vote so overwhelmingly for Kennedy when you have been such a real friend. I think this happened because of a lack of confidence in the Party, not in you. We all are worse off, in my opinion, and I do hope you continue to use your influence whenever possible.

I do hope we can visit soon. There is so much that needs to be done. It is sad to keep hearing Republicans in high offices say we can't win the Negro vote. I hope, at least in the future, they will try to win it. They haven't tried in the past. . . .

Continued good luck.

Very sincerely yours,
Jackie Robinson

NELSON ROCKEFELLER TO ROBINSON

Rockefeller's veto of a minimum-wage bill did not significantly affect Robinson's enthusiasm for the governor.

May 3, 1965

Dear Jackie:

Thanks for your recent letter urging me to sign the $1.50 minimum wage bill, which I was sorry to have to veto.

I am, of course, aware of the need for an increase in the minimum wage, and so recommended to the Legislature in my Annual Message. However, as I pointed out, any substantial increase must be made concurrent with an increase in the Federal minimum wage if New York is to avoid a serious loss of employment and economic opportunity. I am still hoping for the passage of my program bill which would increase New York's minimum wage to $1.50 per hour, effective when the Federal minimum is also increased.

I am enclosing for your information a copy of my veto message.
With personal regards,

Sincerely,
Nelson A. Rockefeller

ROBINSON TO WALTER O'MALLEY

The Los Angeles Dodgers honored Robinson at Dodger Stadium on June 16. It was a low-key event, and joining Robinson for the pregame ceremony was Walter Dorn, a childhood friend then serving as a Los Angeles County supervisor. The following letter suggests that, however strained their relationship continued to be, there was some level of reconciliation between Robinson and Walter O'Malley. The owner of the Dodgers replied on July 15, "It was thoughtful of you to write me and I do appreciate it."

July 2, 1965

Dear Mr. O'Malley:

Thanks for helping to make the Jackie Robinson Day a big success, at least for my family. Red Patterson was of great help and we feel his know-how made things fit better into place.

I am told everyone considered the day a success; much of it was due to your cooperation.

Rachel sends her best and thanks as well.

Regards to Mrs. O'Malley and the family.

Sincerely yours,
Jackie

ROBINSON TO HUBERT HUMPHREY

The conservative John Birch Society was a vigorous opponent of the civil rights movement in the 1950s and 1960s. Robinson suggests here that the growth of the society could lead to the type of rioting that occurred in the Watts area of Los Angeles in 1965.

September 21, 1965

My Dear Mr. Vice President:

Two thousand Stamford, Connecticut residents turned out for a John Birch meeting about a month ago. Last week the papers carried the story that in Washington, offices have been established for the John Birchers. In Los Angeles during my recent visit, friends informed me the growth of the Birchers and the Conservative element is causing still more unrest.

We cannot afford any more riots. Our prestige has sunk to a new level in Colored Nations, due, I believe, primarily to our race problems. What I see, what I hear, and what I know, Mr. Vice President, causes me great concern. I am not an alarmist, but unless we are willing to voice our concern, we are heading for more situations like Watts, California, in the immediate future.

Negroes are not going to let up. We know one of the purposes of the Birchers is to intimidate us and prevent our drive for equality. The growth of the Birchers is being brought to the attention of Negro Americans—some thought and action must be given to this potential problem which could explode as it did in Los Angeles.

Knowing your dedication, I am pleading for you to take the leadership in preventing any further problems. A show of concern will be of great value.

Sincerely yours,
Jackie Robinson

HUBERT HUMPHREY TO ROBINSON

In reply to Robinson's concern about the John Birch Society, Humphrey refers to Johnson's June 4 announcement that he intended to call a White House conference titled "To Fulfill These Rights," with the purpose of helping "the American Negro fulfill the rights which, after the long time of injustice, he is finally about to secure." The conference took place on June 1 and 2, 1966.

September 27, 1965

Dear Jackie:

I appreciate so much hearing from you. I share your concern about the growth of the extreme right-wing in this country. At the same time, one should not ignore the encouraging evidence on the other side, namely, the recent Gallup poll which indicated that a majority of Americans would vote for a Negro for President if he was the most qualified man in the race. This surely could not have happened even a few years ago.

I hope the President's White House Conference on Civil Rights will be a focal point where much of the concern you mention in your letter can be expressed. The weeks and months and years ahead will not be easy, but I believe we should not be overly downcast or feel that control of the situation is slipping away.

The President is as dedicated an individual to the cause of freedom and equality in this country as one could hope for, and this is a fact of life we should never forget. His leadership, and the support of leaders throughout America, will be of great value in these difficult times.

Best wishes.

Sincerely,
Hubert H. Humphrey

HUBERT HUMPHREY TO ROBINSON

Humphrey's prior letter apparently prompted a negative response from Robinson.

October 14, 1965

Dear Jackie:

I appreciate very much having your frank opinions on these important matters. And I am sure you realize that the President, as well as his Vice President, is deeply committed to correcting the social ills you have spelled out so clearly. By noting the progress which has been made, I in no way intended to suggest that nothing more need be done.

I know that the President will not be satisfied until every American is able to exercise his full rights as a free human being.

Throughout the campaign I denounced the John Birch Society on a number of occasions and I will continue to do so. And I know we are not going to be satisfied until this battle has been won once and for all.

Best wishes.

Sincerely,
Hubert H. Humphrey

ROBINSON TO JACOB JAVITS

Robinson registers a complaint with Senator Jacob Javits of New York, a Republican, after reading the following lead of a November 20 article in the New York Times: *"Senator Jacob K. Javits declared today that Governor Rockefeller was 'in trouble' in New York State but could still win reelection for a third term next year." Robinson spoke about Javits's comments with George Lawrence, pastor of Antioch Baptist Church in Brooklyn, and Wyatt Tee Walker, who later served as special assistant to the governor for community affairs. Javits eventually agreed to chair Rockefeller's campaign for reelection.*

November 22, 1965

Dear Senator Javits:

Shocked to read statements attributed to you in the *New York Times* last Saturday, indicating that Governor Rockefeller has to prove himself during the coming legislative season.

What shocks me is that you of all people know full well what the Governor has done. When you speak in this manner, it causes us to wonder if this is not a deliberate attempt to embarrass Governor Rockefeller. You say you are for him, but when I talked about your statement with Reverend George Lawrence and Reverend Wyatt Tee Walker, we could not help but wonder why your statements always seem to undermine the Governor and to project the image of Senator Javits.

We are dedicated to seeing that the two-party system comes about. We feel it can best be done by Governor Rockefeller, for in our opinion, there is no other Republican on the horizon whose background inspires minorities as the Governor does.

If you are sincerely in Governor Rockefeller's corner, I urge you to recognize the harm you are doing, and adopt another tactic. This letter is sent in an effort to promote better understanding instead of creating further problems.

Sincerely yours,
Jackie Robinson

NELSON ROCKEFELLER TO ROBINSON

Jackie, Jr., now in the U.S. Army, left for Vietnam in June. He was wounded in a November 19 attack that left two of his friends dead. Jackie, Jr. dragged one of his dying friends out of the heat of battle, and he was awarded the Purple Heart.

December 2, 1965

Dear Jackie:

I was terribly sorry to hear that your son was wounded in Vietnam; thank heaven it was no worse, particularly in view of the tragic death of his two companions. Please give Rachel my best wishes; I'm sure she met this trial like a champion, but I also know too well how hard it strikes a parent when something like this happens to one of the children.

Let me also express my deep admiration for the balance and restraint of your remarks about those in the country who criticize our servicemen and support the Viet Cong. Such temperance would be hard even without the emotional stress of personal concern; with it, the temptation to lash out violently must have been almost intolerable.

With warm personal regards to you and Rachel,

Sincerely,
Nelson Rockefeller

ROBINSON TO KIVIE KAPLAN

Kivie Kaplan, newly elected president of the NAACP, invited Robinson to reassume a leading role in the civil rights organization. But Robinson declines in the following letter, citing his disagreement with certain NAACP members and the association's "problems of inferiority and fear." This letter foreshadows a 1967 showdown between Robinson and Roy Wilkins.

No date [1966]

Dear Kivie,

. . .

The problem, Kivie, is that the association seeks help, but what are they willing to do in return? There was not a more devoted man until I began to see that the desire is for personal gain, not for the good of the masses. The pettiness of some of the members and the unwillingness to change for the good of all.

Kivie, the shame is that an organization with the ability the NAACP has feels as it does. The association has lost its chance to be respected by the overwhelming majority. You can't be petty and be big. The association will never be big with little me at its head. We have talked about all of this before. I am sorry to feel as I do, but I am at least honest enough to know there cannot be strength in a group that is beset with problems of inferiority and fear. There is no need for it, but it exists and seemingly nothing can change it. I hope all our thoughts can be kept from the public, but they probably won't.

I still feel you are a real credit. You have worked hard and deserve the "honor" of being president. I only wish there were more people as dedicated.

Continued good luck.

Sincerely,
Jackie

ROBINSON TO NELSON ROCKEFELLER

Robinson refused to join public criticism about the insignificant number of African Americans in Rockefeller's administration, mostly because he deeply admired the governor's commitments to various civil rights causes through the years. In his January 8 column Robinson even praised the governor's "fine record," but in this private letter he shares his disappointment over the lack of African American appointees.

January 12, 1966

Dear Governor Rockefeller:

This is one of the most difficult letters I have ever had to write. It is, however, absolutely necessary.

While I sincerely believe there is not a more dedicated politician on the scene, your record toward the Negro regarding political appointments cannot be accepted by any self-respecting Negro. In New York, it seems to me inexcusable that on the state level, excluding a few appointments, you do not have any one of color on your staff. In states far less sophisticated, as far as race relations are concerned, the governor is completely aware of the necessity of having qualified Negroes on his personal staff.

I felt we had made it clear at our meeting some time ago about the importance of appointments of this nature. Little, if anything, has been done, and our group, I in particular, has been left in a most embarrassing position. I can only come to the conclusion that nothing is going to be done, and because of what I stand for, my personal high regard for you cannot stand in the way of my desire to see the progress Negro Americans are making continued.

Your inaction can only mean a lack of interest, which compels me to do whatever I must to bring it to the attention of the public. If I am to be of any use to anyone I eventually support, whatever my value is, I can only be useful if I continue doing what I believe to be right. Unless there is immediate action, Governor, I must publicly answer the challenges which have come to me concerning favorable articles I have written about you—the latest in the January 8th issue of the *Amsterdam News*. The challenges have come from Negro newsmen for whom I have great respect.

I hope you understand my position. I do not put personal feelings above the feeling I have for the masses of our people. I know you hold the greatest position of respect among the Negro. However, as you yourself stated at the meeting, Negroes are not concerned about yesterday, they are asking about today. Lindsay's victory is the best example.

Respectfully yours,
Jackie Robinson

NELSON ROCKEFELLER TO ROBINSON

Rockefeller replied by phone to Robinson's previous letter, and on February 8 Robinson became a special assistant to the governor for community affairs.

February 8, 1966

Dear Jackie:

One of the things I have looked forward to for a long time is the possibility of working with you in close association. Today this becomes a reality and I just wanted to write this note to tell you how much it means to me personally.

Your life has been a fulfillment of the basic principles and goals in which I was brought up to believe. To have the opportunity of working closely with you in the achievement of these goals for all is a source of infinite satisfaction and pride to me. I feel that we can accomplish great things together and I look forward to the close association that will be possible in the days that lie ahead.

With best wishes to you and Rachel,

Sincerely,
Nelson A. Rockefeller

ROBINSON TO JOHN LINDSAY

With assistance from Robinson, Republican John Lindsay won the 1965 mayoral race in New York City, garnering a significant percentage of the African American vote and defeating Democrat Abraham Beame and Conservative William F. Buckley, Jr. The campaign left Robinson and Buckley bitter toward each other, and in his February 12 column Robinson referred to Buckley as "one of the high priests behind the Barry Goldwater candidacy for President." The following telegram is significant mainly because of Robinson's admission that he is a "Rockefeller Republican."

February 10, 1966

Some press reports re my appointment by Governor Rockefeller created erroneous impression I claimed to have turned down job with you because I am a Rockefeller Republican as opposed to a Lindsay Republican. This was a distortion of the type you know too well often arises from the eagerness of some of our friends of the press to get a controversial story. I am a Rockefeller Republican but the Governor and press know that I expressed my sincere high regard for you and did not claim you had offered me a job but appointment to a commission. I also said as I firmly believe that the combined progressive leadership of yourself and the Governor would be the finest stimulant to the two party system in this nation and therefore benefit all the American people. I have sent a copy of this wire to the Governor.

Jackie Robinson

ROBINSON TO NELSON ROCKEFELLER

Robinson's pointed memorandum to Governor Rockefeller reveals his distaste for Republican leaders at the county level, especially as the 1966 gubernatorial campaign was heating up.

May 13, 1966

I would like to emphasize that this is going to be a tremendously difficult campaign among Negroes, especially since it is pretty obvious to me that most of the county chairmen know very little, if anything, about the attitudes and thinking of the Negro in their particular districts.

I would suggest that the first thing that they do is to find Negro Republicans in their areas who are willing to tell them what they should know about the Negro and his attitudes, rather than what they want to hear. I would also suggest that they not try to bluff their way through in the next few months about their knowledge of the Negro and what his desires and ambitions are. If we are to recapture some of this vote, we must show that we are sincere and serious about the problems that have existed over the past few years as far as the Republican party and the Negro is concerned. The first step, therefore, must be the county chairmen's willingness to learn as fast as possible what the desires and ambitions of the Negro are.

Our team is willing to cooperate in any way that it possibly can, for it is our aim to get an even larger percentage of the Negro vote than did Mayor John Lindsay. The reason Mr. Lindsay got some 43% of this vote was his willingness to listen and accept advice. We have, in my opinion, a team that thoroughly knows and understands most of the problems, the aims and desires of the Negro community. If the county chairmen are as dedicated as we are to your reelection, I hope that we can get together and discuss the problems that exist; but before we meet, it is urgent that they find competent and unselfish Negroes who are interested more in the progress of their race than in individual advancement.

I know you understand that this letter is merely to demonstrate my concern about the chances of your getting a larger vote than ever come November.

ROBINSON TO RAY BLISS

The National Negro Republican Assembly (NNRA) was created after African American delegates walked out of the 1964 Republican convention to protest the nomination of Barry Goldwater. The fundamental purpose of NNRA was to advance African American rights and concerns within the party, and its founding members included Clarence Townes, a Virginia delegate who later became director of minorities for the Republican National Committee, and Grant Reynolds, a prominent New Yorker who acted as NNRA's political director. Following the 1966 NNRA convention, Robinson warns Ray Bliss, chair of the Republican National Committee, against interfering in the group's internal administration and policies. One of the highlights of the convention was the appearance of Ronald Reagan, the Republican candidate for governor of California. Reagan stormed out of the convention after he was accused of being a racist during a heated discussion of his views on civil rights legislation. After Reagan won the election, Robinson stated: "The victory of Ronald Reagan in California is, in my view, a tragedy. If I read Reagan correctly, he is another Barry Goldwater—with what the kids call 'smarts.'"

May 23, 1966

Dear Mr. Bliss:

As you are doubtless aware, Grant Reynolds and I have just returned from the 1966 Convention of The National Negro Republican Assembly

(NNRA). We had what we consider to be an excellent and successful convention. The most rewarding development was the virtually unanimous enthusiasm of those in attendance for all-out efforts to help in the building of a strong Republican Party, and the kind of party principle which we can, in good conscience, work for and endorse.

Since Clarence Townes was present in Detroit, you are doubtless aware that we elected Mr. Reynolds National President and we believe he will do a wonderful job. However, in all honesty, I must admit to you that Mr. Reynolds and I and many of our delegates deeply resent what appeared to be the vigorous and determined attempt of persons employed by or close to the National Committee to interfere in our right to independently select and elect our own slate of leadership.

We are proud that the Convention discovered the plot and refused to yield to the pressures involved.

We want very much to work with you for the triumph of the Republican Party and the perpetuation of the two-party system. However, I know that I speak for our new President (who will have read a copy of this letter before you receive it) and for the majority of our membership when I say that we do not intend to be dictated to or taken over. We feel we have a tremendous opportunity to do a significant job for the Negro people, our organization and the Party and two-party system. But, we would not, could not and should not seek to do it wearing the collar of an outside force.

Grant and I have been given a mandate to work with the members of the Assembly to build and strengthen it. Whether you will accept our cooperation or not—and acceptance means on terms which may indicate new grounds for cooperation between the National Republican Committee and Negro leadership—we intend to strive for the accomplishment of ultimate goals in which the National Committee must inevitably be interested. We hope there can be a mutual relationship for the good of all concerned. We are reasonable men but we are men, first of all.

Sincerely,
Jackie Robinson

NELSON ROCKEFELLER TO ROBINSON

This congratulatory telegram indicates that Rockefeller, like Robinson, recognized the connection between civil rights and the creation of business and commerce opportunities for minorities.

June 22, 1966

I am advised you have been elected co-chairman and a director of Hamilton Life Insurance Company. I commend you and your associates on your announced intention to give creative and constructive attention to the development of this company as a totally integrated organization. It is vital that businessmen in our society cooperate to help bring the Negro citizen more importantly into the economic mainstream. Congratulations.

Nelson A. Rockefeller

ROBINSON TO NELSON ROCKEFELLER

Using his August 13 column as a virtual campaign tool, Robinson sketched several reasons for supporting Rockefeller, including his philanthropic contributions to the civil rights movement and a legislative program that favored poor persons in need of education, medical insurance, and housing rights. Robinson's campaign travels took him to predominately African American areas, like Brooklyn, where the attorney Joseph Williams helped to organize grassroots meetings. The meetings convinced Robinson that African American voters would not support the Democratic gubernatorial candidate, New York City Council president Frank O'Connor.

August 16, 1966

Dear Governor:

Last week, for the first time, I felt we could win the Negro vote with an even greater margin than Mayor Lindsay did. My meetings with prominent Negroes in Brooklyn, arranged by Joe Williams, were most encouraging. There are still a lot of questions I tried to answer, but I feel the answers should come from you. Your statements regarding

Dr. King, the insurance problem, and the way you are campaigning, are all most encouraging.

I hope you will soon take the time to join me with the Brooklyn people. I believe this will be a must, for, as you must know, we don't trust O'Connor at all. It appears he will be your opponent, and his image in Negro circles is bad. They haven't forgotten his efforts as a state senator. (We feel he will do well in Queens, and other conservative areas.)

Without bragging, I feel I have made great gains for you. The door is open in Brooklyn, and you have a chance to move in and grab this vote. Let's move to solidify it.

I believe we can do the same all over the state. It must take the same courage you showed on 125th Street. It wasn't easy, but I believe you made much progress.

I am proud to be working with you. I can speak about you with complete conviction, and I think it shows up in my talk.

Sincerely yours,
Jackie Robinson

ROBINSON TO BARRY GRAY

Robinson criticizes Barry Gray, a radio personality on New York City's WMCA, for supporting an attempt by the Patrolmen's Benevolent Association (PBA) to thwart Mayor John Lindsay's creation of a police review board comprised mostly of citizens. Robinson's main New York City nemesis, William F. Buckley, Jr., also opposed the review board, and PBA president John Cassese garnered enough signatures for a ballot measure that resulted in prohibiting civilians from serving on the oversight board. Robinson uses hyperbolic rhetoric to question Buckley's racial and religious views.

August 17, 1966

Dear Barry:

Last Thursday I heard for the first time that you had consented to be one of the three co-chairmen aiding the PBA fight against the Civilian Review Board. I told my informer I did not believe the information was true.

"I know Barry to be a true liberal in the purest sense of the word," I insisted.

I hope I am right, Barry. For, in my opinion, only the bigots and those who have something to hide are afraid of a Civilian Review Board. All the excuses given by Mr. Cassese and his ilk seem to form a smokescreen to camouflage their own personal prejudices.

It is difficult for me to believe that you would be a party to this kind of deception. For so many years you have been advocating so many positions which you now appear to repudiate. You have aligned yourself with the Bill Buckley types and others who are as capable of seeking to eliminate persons of your religion as fast as they would eliminate persons of my race.

If it is true that you have accepted leadership in this fight against the Civilian Review Board—and in the passing days there has been no indication that you have not—I must refuse, in the future, to have anything to do with your program. I would hope other Negroes would feel the same way. That is why I have sent copies of this letter to persons whose names are herewith listed.

I hope I am wrong, Barry. I could not in good conscience call you a bigot. But you know the logical conclusion about the man who lies down with hogs. The hogs do not end up smelling like men. The concept of you and Bill Buckley fighting shoulder to shoulder would be ludicrous if it were not tragic. I can understand Buckley, Barry. I cannot understand you.

Sincerely,
Jackie Robinson

ROBINSON TO NELSON ROCKEFELLER

Robinson helped to arrange a public meeting between Rockefeller and residents of St. Albans, Queens, the neighborhood where Robinson had lived while playing for the Brooklyn Dodgers.

September 19, 1966

Dear Governor Rockefeller:

I was proud again to be associated with you as you did a magnificent job of answering tough questions at the St. Albans meeting on

Saturday. I am positive that you gained considerable support from this meeting.

I would suggest, Governor, that you be tremendously careful about your habit of saying "attaboy." Although all the people who know you look upon your use of the expression as perfectly harmless, the word "boy" is practically a dirty word to all Negroes.

If you are again challenged, as you were at the meeting, I would suggest, Governor, that you do not attempt to justify it by the example you used in Queens. You see, those people who heard you simply cannot equate the habits of a Rockefeller family with their own bitterness over the traditional use of the word "boy" in addressing Negro male adults.

Again—you were great!

Sincerely yours,
Jackie Robinson

NELSON ROCKEFELLER TO ROBINSON

September 23, 1966

Dear Jackie:

You are right—I should not use the expression "attaboy." I shall be more careful in the future.

Thank you so much for bringing the matter to my attention.

With warm regard,

Sincerely,
Nelson A. Rockefeller

ADAM CLAYTON POWELL, JR. TO ROBINSON

In his October 22 column Robinson praised Powell for publicly dissociating himself from the definition of "black power" set forth by SNCC's Stokely Carmichael. Rather than focusing on black separatism and the right to bear arms, as Carmichael had done, Powell described black power as a form of black initiative and responsibility, pride and productivity, and the belief that God created all of humanity to live as a family. After lauding Powell's "strong and courageous stand," Robinson added his own definition of "black power"—"when we use our ballot and our dollars wisely, we are exercising black power without having to define it"—and called for Powell, Wilkins, King, Randolph, and Whitney Young to work together to advance this type of power.

November 10, 1966

Dear Jackie:

Belatedly, but certainly no less gratefully, may I thank you for the very generous remarks in your column concerning my recent sermon, "Black Power: A Form of Godly Power." Your assessment of what I attempted to say and your support of those words is warmly appreciated.

You discussed both the logic and the need for a "Summit Meeting" and I am wondering if you would take the leadership in convening, perhaps a "Summit Meeting of 100" or the top infrastructure of Negro political, business, civil rights, religious and civic leadership. I think it is time for the Negro leadership to sit down together and have a serious discussion on the future direction of our collective efforts in these major areas, where Negroes are headed and at what pace.

Your assuming the responsibility along with somebody like our distinguished colleague, A. Philip Randolph, for such an undertaking could greatly contribute to its success. I would be happy to assist in any way you feel I could materially contribute to the summit meeting's implementation. Could I tentatively suggest such a meeting in December or January in Miami, depending upon commitments and schedules of other persons.

Congratulations on the fine work you did in this election and I was pleased to note that the governor publicly recognized the success of your efforts.

With every good wish.

Very truly yours,
Adam C. Powell

ROBINSON TO ADAM CLAYTON POWELL, JR.

The following is a draft of Robinson's reply to Powell. Robinson forwarded the draft to Rockefeller before mailing the final letter to Powell.

No date [November 1966]

Dear Congressman Powell:

Thanks for your letter concerning my remarks in the *Amsterdam News*. We were delighted with your sermon and prayerfully hope it was sincere and that you will work for a concept of "Black Power" that could bring gains to our Race as we have never had before. I, too, believe it is time that Negro leadership sat down to discuss the direction of the Negro and to plan programs that can effectively involve the masses of people.

I wish I would believe you were dedicated towards this goal, for in my opinion, a sincere and dedicated Adam Powell could contribute more to our progress than any leader we have. In my opinion, however, you are not really concerned about our people and couldn't care less whether a "Summit Meeting" of 100 was successful or not.

Prove me wrong and I will be most anxious to do whatever I can to help. I believe we could get support from men such as Rockefeller, Kennedy, Romney, Humphrey and many more people I consider honest in their stand on civil rights. We would have to be so well organized and so above board no one could question our motives. If I were certain of your motives and if we were able to organize a group, I would be most willing and anxious to become involved. I cannot participate, however, if the same self-aggrandizing leaders attempt, as in the past, to take over for personal glory rather than for the good of all.

If you and the others are ready to work, then all I can say is we waited too long. The need is now and our position has never been better.

Thanks for your remarks on my role in the election. What pleased me most was the recognition by all in the campaign that I was "not only loyal to the Governor but also loyal to my people." I believe both major parties are ready for the kind of meeting you suggest—the question is—are we?

Sincerely,
Jackie Robinson

ROBINSON TO NELSON ROCKEFELLER

Robinson pressures Rockefeller, now elected to his third term as governor, to offer political appointments to African Americans who campaigned for him. The memorandum refers to Senator Robert Kennedy's efforts to redevelop the Bedford-Stuyvesant area of New York.

December 14, 1966

It has been a long time now since the election and many key appointments have been made. There are many people who worked hard in the campaign and have contacted me regarding the future. My response has been I supported the Governor because I believe in him and whatever he decides is fine with me. In all fairness, however, I believe I should be able to say to them exactly what is to happen. I can accept it if you feel there is nothing available for those who, in my opinion, were more loyal than any group connected with the political campaign.

I believe this can be substantiated by any of the campaign staff . . . I think there should be some key minority appointments to insure the gains that have been made. Bobby Kennedy's move in Bedford-Stuyvesant is obvious. Your immediate action will determine whether he stems the tide and regains the plurality the Democrats used to hold, or whether the moderate philosophy of the Republican Party prevails. Many people—those who worked and others who are interested in the role that the minority played in your victory—are looking and wondering.

Please give us some answers one way or another.

ROBINSON TO NELSON ROCKEFELLER

This is a handwritten note in Robinson's Christmas card to Rockefeller. In his November 19 column Robinson wrote, "In my book, Ronald Reagan is as much bad news for minority people as Governor Rockefeller is good news."

No date [December 1966]

Dear Governor,

Because I have worked for and with you in 1966, my life is much richer. Because I have had the chance of knowing Mrs. Rockefeller just a bit more, the future is brighter. Still—so much has to be done. Progress has been made. The two party system has been strengthened and the steep hill of doubt is leveling off. How fast and how far we go is up to you. Your instincts are perfect. I beg you to lead us forward—make America the place we dream of it being. You in my opinion can do it by being yourself. By doing what I constantly hear you say—"if it's right."

I am honored with my association. I seek no special favors. I hope I can help in making the next four years years New Yorkers will *remember* Gov. Rockefeller as the greatest Gov. the state has ever had.

I admire you for what you are, not for what you have. I think you are a great man. I believe you will prove it.

Sincerely,
Jackie

11

SHARP ATTACKS, SURPRISING DEFENSES

· 1967 ·

ROBINSON TO NELSON ROCKEFELLER

At the beginning of the Ninetieth Congress, Representative Gerald Ford of Michigan, the Republican minority leader, actively supported House Resolution No. 1, which prohibited Adam Clayton Powell, Jr. from taking his seat and called for the appointment of a select committee to decide on his eligibility to serve in the session. The resolution was a response to allegations that Powell had misused travel funds and directed staff members to make illegal salary payments to his spouse. In this memorandum to Governor Rockefeller, Robinson points out the ominous subtext of the congressional action.

January 11, 1967

I am very much concerned about the role Congressman Ford played in Powell's punishment. While I basically agree that Mr. Powell's conduct is cause for punishment, it seems to me the Republican Congressmen leaned over backwards to show the white masses that they too are involved in the white backlash that is being exhibited around the country.

Great pains have been made in bringing back minorities into the Republican ranks. The time is ripe for continuation. My concern at this point is whether or not Ford and the Republican Congressmen's action will stem this tide.

It is something that you and the other top Republicans should take into consideration. I feel careful evaluation of the situation should be made.

ROY WILKINS TO ROBINSON

Wilkins defends the NAACP and responds to Robinson's charge that his leadership was "a kind of dictatorship, insensitive to the trend of our times, unresponsive to the needs and aims of the Negro masses—especially the young—and more and more, seeming to reflect a refined 'Yessir, Mr. Charlie' point of view." Angered at Wilkins's alleged efforts to squelch dissent within the NAACP, Robinson publicized this critique in his January 5 column. "This determination to keep things as they have been instead of the way they ought to be," Robinson added, "may be gaining Ford Foundation money, but it is not gaining respect of the younger people of our race, many of whom feel the NAACP is archaic and who reject its rigid posture completely." Gloster Current, who had coordinated Robinson's 1957 tour for the NAACP Freedom Fund, replied to Robinson's criticism in an earlier letter.

February 8, 1967

Personal—Not for Publication

Dear Jack Robinson:

I had not intended to comment on your recent column about the NAACP and myself because for anyone even faintly acquainted with the workings of the NAACP, it proceeded so obviously out of either gross misinformation or deliberate distortion. Your letter to Gloster changed my mind.

It is, of course, laughable to maintain that the NAACP, under my direction, is a "dictatorship," political or otherwise. Whatever its shortcomings or those of myself, "dictatorship" is not one of them.

Up to this moment, the evaluation of expert observers and students of organizations like the NAACP has been that the political democracy within the NAACP is genuine and, accordingly, opens opportunity to manipulators, local and national, and thus to a diffusion and weakening of its central purpose. Also this democratic process permits the elevation of people to positions of influence on a purely political basis, irrespective of their concomitants of skill, dedication, prestige and/or influence, and thus threatens the direction, strength and effectiveness of the whole program.

These critics have marveled at the continued life of the NAACP in the face of the development of competitive organizations which do not have an elective process.

CORE is run by a tightly-knit group. SNCC runs its miniscule combination of members and staff on policies debated by the entire

150–200 members-workers for days and nights on end. SCLC does pretty much what Dr. King and his close advisors desire.

The NAACP Legal Defense and Educational Fund has a self-perpetuating board of directors, none of whom has to "come up through convention and regional politics, trades, pledges, etc.," as do our board members.

The National Urban League is governed by a self-perpetuating Board, and is supported almost totally by large contributors, foundations, corporations and trade unions, all predominately white.

Only the NAACP has a democratic electoral process. Only in 1966, when that process turned up five defeats out of six nominees by a political faction that gloated in the press in Los Angeles that it had "captured" in a "clean sweep" the nominating committee elected at the convention, did you or anyone else dream up the "dictatorship" bit.

I was prompted to write you by the self-revelatory question in your letter to Gloster: "why should the NAACP be dependent upon the Ford Foundation?"

The NAACP is not dependent upon the Ford Foundation. If you took the trouble to glance at our year-end financial statement, you would have found that the NAACP (exclusive of the Special Contribution Fund) raised in 1966 a rough total of $1,408,000. Of this amount, *$1,159,000 or about 82 percent* came from NAACP members.

All other civil rights organizations have depended upon the general public (which means white people) for their funds. Thus the hateful remark about Jews, made in Mt. Vernon by a local CORE officer at a school board meeting, sheared instantly $200,000 from the CORE income. Dr. King is dependent upon mail solicitations and his own personal appearances. SNCC depends upon various contributors, mostly white.

Every single one of these organizations, which, according to your implications, are preferable to the NAACP, has been to every prominent foundation repeatedly, seeking a grant.

The NAACP went to the Ford Foundation not to stay alive, but to enable it to expand. You ought to be glad that in addition to granting millions of dollars to various cultural efforts and to vague projects overseas, the Ford Foundation committed a tiny sliver of its enormous wealth to the civil rights fight through the NAACP. Instead, you talk as though such a grant were a badge of shame.

For all the glib talk about "the masses," no one with two minutes of experience ever contended that "the masses" (the kind you refer to) finance anything. They don't have money to give. As for joining, anyone who knows about organizations knows that the great body of people does not join anything. They may believe in a cause and they may shout, but they do not join and do not put up money. Even so, which of the civil rights groups is more representative of "the masses" than the NAACP? Our 441,139 membership in 1966 is more than four times the combined claimed memberships of all the other organizations.

Until the labor unions secured the right in law to have the employers collect dues in a check-off system from payroll checks, even union members, with their jobs depending upon their membership, did not consistently pay their dues.

One of these days before you are seventy, some down-to-earth wisdom will find its way into your life. If it does nothing else except stop you from believing that "because I see it this way I have to say it," it will have done a great service. The basis of informed comment is not simple, self-serving personal reaffirmation, but truth arrived at through reasoning, not feeling.

If you had played ball with a hot head instead of a cool brain, you would have remained in the minors. You need that cool brain in the weighing of issues in the critical area of civil rights.

Very sincerely yours,
Roy Wilkins

ROBINSON TO ROY WILKINS

February 15, 1967

Dear Roy Wilkins:

It took longer to hear from you than I expected. I was sure Gloster had your blessing and only signed the other letter. Perhaps it would have been better if you had let it go as Gloster's letter. I am sorry you cannot accept honest criticism. For whether you choose to believe it or not, it was honest criticism. While I am sorry you chose to become "hot headed" yourself about this matter, it does not change the opinion I have had for a long time.

I saw for years, first hand, what was going on and it is obvious things have not changed. I don't intend to remain silent when I see things I believe to be wrong. I have to laugh when you talk of down-to-earth wisdom. When I speak it's because I know what I am doing. I am sorry the truth hurts so much. I don't really have to answer to you for what I have done and I certainly will not apologize. It seems to me I remember a number of statements Roy Wilkins made that made people wonder, but they don't challenge your right to an opinion. Criticize, yes, but it is your opinion.

I have not said the vote by the Board was not democratic. Every election needs electioneering. You have good control over the Board. I don't fault you for it. It is the same kind of control Goldwater had over the Republican Convention in 1964. He won with it—so have you.

I don't intend to get into a further hassle with you. Whenever I feel criticism of you, the N.A.A.C.P. or any other organization is justified—expect it.

Very sincerely yours,
Jackie Robinson

ROY WILKINS TO ROBINSON

Wilkins indirectly criticizes Robinson for using ghostwriters and directly accuses him of not understanding the governing procedures of the NAACP.

February 17, 1967

Dear Jack Robinson:

Thanks for your letter.

I wish to say that I did not know about Gloster's letter until after he had received a reply from you, so his letter was not mine signed by him. I do not operate that way. What I write I write—letters, statements, columns and what have you.

I am not disturbed about your opinion of me. That is something one must deal with in public life and I long ago learned to live with it. My prime and overriding interest is the NAACP. What disturbs me is your sweeping assumptions about the NAACP. I do not, for example, "have control over the Board." If I had such control, the NAACP would either be farther along the road or gone under. Indeed, my best friends are strongly of the opinion that I am weak because I do not have and do not seek to exercise control over the Board.

The comparison with Goldwater is hardly valid since he got control through the precinct and county and state units of the Republican party beginning in 1960. If I had had that in the NAACP I would not be in the "democratic" hassles in which I and a staff trying to do a job find ourselves.

I am at a loss to understand why you asserted so positively "I will certainly not apologize." I did not ask any apology. I did not even ask you to change your mind. I was simply setting forth the record from the records. It is entirely up to you to go from there.

If a man bats .303 and some loud critics keep repeating that he is batting .213, in the end the record will be there and the critics will be just critics.

By all means, if you see anything to criticize, feel free to do so. I expect it, only now I know what kind of criticism to expect.

Very sincerely yours,
Roy Wilkins

ROBINSON TO ROY WILKINS

February 20, 1967

Dear Roy Wilkins:

Thank you for your letter of February 17, 1967.

The only criticism that you can expect Roy—is the truth. I am sorry we cannot get together on this, but just as you feel you are right I feel the same. It is because of my concern for the N.A.A.C.P. that I write as I do.

I am not proud of the progress we have made and cannot see why you should be. The Association needs new blood. It needs young men with new ideas and a mind of their own. Unfortunately, I don't think this is true of the present Board.

This is my last say on the matter to you. My opinion has always been honest and will continue to be.

Sincerely yours,
Jackie Robinson

ROBINSON TO NELSON ROCKEFELLER

This is the second half of a memorandum that Robinson wrote to Rockefeller after the House had voted to exclude Powell and declare his seat vacant. The memo continues the themes of Robinson's January 21 column, in which he argued that although he was no fan of Powell, "what the Congress did to Adam seemed to me to be a blatant announcement that the thumping majority in the House has every intention of being enrolled in the white backlash column . . . Adam Powell is a tragic figure today. But more tragic is what has been done to his people and how he was used as an excuse for doing it."

March 6, 1967

. . . Secondly, after careful consideration over the weekend, I must say I understand your position, but must stick to my belief that those of us who have become Republicans because of you must look at the complete picture. I believe the efforts of the members of the House were racial rather than political. While in my personal opinion Powell is a disgrace to his race, the Congress and the church, we cannot join with the Democrats and the Republicans in their conspiracy. If it were only a situation where Powell was involved, I would do all I could to help defeat him.

Governor, in the minds of most Negroes, it is not a race between Republicans and Democrats, but a race of white against black. In my opinion Adam Powell does not deserve a seat in Congress, but neither can the Negro afford to accept the decision without a fight because of what the implications are.

Politically, Governor, you are right in your position. This situation, however, I repeat is not political and I believe it would be morally wrong to join with the other Republicans and Southern Democrats who have conspired against the Negro whether this was their true intention or not.

ROBINSON TO NELSON ROCKEFELLER

After Powell was unseated, New York Republicans successfully recruited the civil rights activist James Meredith, then a student at Columbia University School of Law, to run against Powell in a special election. On March 9 the New York Times *reported that Robinson had "castigated his party" for enlisting Meredith. The article also claimed that Robinson had tried to dissuade Rockefeller from supporting Meredith, and that Robinson was "shocked that the Republican party would ask him to join what we consider a conspiracy" against Powell.*

March 9, 1967

While the *New York Times* article was distorted and confusing, I can understand where it would cause you concern. One of the reasons I swore I would not align myself with a political party was that it expected a person go along with Party line decisions.

As you know, Governor, I am not made that way. While I regret the writer, James Clarity, slanting the article to make it appear you were the decision maker, I did emphasize that you had nothing to do with the decision as to who was to run. He still made it appear that you did. He did not make it clear that I said I was shocked the Party asked "him" (Meredith) to join the conspiracy started by Southern Democrats and Republicans in the House. I did not say anyone had asked me to join in.

I am sorry the writer chose the angle he did, but I must again say I must in good conscience express myself as I believe. This may sometimes cause embarrassment and bring on an intolerable situation, but it is a chance a *man* must take.

I am sorry you were played up. It was not my intention. It was not done so in the interview, only in the story.

ROBINSON TO GEORGE FOWLER

In the following letter to George Fowler, chairman of the State Commission for Human Rights, Robinson's confrontational personality is in full bloom. The letter is equally significant because of Robinson's claim that his "interest has always been the growth of the Negro into the mainstream of our economy." Robinson uses hyperbolic rhetoric to express his opinions about Fowler's character and conduct.

March 15, 1967

Dear George:

I have received word that you are disturbed because I didn't touch base with you regarding the meeting I had with the Long Island Group. I am certain, since I was asked to meet with them, that had the Governor wished to have a representative from the Commission at the meeting, he would have so advised.

I want at this time, George, to put you straight once and for all. I couldn't care less whether you are Chairman or not. I believe it to be a tragedy in light of the loyalty to his staff by the Governor that you would so conduct your Commission in a manner that would bring the number of complaints we have seen. It seems to me that you should be knocking yourself out to help a man that has been the friend the Governor has been. The apparent friction by Commission members is cause for concern and makes one wonder. Since I have felt you have great ability, I can only come to the conclusion that either I was wrong about your ability or you don't care. I believe the latter to be the case.

So, George, you can be angry if you please. I have tried to work with you, but your apparent insecurity and what appears to me to be jealousy has caused you to lose sight of the overall objective—service to the Governor. I think you know my interest has always been the growth of the Negro into the mainstream of our economy. Our breach has not helped, but it certainly was no fault of mine.

I wish you luck, George, and if you do remain as Chairman, I hope you do the job that is required and certainly with the broad powers of the Commission. You have the authority. It does take courage and integrity. So far, I have seen little of either.

Sincerely,
Jackie Robinson

ROBINSON TO AVERY BRUNDAGE

In this letter to Avery Brundage, president of the International Olympic Committee (IOC), Robinson threatens civil rights action should the committee decide not to bar South Africa from the 1968 Olympics. In May 1968 the IOC announced that it had voted overwhelmingly to exclude South Africa from the Mexico City Olympics.

March 21, 1967

Dear Mr. Brundage:

It has been brought to my attention that the International Olympic Committee will be reviewing its decision which barred South Africa from the 1964 Olympics because of its racist position.

I must alert you that if there are any changes in this decision we will do everything within our power to have all civil rights organizations urge Negroes to withdraw from any competition as far as the Olympic Games are concerned.

America cannot in 1967 condone the racist policies of South Africa. Certainly no athletic body in America can place itself in the position of supporting South Africa. We hope that unless there is a change in the South African policy, the United States delegations will fight vigorously any changes from its present position.

Very truly yours,
Jackie Robinson

ROBINSON TO LYNDON JOHNSON

Robinson assures President Johnson that Martin Luther King, Jr.'s dissent from the war in Vietnam is not representative of all African Americans. King publicly condemned the war during his April 4 speech to Clergy and Laity Concerned, an antiwar group, at Riverside Church in New York City. Before sending this letter, Robinson also used his April 8 column to suggest that King's public resistance to the war detracted from his civil rights work. "Let us hear from Dr. King on the DOMESTIC situation," Robinson stated. "I concede his right as an individual and as a man of God—to oppose war. But we do need his voice to cry out in the American wilderness."

April 18, 1967

Dear Mr. President:

First, let me thank you for pursuing a course towards Civil Rights that no President in our history has pursued. I am confident your dedication will not only continue, but will be accelerated dependent on the needs of all Americans.

While I am certain your faith has been shaken by demonstrations against the Viet Nam war, I hope the actions of any one individual does not make you feel as Vice President Humphrey does, that Dr. King's stand will hurt the Civil Rights movement. It would not be fair to the thousands of our Negro fighting men who are giving their lives because they believe, in most instances, that our Viet Nam stand is just. There are hundreds of thousands of us at home who are not certain why we are in the war. We feel, however, that you and your staff know what is best and we are willing to support your efforts for an honorable solution to the war.

I do feel that you must make it infinitely clear, that regardless of who demonstrates, that your position will not change toward the rights of all people; that you will continue to press for justice for all Americans and that a strong stand now will have great effect upon young Negro Americans who could resort to violence unless they are reassured. Recent riots in Tennessee and Cleveland, Ohio are warning enough. Your concern, based on causes and not on whether it will hurt the Civil Rights effort, could have a wholesale effect on our youth.

I appreciate the difficult role any President has. I believe, also, yours is perhaps the most difficult any President has had. I hope God gives you the wisdom and strength to come through this crisis at home, and that an end to the war in Viet Nam is achieved very soon.

Again, Sir, let me thank you for your domestic stand on Civil Rights. We need an even firmer stand as the issues become more personal and the gap between black and white Americans gets wider.

Sincerely yours,
Jackie Robinson

CLIFFORD ALEXANDER, JR. TO ROBINSON

Clifford Alexander, Jr., White House deputy special counsel, informed President Johnson of Robinson's April 18 letter. "I think it may be one of his grandstand political plays," Alexander wrote, "particularly his inference that during your Administration the gap is widening between Negro and Whites." Alexander had expressed reservations about Robinson in an earlier White House memorandum dated November 22, 1965: "While it is true that Jackie Robinson supported the President with his right hand, he was doing everything with his left hand to defeat a variety of democratic senatorial and congressional candidates across the country."

April 20, 1967

Dear Jackie,

The President has asked me to thank you for your kind letter of April 18th. Please be certain that the President's commitment to equal opportunity for every American has not, and will not, falter.

We regret that you feel the gap between black and white America is widening. This Administration does not share this feeling, and will continue to do all that is possible to continue to close the gap and encourage more communication and good will between Americans from every background.

We deeply appreciate your commitment to, and support of, the President's programs. As you know, the President can only go as far as the support he receives from leading Americans such as yourself.

With personal good wishes.

Sincerely,
Clifford L. Alexander, Jr.

HUBERT HUMPHREY TO ROBINSON

April 29, 1967

Dear Jackie:

Thank you for sharing with me a copy of your letter to the President of April 18.

Let me share with you a copy of a letter that I have sent to one of our fellow citizens who was concerned about my recent visit to Georgia and Governor Maddox. I believe the letter is self-explanatory.

You have made comment about my remarks concerning Dr. King. I do regret that Dr. King has fused Vietnam policy with civil rights. I know that this causes trouble and concern in Congress. Only recently Congressman Celler of New York, Chairman of the Judiciary Committee, where all civil rights legislation must originate, stated that Dr. King's actions had made the passage of any civil rights legislation impossible. I cannot agree with Congressman Celler, but I do feel that the situation is more difficult.

I have long admired Dr. King, and my remarks were said in sadness rather than criticism. My comment was that I thought he was making a mistake. Nevertheless, he is entitled to his views and whatever position he wishes to follow.

Every day I continue my work in the field of human rights. As your Vice President and friend, I keep asking our federal agencies to use every means at their command to guarantee equal opportunity in jobs, in education, in housing, in protection of the laws—yes, in every activity of life. I am sure you know that I am spending a great deal of time these days trying to make our program—the War on Poverty—more effective; trying to design a summer program that will be helpful to disadvantaged young people; in other words, trying to carry out the spirit and the letter of the civil rights laws.

Be assured that, regardless of the stand of any person involved in the civil rights movement, neither President Johnson nor Vice President Humphrey will ever relax or weaken their efforts toward guaranteeing full and equal rights for all Americans. The American Negro is displaying great courage and patriotism in Vietnam. He has suffered many injustices here at home. He has been patient beyond human understanding. As long as I have any opportunity to serve this country, I will do everything within my power to remedy these injustices and to do honor to those who have served this nation so honorably.

You know of my great admiration for you. It continues to grow every year.

Sincerely,
Hubert H. Humphrey

ROBINSON TO MARTIN LUTHER KING, JR.

In this open letter, published in his May 13 column, Robinson criticizes King for demanding a cessation of bombing in Vietnam and for praising Muhammad Ali's April 28 refusal to be drafted into the U.S. Army. King replied in a late-night call that left the two on good speaking terms. But King did not change Robinson's belief that the United States must halt communists in Vietnam, and five months later Robinson argued that Johnson "is the third president who has acted out of the conviction that it is better to fight this fight in Vietnam than to wait until we must fight it closer to our shores. I believe the President deserves the support and confidence of the American people on the Vietnam issue."

May 13, 1967

Dear Martin:

I am confused.

In my book, you've always been the greatest civil rights mastermind and leader which the movement has ever had.

That is why I and my wife, Rachel, have been thrilled to give time and energy to raising several hundreds of thousands of dollars for The Southern Christian Leadership Conference. I do not refer to this to brag. I wish we had been able to raise millions because we felt, and still feel, that you are a dedicated man, working unselfishly in a vital cause.

But I am confused. And so is Rachel, and so are our youngsters to whom you have been an idol also.

Our youngsters have started asking us questions which we find ourselves unable to answer. So, I thought I ought to turn to you for the answers.

Maybe I am wrong. But I feel you are utterly on the wrong track in your stand on Viet Nam.

RIGHTS

I am not one of those who feels you have no right to express your own convictions on Viet Nam. You have such a right—as a citizen, as a minister, as a human being and as a Nobel Peace Prize Winner. You are for nonviolence and it makes as much sense for you to oppose wars throughout the world as it did for you to oppose violence in Montgomery and Selma and Birmingham.

So I am not questioning your right to speak out and speak up about this war.

What concerns and confuses me is some of the positions you have taken and some of the statements you have made regarding this war.

Maybe I am wrong. But I have a deep respect for our country. I know that our country is not always right and that, in fact, on the domestic front, our country has been and is so terribly wrong with respect to its treatment of the Negro, and I know this is a war we could do without.

WHAT ABOUT THEM?

But, Martin, aren't you being unfair when you place all the burden of blame upon America and none upon the Communist forces we are fighting. You suggest that we stop the bombing. It strikes me that our President has made effort after effort to convert the confrontation from the arena of battlefield to the atmosphere of conference table. But why should we take the vital step of stopping the bombing without knowing whether the enemy will use that pause to prepare for the greater destruction of our men in Vietnam?

Won't you admit that, whenever there has been a lull or a ceasefire, our opponents have used this time to regroup and rebuild and to make themselves stronger so they can kill more of our boys? Yet, you have called the United States—and unfairly, I feel—the greatest purveyor of violence on earth. There was, you will recall, one 39-day period of cease-fire during which the Viet Cong built roads and tunnels and stored food in order to further their murder of our boys and their own fellow countrymen. Why is it, Martin, that you seem to ignore the blood which is upon their hands and to speak only of the "guilt" of the United States? Why is it that you do not suggest that the Viet Cong cease, stop, withdraw also?

I am firmly convinced that President Johnson wants to end this war as much as anyone. If you want to be very cynical about it, you have to admit that the termination of the war would be in his best political interest in the coming elections.

There is another point upon which I am confused, Martin. That is your praise of Cassius Clay. I admire this man as a fighting champion and a man who speaks his mind. I can't help feeling he wants to have his cake and eat it too. I can't help wondering how he can expect to make millions of dollars in this country and then refuse to fight for it. What values do you have in mind when you praise him and say he has given up so much? I think all he has given up is his citizenship. I think his advisors have given him a bum steer. I think the only persons who will come out well in his situation are his lawyers.

I am confused because I respect you deeply. But I also love this imperfect country. I respectfully ask you to answer this open letter and give me your own point of view.

With the deepest regard and the deepest confusion.

ROBINSON TO THE EDITOR OF THE *NEW YORK TIMES*

In a July 24 editorial on black power militants, the New York Times *attempted to give "the other side of the story" about the advancement of African Americans in the United States. "They are economically the most prosperous large group of nonwhites in the world, enjoying a higher average income than the inhabitants of any nation in Africa, Asia, or Latin America," the editorial stated.*

July 30, 1967

To the Editor:

Your fine editorial "Black Racism" was ruined in my view by the complete lack of understanding of the desires and the ambitions of Negro Americans.

I resented your comparing the status of the American Negro not with the status of other Americans by saying we are better off than nonwhites in Africa, Asia and Latin America. What you are saying is, "We never had it so good." It's high time that you understand that we are interested in comparing ourselves with the standards of our own country and not with the peoples of other lands.

Most of us recognize the opportunities we have, and this is the reason why there are the kinds of demands by people of our race. I am somewhat surprised that *The New York Times* and its editors do not understand these ambitions and desires. As I said at the start, yours was a fine editorial, spoiled only by your lack of understanding of our problems.

Jackie Robinson

ROBINSON TO ALTON MARSHALL

Robinson spoke before the Buffalo Junior Chamber of Commerce on September 21, and he criticized Tom Yawkey, owner of the Boston Red Sox, during the question-and-answer session. "Anyway," Robinson stated, "because of Tom Yawkey, I'd like to see them lose. Because he is probably one of the most bigoted guys in organized baseball." The Red Sox were the last major-league team to integrate; it was not until 1959 that the club brought up a black player. The comment prompted a letter of complaint from Gerald L. McInnis, a Rockefeller supporter from Massachusetts, who defended Yawkey and suggested that Robinson clear his statements with the governor before making them. Below is Robinson's reply to Alton Marshall, executive secretary to the governor.

October 2, 1967

In a question and answer session after my speech in Buffalo I gave my honest opinion. If I am ever asked the question again, I will repeat my beliefs. I am sorry but in my opinion Yawkey is one of the worst bigots in Baseball. I do not go around saying things for the sake of saying them, nor will I clear statements as McInnis suggests.

I do not know where McInnis gets his information but I once tried out for the Red Sox and was rejected. I was informed that Yawkey would not hire Negroes regardless. His record indeed proves what I said to be true.

ROBINSON TO NELSON ROCKEFELLER

In October 1967 representatives from the New York State Careerists Society, the Federation of Negro Civil Service Organizations, the NAACP, and the Urban League sent Rockefeller the following grievance: "We are angry and disturbed about the fact that discrimination in New York State Civil Service is rampant and has deprived the Civil Service career Negroes and Puerto Ricans of equal opportunity in the entry, promotional and policy making jobs in State Government." The aggrieved parties faulted Rockefeller for the alleged pattern of discrimination and called for him "to take personal command in effecting immediate correction." Robinson represented Rockefeller in an October 23 meeting, and it was this type of work—which pitted him against civil rights organizations—that led some critics to see Robinson as more heavily invested in Rockefeller than in the everyday concerns of minorities.

October 24, 1967

We had a turbulent meeting yesterday afternoon with the representatives of the Careerists Society, of the NAACP and of the Urban League which ended in a walkout and a promise that the picketing will definitely take place.

Throughout the meeting tempers were hot. The Careerists say they are tired of being ignored and of not being able to air their grievances but of getting the run-around from State representatives they allegedly have met with during the past twelve months.

We were told that nothing short of a meeting with you will appease them at this point. I told them it would have to be after November seventh.

Sam Singletary knows the background and will send you further material prior to your meeting with the Careerists.

ROBINSON TO NELSON ROCKEFELLER

Robinson laments the possibility of Reagan or Nixon winning the 1968 Republican presidential nomination—a position he had publicly staked out at least six months earlier, in his March 18 column. "It would be a sin and a shame," he had stated, "for Dick Nixon to be able to make a comeback, particularly if he rode the backlash. It would be virtually a crime for Mr. Reagan to be the standard-bearer." Robinson returned to this theme in his September 22 column: "If the GOP should nominate Nixon or Reagan, it would be telling the black man it cares nothing about him or his concerns."

October 31, 1967

I think you know my position regarding the possible nomination of Ronald Reagan or Richard Nixon. I do not want to embarrass you on this issue, but whenever I am asked, I must emphatically state that under no present conditions would or could I support either of these men. As a matter of fact, I am letting it be known that if the Republican Party does not want the Negro vote, they will have difficulty getting it.

A nomination of either of these Goldwater men, in my view, will be a renewed rejection of Negro support, leading us once again to turn to the Democratic Party as we did in the '64 election. I believe that such a nomination would set back the progress Negroes and liberal white Americans are working for.

My reason for writing is to spare you possible embarrassment because of our relationship. However, I cannot support anything that would hurt what I stand for and what you have been doing to make it better for all Americans.

I hope the Party wants to win and persuades you to accept. We could get the independent and Democratic votes needed for a win. Everywhere we go, people seem to want you and do not hesitate to say so. We would have no trouble getting minority support.

I trust you understand my concern.

ROBINSON TO GEORGE HINMAN

George Hinman, one of Rockefeller's closest associates, served as special counsel to Rockefeller Family & Associates. The article that Robinson refers to below reported on a Negro Political Action Association dinner in Phoenix, where both he and Goldwater delivered speeches. The mostly African American attendees heard Goldwater announce that he was finding it "reprehensible and a little more difficult" to undertake speaking engagements in the segregated South. "America has come of age," Goldwater declared, adding that the time had come to end racial discrimination. Just five months earlier, in his June 3 column, Robinson had criticized Goldwater for making negative remarks about Martin Luther King, Jr., and for failing to see the disproportionate deaths of African American soldiers in the Vietnam War as an example of racism.

November 13, 1967

Dear Mr. Hinman:

Enclosed is a copy of an article on the meeting I attended in Arizona. Barry Goldwater surprised me by his remarks and friendliness. He has asked that we get together on one of his visits to New York.

While I found it hard believing him, I kept remembering your advice, "If someone makes an attempt, you work with him." I believe we started some communication and I will do all I can to cultivate it. We must check sincerity when it is spoken by Goldwater or anyone else.

I am writing the Senator to thank him for the meeting and suggest his remarks could lead to much greater understanding. I am saying, because of his leadership role he can, without taking sides, close the communication gap and do a great service to America. I believe his remarks at the dinner at least demonstrated thinking on the subject. If you have any suggestions, I would welcome them.

Sincerely,
Jackie Robinson

ROBINSON TO BARRY GOLDWATER

November 21, 1967

Dear Senator Goldwater:

First let me say it was indeed a pleasure meeting you. I was impressed with your speech and what appeared to be a deep sense of understanding and sincerity. I couldn't help but feel how effective you could be in bridging the communication gap between the races. We have reached a crossroads and it will require leadership from men and women such as yourself if we expect to take the right path. If we could get people of this country talking together, it is my opinion many of our problems could be solved.

The people of Phoenix, Negro and white, who were at the dinner impressed me with their understanding; it was a good start. I hope you are willing to continue and help make the American dream become a reality.

Thanks also for your personal attitude; we have had a wide disagreement. I believe, however, we both are dedicated to a better America and I would like very much to discuss our differences so we might find answers.

I sent a copy of your statement to Governor Rockefeller and Mr. George Hinman. They were pleased to note we had a chance to meet and perhaps a chance to better understand what motivates us. Thanks very much, once again.

Sincerely,
Jackie Robinson

ROBINSON TO HUBERT HUMPHREY

November 28, 1967

Dear Mr. Vice President:

I assume you know it is always a pleasure hearing from you. Since I had the opportunity of working for you in 1960 I have felt that your dedication and sincerity is worthy of support. Your many years of service to people is making our society a better place to live and work.

I am impressed with President Johnson's desire in furthering race relations and am proud I supported him in 1964. I am not committed to either political party but whenever I recognize good and decency in any individual, I must speak out. That is why I have let it be known that unless the Republican Party nominates someone who can enhance the two-party system, I must again support the Johnson-Humphrey ticket. For, in my opinion, there has not been a President who has contributed as much as Mr. Johnson has in terms of race relations. I believe his growth in this area comes from your closeness to him. I am sure it will continue.

Best wishes. It was nice hearing from you again.

Sincerely,
Jackie Robinson

BARRY GOLDWATER TO ROBINSON

Coupled with Robinson's earlier correspondence, the following letter suggests that the two antagonists, even with vast policy differences between them, were working to establish a personal relationship marked by civility and cordiality.

November 30, 1967

Dear Jackie:

Having never heard you called anything but Jackie, I am afraid I would never reach first base if I addressed you as Mr.

During the whole period of my life I have been working, not as a politician, but as a citizen to try and impress upon people that understanding will come between men only when they try. No legislation can do it. It might help and probably does, but only when we can erase discrimination, regardless of who it is between, will we see the kind of world that God intends it to be some time. I will continue to work in this way and I think that we in Arizona have made good strides and are making them, and I see no reason why we shouldn't continue.

Just as I left the dinner the other night I asked if I might call you for a personal chat some time when I am in New York, and your having said yes, I am going to take you up on it, but I don't know just when that might be. Probably around the 20th of December I might be in your city, and if I am, I will give you a call. It was great meeting you.

With best wishes,
Barry Goldwater

ROBINSON TO NELSON ROCKEFELLER

On December 6 Robinson sent Rockefeller a note of appreciation. "The more I see of you and work with you," he wrote, "the more impressed I am with your dedication, sincerity and fantastic ability." Now, one day later, Robinson asks the governor to purchase shares of Freedom National Bank in Harlem. While shoring up financial support for the bank—work that he interpreted as empowering African Americans for economic freedom—Robinson also favored an increase of funding for Johnson's War on Poverty.

December 7, 1967

Dear Governor:

I am doing something that I promised myself I would never do. However, as Chairman of the Board of the Freedom National Bank, recognizing the tremendous needs that we have to fulfill the promise that Freedom National Bank was established for, I am asking you to look at this letter. If you know of anyone, including yourself, who might be interested in taking some of these shares I would be tremendously grateful.

I want you to know that I do not like making this request but for the good of our community, and I feel it is also a very sound business and political venture. I think it is worth going against my promise to myself in this case.

Please let me hear from you on this. If it is against policy, I certainly understand. But under the circumstances, it just had to be done.

Sincerely,
Jackie Robinson

12

THE POLITICS OF BLACK PRIDE

· 1968 ·

ROBINSON TO NELSON ROCKEFELLER

Rockefeller's attorneys advised that the purchase of Freedom National Bank stock would create a conflict of interest, and the governor decided not to accept the offer that Robinson had set forth in his December 7 letter. In the following letter Robinson hints at yet another new business venture, this one with a potential to pull him away from his salaried position with Rockefeller. Indeed, two weeks before Robinson wrote this letter, Sea Host Incorporated had hired him for a public relations campaign designed to increase the sales of its franchised seafood restaurants. Robinson later told Rockefeller that this new position was another business-based attempt to aid African Americans and other minorities in gaining economic freedom. Unlike civil rights leaders with democratic socialist inclinations, Robinson remained an advocate of U.S. capitalism throughout his lifetime.

January 18, 1968

Dear Governor:

Thank you for your letter of the ninth. I am aware of the requests you receive and the problems involved, and I understand and respect your position. That is why I hesitate in joining the many people who constantly seek assistance. I will only do so if I feel that such a request will benefit you as well as the organization. Thank you for considering the purchase of stock in Freedom.

I also want you to know that 1967 has been one of the most rewarding years of my life because of your understanding, commitment and direction. Since I have known you, my life too has been enriched and I hope to be associated with you for years to come, although it may not be on a basis where my services call for a salary. I want to offer to you these services even though I may have to seek employment that will take care of my financial needs. I would like to talk to you about this when time permits.

I just want you to know it is a privilege knowing you. There is no one I admire and respect more and, like thousands of people who know you, I feel our country would be blessed if you were our President. It is hard writing this as it sounds mushy, but I believe you know I would not write if I did not feel it.

My regards to Mrs. Rockefeller, for whom I have the same respect. I think she has been to you what Rachel has been to me and feel we are both fortunate.

Sincerely,
Jackie Robinson

ROBINSON TO THE EDITOR OF THE *NEW YORK TIMES*

The singer Eartha Kitt lashed out against the Vietnam War at a White House luncheon hosted by Lady Bird Johnson on January 18. "You send the best of this country off to be shot and maimed," Kitt stated. "They rebel in the street. They will take pot and they will get high. They don't want to go to school because they're going to be snatched off from their mothers to be shot in Vietnam." The first lady, visibly shaken by the outburst, replied: "I am sorry. I cannot understand the things that you do. I have not lived with the background that you have lived." The incident received widespread publicity, and the New York Times *commented on the exchange in an editorial published on January 20. "This is the heart of the matter," the editorial stated. "White people have not experienced the hurts and humiliations at the hands of the whites that are the lingering heritage of hundreds of millions of people of color around the world. Because whites have not experienced the anguish, they do not understand the anger." Below is Robinson's response to the editorial, published in the January 27 issue.*

January 27, 1968

To the Editor:

Congratulations on your Jan. 20 editorial "From the Heart of Eartha Kitt." It is the kind of understanding that has made the *Times* the great newspaper it is. Your understanding of how Negro-Americans feel about the scars of centuries of injustices is most encouraging.

I hope it means white America must be willing to look at the causes that brought about Miss Kitt's comments. Perhaps it will make more non-Negroes understand why some young athletes are willing to sacrifice prestige and glory to boycott the Olympic games. This kind of understanding can and, I am sure, will help bridge the gap between the races.

Jackie Robinson

ROBINSON TO NELSON ROCKEFELLER

Robinson suggests the possibility that Goldwater would support Rockefeller in the race for the Republican nomination for the presidency. He also reiterates his opposition to Nixon and Reagan.

February 26, 1968

My weekend was quite full what with the Saturday Goldwater breakfast meeting and a Sunday TV program which gave rise to a great deal of news comment Sunday night and this morning.

The Saturday breakfast was interesting. There is no doubt that the Senator is strongly pro-Nixon. However, I got the feeling that he doubts Nixon's ability to win. As a matter of fact, he seemed skeptical that any Republican can defeat President Johnson. On the subject of Ronald Reagan, Goldwater's comment is that "Johnson would chew him up." He seemed interested in my contention that no Republican has much of a chance winning without the Negro vote. I emphasized that you could get it, because of longstanding family tradition in helping Negroes get education.

I let him know my concern about the open occupancy housing bill and the harm I feel Senator Dirksen is doing the Republican Party with our people and the many non-Negroes who support open housing. My attitude toward Senator Goldwater was one of caution and, although I tried not to show it, distrust. I must admit, however, that he is a charmer and, although we had many differences, he really poured on the charm.

As I saw it, his greatest problem with you is more one of outraged feelings than political antagonism. He claims that you made a strong statement, some years ago, regarding Conservatives in the party, comparing them to the Klan and other anti-American elements. He says he would not have been so disturbed if you had told him you were going to make this statement. He claims you and he have much in common. I really got the feeling that he wants the GOP to name a winner, even though he thinks LBJ is practically unbeatable. Along these lines, Mr. Goldwater conceded the fact of your public popularity, but he says your problem is the Republican Party and winning the nomination. I deduce that he could be influenced if stress were placed on his desire to see a winner nominated. Specifically, I believe he would be interested in your cause if he felt you could defeat Johnson. Perhaps we need a groundswell of Negro sentiment with a pledge of support should the GOP nominate you.

The Sunday broadcast "Direct Line" is pertinent only to the point that I emphasized my position on Nixon and Reagan. I cannot support either and I said so. I realize that this may not be the best politics, but my conviction is awfully strong. I cannot work for a party which is unwilling to take the Negro vote seriously. Nomination of Nixon or Reagan could only mean, once again, that the GOP is not interested in the Negro vote. My self-respect will force me to do all I can to see that my people do not vote for a party which has no respect for them. Negroes gave 6% of the vote in 1964. Why should we change in 1968, if the Party doesn't change? To do so would be to go backward since I feel that Nixon supporters in 1968 are Goldwater supporters of 1964.

If the Party wants to win, its only chance, in my view, is your nomination. You can get our vote, and labor, independents and some disgruntled Democrats will give you support also. What other Republican can truthfully make that claim?

I hope you understand why I take that position. I said two things on which you might get some flack. I said I believed the Party is too stupid to nominate a winner. Also, asked what I would do if (since you had been quoted as saying you would support Nixon if he were the nominee)—what I would do if you were campaigning for Nixon. I said that if you were in one state campaigning for Nixon, I'd be in another state campaigning for Johnson. When I said that, some people accused me of being prejudiced, but I also said that I consider you the greatest American. I meant that too.

BARRY GOLDWATER TO ROBINSON

One day after Goldwater wrote this note, Senator Dirksen announced a reversal in his longtime opposition to open housing and began to engineer successful passage of the Open Housing Act of 1968. Dirksen changed his mind only after his son-in-law, Senator Howard Baker of Tennessee, informed him of a possible revolt among Republican senators.

February 26, 1968

Dear Jackie:

It was a real pleasure to have that long chat with you the other morning and I thank you for giving me so much of your time. I later that day saw you on television going over the same ground we discussed and I must say that in both instances I agree with you.

There seems to be some indication that the Republicans in the Senate might be relenting on their stand on open housing but, not having visited there since talking to you, I can only report it as a hunch.

If you are ever out this way, please feel free to call on me as it would be an honor to see you again.

With best wishes,
Barry Goldwater

ROBINSON TO BARRY GOLDWATER

Robinson's March 23 column echoed the friendly theme of the following letter. "I must confess," Robinson stated, "that, although we still disagree sharply in some areas, my personal anti-Goldwater feelings have ebbed considerably."

February 27, 1968

Dear Senator:

Thank you for the breakfast and for a most enlightening meeting. We still have our differences, but it seems to me we really are not too far apart, and if we are able to communicate as we did last week, a better understanding of many of our problems would resolve.

I will continue to express my views, but please be assured that they are no longer personal but relate to my feeling that much still needs to be done. I am certain you realize how you can be a momentous force in bringing about a better relationship. I hope we are able to meet again soon. I feel certain more can be accomplished.

It was good getting a chance to know you better.

Sincerely,
Jackie Robinson

ROBINSON TO CLARENCE TOWNES, JR.

Clarence Townes, director of minorities for the Republican National Committee, was one of the few African Americans prominent in the Republican Party at this point.

February 29, 1968

Dear Clarence:

Recent reports indicate that the Republican Party would like to get 35% of the minority vote. I assume this means the Negro vote. In view of Senator Goldwater's latest statement that the campaign for nomination is strictly a liberal vs. conservative race, in view of the fact that the same people who supported Goldwater are now Nixon supporters and because in the last election Negroes voted overwhelmingly for President Johnson, I wonder how the GOP can expect Negroes to go backward.

Clarence, I suspect that unless the party shows a desire to win our vote, it may rest assured that I and my friends cannot and will not support a conservative and will do whatever is necessary to see that the 6% the Republicans received in '64 does not improve.

We need a two-party system, but only if our vote is wanted. I am sure you understand.

With best wishes,

Sincerely,
Jackie Robinson

ROBINSON TO NELSON ROCKEFELLER

Four days before drafting this memorandum, Robinson learned that his son, Jackie, Jr., was arrested for possession of drugs. Rockefeller sent his personal concerns and an offer of assistance when he heard of the arrest—a move that most likely deepened Robinson's faith in the governor's character and integrity. With the help of Daytop Rehabilitation Program in New York, Jackie, Jr. eventually beat his drug addiction.

March 8, 1968

First, let me thank you for your understanding of my present position and for your most generous offer to help. It is so typical of you and we appreciate it very much.

Second, I must say to you something in which I have the deepest conviction. I appreciate the enormous pressures which have been added to your already arduous responsibilities but when you decided many years back to lead a life of public service, I am sure you recognized what heavy crosses you would be forced to bear. I do not try to speak for anyone else. I am not now nor have I ever been a spokesman or a leader. Speaking from the heart of Jackie Robinson, I must tell you several of my strong beliefs.

I believe there never was a more critical time in the life of America and the history of the world. We are faced with the possibility of total polarizations among the Communist and non-Communist societies, polarizations between black and white Americans, polarization between those elements of Republican thought which would march forward and those who would push back the hands of time.

I believe that each man is placed upon this earth with a destiny to fulfill. I feel strongly that you were meant to lead in world councils, in national affairs and domestic problems, and within a political party which was born slanted towards freedom, but which in recent times has turned its back on its own heritage. I believe that the statement of Barry Goldwater (particularly in light of his personal observation to me) clearly demonstrates that the leaders of the party seek another clash and confrontation between the liberals and moderates and the conservatives. Personally, I cannot and will not work for the victory of a party which told my people in '64 that they did not care about us or our votes and who want to repeat that defeatist insult which led the Republican Party down the road of ruin. The people who rejected the black man in 1964 and carried the Goldwater standard are the identical people who desire the all-things-to-all-men phoniness of a Richard Nixon and his crowd.

I will not bore you with statistics which you have so often read, statistics which prove beyond doubt that the party which gets the black vote will also gain the victory.

I say to you simply, honestly, and as much from my mind as from my heart, that you are the one Republican who can get the winning vote. I believe overwhelmingly that you are THE Republican with a decent chance to win over Mr. Johnson, that you are one of the few Americans who by integrity, by vigor, by temperament, by philosophy and by persuasive power can help the Republican Party, our nation and the world to rise to the awesome challenges of our time. I believe you have no alternative but to go firmly forward to acceptance of your rightful role in our society.

As for your question about the Oregon primary, I certainly feel a definite yes is the answer.

We would like to sit down with some of your advisors in order to polarize our group.

ROBINSON TO BARRY GOLDWATER

Goldwater also responded to news of Jackie, Jr.'s arrest.

March 26, 1968

Dear Senator:

I can hardly tell you how much it has meant to me to have such a note of encouragement and support. Rachel joins me in my thanks and we both have come to believe that with God's help things will right themselves for Jackie Jr. in the days to come.

My best wishes to you.

Sincerely,
Jackie Robinson

ROBINSON TO NELSON ROCKEFELLER

In reply to a February 24 press inquiry about a possible run for the presidency, Rockefeller stated: "I'm not a candidate. I'm not going to be a candidate. I'm supporting [Michigan] Governor [George] Romney and I think he's the best man." Rockefeller added that he would support Richard Nixon if he won the Republican nomination. For his part, Robinson was disappointed not only with Rockefeller's apparent withdrawal from the race but also with the looming candidacy of Senator Robert Kennedy. While pleased with Kennedy's fight against New York City slums, Robinson harbored resentment at Kennedy for moving to New York and defeating the incumbent senator, Kenneth Keating, a racially progressive Republican.

March 27, 1968

Dear Governor:

Your surprise announcement has left me disappointed, hurt and utterly confused. I am disappointed because I have pictured a Republican victory with Negroes giving overwhelming support to your candidacy and the dream of the two-party system becoming a reality.

I am hurt because Negroes desperately need the kind of positive leadership your dedication can bring. I am confused because I now must search for a candidate and the choice is difficult.

As much as I want to support the Republican Party, I strongly feel, for several reasons, that Negroes cannot support Richard Nixon as he projects himself. I am also confused about President Johnson. While, in my opinion, he has been the greatest influence in our domestic racial policies, he leaves so much to be desired on the foreign policy level.

I cannot help but feel that Robert Kennedy is a vindictive opportunist. I wonder if it would be good for the country if the power of the Presidency were in his hands. Nevertheless, I would have to support him over Richard Nixon.

How any man in 1968 seeking the Presidency representing a Party that has only 27% of the total vote can put forth the programs or non-programs he espouses is beyond my comprehension. I believe his attitude is dangerous and would cause more frustration than ever before in our ghettos. His statement, "order before progress," will be a constant reminder to Negroes of where Richard Nixon stands. I pray that he gets less than the 6% Negro vote that Goldwater got.

While I admire you all the more for having the courage and strength to say "no" to the opportunity of being a Republican nominee, as a

Negro I cannot feel good knowing there is no choice in the Republican Party. I want you to know that I feel compelled to do all in my power to get Negroes to see Nixon as he is. While I do not consider myself a man with a great following, I am convinced from our 1966 campaign that I am a pretty good campaigner.

I am sure you will understand my frustrations and while this may have an effect upon our official relationship, I am sure you know I must do what I consider right even at the expense of losing an association I cherish more than you know.

I shall await word from you before I take any step at all. As I said earlier, I am greatly confused and I am also very much concerned about the future of all children, black and white, in this country.

Sincerely,
Jackie Robinson

HUBERT HUMPHREY TO ROBINSON

Humphrey writes one day after the assassination of Martin Luther King, Jr. and one week following Johnson's March 31 announcement that he would not seek or accept the Democratic nomination for president. Like so many others, Robinson was crushed by the news of King's death. He flew to the funeral services in Rockefeller's private plane and devoted several columns to the man he considered to be "the greatest leader of the twentieth century."

April 5, 1968

Dear Jackie:

I have been thinking of you a great deal in these recent weeks. I know that you have had many burdens. As I write this letter, our country is in such trouble. The terrible tragedy of the assassination of Dr. Martin Luther King, Jr. has cast a shadow over our land. I do hope that reason can overcome the emotion and bitterness, and I do hope that the American people will respond to the challenge that is everywhere evident in our cities and amongst our poor. Words will no longer suffice. Deeds are required.

I saw your article of recent date in the *Daily Defender*, where you have made it quite clear that you cannot vote for Mr. Nixon. I do hope that if I should decide to be a candidate that I would be privileged to have your support. I know how much you helped me before. I really believe that this time we could succeed.

Do let me hear from you. Your support would be that added measure of strength that can mean so much. Above all, my thanks for your friendship.

Sincerely,
Hubert H. Humphrey

ROBINSON TO HUBERT HUMPHREY

May 3, 1968

Dear Mr. Vice President:

I am honored that you would want my support. There are few men I have had the pleasure of meeting who I respect more. However, Governor Rockefeller's desires dictate my actions. I fully expect he will be the Republican nominee and I will do everything I can for him. I find him to be a man of great integrity and ability.

If, by chance, things do not work out and you feel I can help, I will be happy to do so, for I believe Vice President Humphrey to be one of the best qualified men of any I know.

I am sure you understand my position.

Sincerely,
Jackie Robinson

ROBINSON TO ROBERT DOUGLASS

George Romney withdrew from the Republican primary campaign in February, and Rockefeller became the main challenger to Richard Nixon, the apparent front-runner. Rockefeller defeated Nixon in the Massachusetts primary on April 30, and by the time Robinson drafted this memorandum, Rockefeller's team still had hopes for a victory. But the governor's candidacy quickly faded, and Ronald Reagan replaced Rockefeller as Nixon's major opponent. What follows is the second part of a memorandum in which Robinson complains to Robert Douglass, the manager of Rockefeller's 1968 presidential campaign, about the governor's decision not to meet with local representatives of the Poor People's Campaign—SCLC's effort to eliminate poverty in the United States—during a visit to Pittsburgh.

May 17, 1968

. . .

If the Governor gets the nomination, Bob, I am positive we have a winner. Being an ex-athlete I am always aware that a good offense is the best defense and when you are behind you pull out all stops and go with your strength. I feel, even though I am not privy to strategy, we are trying to out Republican Nixon. It can't be done in three months. We must go to the Governor's strength, for it is my belief those who control the party want a winner, but they will not believe the Governor has changed to their way of thinking. You could very well win the battle and lose the war by being too reluctant or, if you will, being conservative in your approach.

The refusal of the Governor to make an effort to see the representatives of the Poor People's March in Pittsburgh has to hurt. I can't imagine why he did not see them but these are the people we are going to need.

Continuance of our present course cuts our effectiveness a great deal. I am certain you know why I feel I must write this way. I want a winner. I am not interested in anything personal, for I am in the process of lining up something that secures my future as I know there isn't much more time with the State.

So, Bob, I may sound blunt but it's only because of my strong feeling for the Governor and because I am sincerely concerned. It is nothing personal. I know you believe that. Look at Reagan on television taking a position saying bigots in California must change, threatening to veto legislation unless a hospital is approved for the Watts area, hiring more and more Negroes to responsible positions and getting praise from Negroes who are marveling at the positions he is taking. If Reagan sees the handwriting, why can't we? This is the area where the Governor has his greatest impact. Governor Rockefeller has to be Governor Rockefeller. His personal approach, his personality, which is infectious, must be projected.

Bob, there should be a black person in a high level policy making position walking into the meetings you have. He may not open his mouth, but he should be there. (Not me, I am already committed.) Please don't feel I am treading where I should not be treading. You know you will hear from me what I believe is right. At least check it out.

HUBERT HUMPHREY TO ROBINSON

On July 8 Senator Fred Harris of Oklahoma informed Humphrey that, should Rockefeller lose the Republican nomination, Robinson stood ready to help Humphrey campaign against Nixon. Robinson had consistently supported Humphrey over Robert Kennedy in the run-up to the Democratic nomination. Robinson had clarified his preference in early June, stating that while Kennedy offered "some commendable contributions," his record was "damning": he "upheld the appointment of segregationist judges in the South . . . urged the Freedom Movement to 'wait' and to 'cool off' . . . and Bobby's Justice Department persecuted the Martin King forces in Albany, Georgia." At the same time Robinson stated that "Hubert Humphrey is no Bobby-come-lately to the cause." Kennedy was assassinated in Los Angeles shortly after Robinson wrote these words, but just two days before they were published in his June 8 column.

July 10, 1968

Dear Jackie:

I understand that you have been in touch with my friend and Co-Chairman, Senator Fred Harris. I was so pleased to have Fred's report of your willingness to help me in case Governor Rockefeller does not succeed in his efforts to win the nomination.

I am sure you know of my deep and sincere respect for you. Your support would be not only highly significant in terms of voter strength, but a personal honor to me.

With warm regards.

Sincerely,
Hubert H. Humphrey

BARRY GOLDWATER TO ROBINSON

Goldwater complains about "reverse segregation"—a popular phrase of the white backlash movement—and about Robinson's decision not to support Nixon in the 1968 presidential campaign. Angered especially by reports that Nixon had given veto power over the selection of the vice president to Senator Strom Thurmond of South Carolina, an avowed segregationist, Robinson announced his resignation from Rockefeller's staff and his plan to campaign full-time for the Democrats. Robinson did not mince words when announcing his shift on August 11. About Nixon, he said: "Now he's sold out, he's prostituted himself to get the Southern vote." The Nixon-Agnew ticket, Robinson added, was "racist in nature" and "inclined to let the South have veto powers over what is happening."

August 22, 1968

Dear Jackie:

As a man who has respect for you and who has enjoyed very much the few chances we have had to talk, I am rather disturbed by your decision not to support Nixon, presumably because of his acceptance of Governor Agnew as a running mate.

I just want to mention to you what was in the Emancipation Proclamation issued by Abraham Lincoln, January 1, 1863: "And I hereby enjoin upon the people so declared to be free to abstain from all violence, unless in necessary self-defense; and I recommend to them that, in all cases when allowed, they labor faithfully for reasonable wages."

I do not believe that anybody could call Abraham Lincoln a racist, and yet, as I read some of your remarks and the remarks of some of your colleagues, anyone who condemns violence and rioting is a racist. I can't believe that you intend this interpretation to be placed on your remarks.

Sometime when there is more time, I would like to visit with you on what I feel we call a reverse twist on segregation. Let me explain it briefly. I am not going into any detail about my past history or my lifetime position relative to discrimination, but I want to comment again that I voted against only one civil rights bill.

Now, let's see what has happened because of what I will classify as reverse segregation. I think I was one of the first to comment in a public hearing before the House Committee on Education that one way to speed up integration in the South or anywhere would be to deny federal funds. I am practically certain that Roy Wilkins was at that meeting and when he heard it, he congratulated me on it, but that was the last I ever heard from him.

I have never been invited to address a meeting of the NAACP outside of my State, although I have been a member of it. I came back to Arizona after my defeat and, as a founding member of the Urban League in Phoenix, I offered my services and even offered a rather large sum of money for a project they had in mind. After one or two contacts, I have not heard from them in over two years.

The running example continued just two days ago. A group of young Negro men in their late twenties and early thirties have formed a training group for young Negroes in the age groups of twelve to sixteen, and they approached me, seemingly at the request of their group, to see if I would meet with them this Sunday at my home. Of course, I agreed to do it. I had made all the plans for a swimming party, hamburgers, cokes, etc., and had set everything else aside, including my family, for that day. I was called yesterday and told that the youngsters involved in the program had decided that they would not visit with Mr. Goldwater.

Let me cite one more example before I close and then I will patiently await the chance to sit down and talk with you about it because, from what I hear, this is not applied only to me but applied to everyone who has not complied one hundred percent with every wish and demand of Negro leaders at every and any level.

About four years ago, my younger daughter was married in the Trinity Cathedral in Phoenix and, as with all of our family marriages, a number of Negro friends were invited. They were also invited to the reception at the Country Club and they all came, but one man, a friend of a lifetime, who has known and worked with five generations of my family in this State, was molested by other Negroes because he attended the Goldwater wedding and reception. This man, at that time, was well up into his late seventies.

Jackie, this whole thing disturbs me because there is nothing right about two wrongs. This isn't going to affect my feeling toward the Negroes or any other group, majority or minority, but if it is wrong for the White to act toward the Negro as the Negro has acted toward many in the cases I have recited, then aren't we both on a very wrong and dangerous path?

Please think this over as I am sure that upon reflection you will agree with me because you are a man of fairness and judgment. I do hope that this finds you and your family in the best of health.

With respect,
Barry Goldwater

ROBINSON TO BARRY GOLDWATER

Robinson explains his decision not to support Nixon and suggests that Goldwater has not fully understood "the drive of the black man for human dignity." More conciliatory than he was in his 1964 correspondence with Goldwater, Robinson by this time had shifted his most vocal attacks away from Goldwater and toward Richard Nixon and William F. Buckley, Jr. In his September 7 column, Robinson stated: "I am proud to be black. I am also embattled because I am black. For, white America—and particularly white Americans of the Buckley ilk—has been walking over Black America too long . . . Give America a President like Nixon—with advisors and enthusiasts like Prima Donna Buckley—and you can make book on serious trouble immediately down the road."

September 5, 1968

Dear Senator:

I am in receipt of your troubled, though sincere letter and permit me to say that I, too, enjoyed our chance to talk. I must honestly say that I gained a great deal from our meetings. I believe that you are really trying and you are sincere. Senator, I, too, am sincere.

It must be apparent to you by now that the process of talking and inviting "numbers of Negro friends" to your daughter's marriage means little in the total context of the problems of black people. Black people are looking for something concrete to hold onto. We want people to reach out with a dedication that is apparent for all to see.

Now, I would like to make it as clear as possible that Governor Agnew's selection as a running mate for Nixon had nothing to do with my decision not to support Nixon. For it was Richard Nixon, alone, who made the deal with Strom Thurmond. It was Nixon who obviously promised the Old South that it would have nothing to fear from him. It was Nixon who gave assurances that his Vice President would be a man satisfactory to them.

I ask that you picture yourself as a black man, standing before your television set hearing Strom Thurmond, whose racial views are all too clear, telling the country of his veto powers over the Vice Presidential choice. Picture, if you will, these Old South delegations saying that we don't fear Nixon's choice; "We know he won't let us down."

Did you read Evans and Novak on Nixon? Did you read Drew Pearson's column? Pearson said that on June first Nixon met with

Thurmond and gave veto powers to him on Supreme Court justices—presumably because he, Thurmond, does not approve of the liberal attitude of the present Court. I have yet to hear a denial of these allegations from Mr. Nixon. So, Senator, my opposition is Nixon. Agnew is immaterial. I condemn riots and violence as vigorously as does Nixon or you. But my emphasis is on law and justice. For without the presence of justice, order is placed in jeopardy. And the mood in the black community is one of impatience over the painfully slow pace of full justice.

Your desire to understand and learn more regarding the problems we face in race relations is heartening. It reminds me of people such as President Johnson, whose record as of 1958 was one that those of us in the civil rights movement were less than enthusiastic about. Today, however, his administration has proven to be the best of any previous administration on these matters, regardless of party. I personally believe that much of it is due to the late President Kennedy and now to Vice President Humphrey.

Mr. Nixon, on the other hand, impressed me in 1960, but in 1968 his dealing with Thurmond made a kingmaker out of the former Democrat who quit the party allegedly over his failure to control its liberal views.

Because I am proud of my blackness and the progress we have made, and because I can't feel that America will continue this progress under Nixon-Thurmond rule, I refuse to support the ticket. Governor Agnew is a mere tool in the total equation—thrown in to appease the South. For what other reason would the party deny second spot to such outstanding choices as Mayor Lindsay, Senator Hatfield or Governor Romney?

Senator, I understand your dilemma of the "reverse discrimination." I understand it so much, because as a black man, I feel that it is the failure of persons as yourself to recognize the depth of this problem. If you offered not a single invitation, nor donated a single dime or service, but you were fully able to comprehend the drive of the black man for human dignity, then you would have made a far greater contribution. This dignity comes with an understanding of self-determination and a realization of the imperatives that compel me to reject Nixon as a black man and your ability as a white man, to accept him.

I could not agree more that we are at a "dangerous crossroads." The future of America is at stake. Let me, too, quote Mr. Lincoln, who said:

"A house divided unto itself cannot stand." And let me say further that the subtle threats of "law and order" implied in the Nixon-Thurmond approach do nothing to heal the breach. Anyone with a broader concept of history and a more perceptive mind must see the futility of repression to contain the seething cauldron of social unrest. Only the application of *justice* with law will bring about an ultimate and lasting order. This is what the Nixon-Thurmond team refuses to see.

Blacks and whites of this country cannot afford the luxury of a further widening of the racial gap. We must elect a man who can bring confidence to the whole country. Because of the distrust for Nixon, I don't feel he has the capacity to understand let alone generate confidence.

Senator, when all of this is over, I hope that we can find the time to sit down and just talk. From our previous meetings I believe you would like very much to build a better America, an America that truly is representative of all its people.

Sincerely,
Jackie Robinson

ROBINSON TO NELSON ROCKEFELLER

The front page of the September 9 issue of the New York Times *included a story about Nixon's speech at a B'nai B'rith convention in Washington, D.C. Nixon took the occasion to reemphasize, clarify, and defend his law-and-order approach to domestic politics. "When an individual talks about the necessity for law and order," he explained, "people think it is a code word for racism. But order without progress is tyranny." Nixon also stated that although he understood Rockefeller's reservations about passing a nuclear nonproliferation treaty in light of Soviet aggressiveness in Czechoslovakia, he believed "that we should negotiate" such a treaty. Below is a short note that Robinson sent to Rockefeller after reading this story about Nixon.*

September 9, 1968

I received a letter from Senator Goldwater and I wanted you to see my answer.

In view of the Vice President's speech before the Anti-Defamation

League yesterday, I am sure it must be difficult for you to support Mr. Nixon.

I hope all goes well with you.

BARRY GOLDWATER TO ROBINSON

Shortly before Goldwater wrote this letter, Robinson delivered a speech to the Black Panthers based in Harlem. Speaking at a news conference just before the speech, Robinson depicted the black militants as peaceful, criticized a group of off-duty police officers who had recently attacked a group of Black Panthers in a Brooklyn courthouse, and suggested that police brutality justified the use of force by blacks seeking to defend themselves. Given his earlier letter about black violence, Goldwater must not have been pleased with Robinson's statements, but the senator makes no reference to this point of disagreement.

September 16, 1968

Dear Jackie:

Thank you for your letter and it certainly has cleared up the question I asked you in my other letter.

I am not cognizant enough of any discussion held between Mr. Nixon and Senator Thurmond, so I can't deny or agree that any so-called commitments were made.

I think that I understand the problem of the black man as I have always known that what is sought for human dignity, which is the same all people seek or should seek.

I look forward to the chance for another visit with you, so after the election and a short vacation, win, lose or draw, I will be in touch with you.

With best personal wishes,
Barry Goldwater

HUBERT HUMPHREY TO ROBINSON

On November 5, Nixon defeated Humphrey for the presidency. Six weeks later, Humphrey sent Robinson this note.

December 14, 1968

Dear Jackie,

I talked to you on the phone today, and you know of my sincere appreciation for your support, your confidence and trust. You were a tower of strength for me and the causes that we worked for.

Remember, Jackie, if ever I can be of help to you I stand ready to respond to your call. I know that we shall work together to help make this country a better place in which to work and to live. Our dedication to people—to human rights—goes far beyond just personal friendship or partisan program. I want you to know that I will continue to work as I have in the past, and I look forward to standing alongside of you.

My best wishes for a Merry Christmas and a Happy New Year to you and to your loved ones.

Sincerely,
Hubert H. Humphrey

13

MOVING FORWARD IN OUR STRUGGLE

· 1969–1972 ·

ROBINSON TO DOROTHY SCHIFF

Robinson talked with Dorothy Schiff, publisher of the New York Post, *at a party celebrating the twenty-fifth wedding anniversary of Whitney and Margaret Young on January 2. In the following letter Robinson recounts Schiff's backing of James Wechsler's 1960 decision to terminate his column, and complains about a recent column written by William F. Buckley, Jr. Robinson uses intemperate, hyperbolic rhetoric to criticize Buckley's views.*

January 9, 1969

Dear Mrs. Schiff:

I was a little surprised when you said at Whitney Young's party I had not knocked you in two years. I don't hold grudges, Mrs. Schiff. However, I must admit your action in 1960 surprised me. You must know that I will not do things to please others for personal gains.

Now to the real reason for this letter. Friends have requested that I answer the lies of your columnist, William Buckley, when he said recently that I called a press conference and intimated I had certain influence over Republican leaders. He left the impression that I have called for rioting in cities and that the likes of Whitney Young . . . is scared off by people like me.

While I recognize those who are Buckley supporters are not Robinson enthusiasts, I know in areas and with people who count, every knock from a Bill Buckley is a boost. I would be concerned if men of *his* character were writing words of *praise*. I deem it a tragedy, however, that this man is allowed the media to project his bigoted views, especially when he does so with impunity.

If being what I am indicates to Buckley I am playing Walter Lippmann, whatever that means, so be it! However, I think it should be made infinitely clear, I am not in a popularity contest and am not trying to please the likes of Bill Buckley. I will not be intimidated by him or anyone else when my rights or the rights of my people are in jeopardy. Mr. Nixon's Administration, while not yet in office, has not given Black America any hope. As far as many of us are concerned, the next four years offer little in terms of racial harmony. As Mr. Finch said, the new administration hardly owes our community anything. From what has been offered it looks as if they don't plan to include us, which could very well be a serious mistake. Buckley wrote as if Mr. Whitney Young, Urban League Director, had been offered a cabinet position. It would have been so easy for a man of principle to check the facts. Buckley, in my opinion, is not a man with principle and therefore used the big lie to impress his readers. Mr. Young could hardly have rejected the position out of fear, for as Whitney said, no position was ever offered to him; therefore he had nothing to reject.

Knowing Whitney Young as I do, he is not a person to be influenced or intimidated, unless it's right. He is in my opinion a dedicated leader of a great organization and wants to help improve relations and to ease the fears that exist. Men like Buckley do more to widen the gap and spread hatred than the "extremist" in any area. Racists like him shall have no role in building America.

Finally, I believe the reason Governor Rockefeller does not attempt to censor me is he knows I do and say what I believe. It does not mean I am right, but it is what I believe. He knows he cannot inject his will over my thoughts and feelings. It should be obvious that I will not allow a bigot like Buckley to influence my thinking, regardless of who reads him or how often he uses his column in any attempt at character assassination.

Very truly yours,
Jackie Robinson

ROBINSON TO RICHARD NIXON

Robinson responds to Nixon's inaugural words—"To go forward at all is to go forward together. This means black and white together, as one nation, not two"—by urging the new president to disregard the lack of African American support for his election and to pursue racial justice "for my people."

January 22, 1969

Dear Mr. Nixon:

In 1960 I gave my wholehearted support to your presidential bid because I felt then your views and ideas would be better for America and for the hopes and aspirations of Black Americans than the views of the late President Kennedy.

I opposed you as vigorously in the last election because I felt strongly that your position regarding the old South, the rumors re Strom Thurmond, and the reports from the convention would adversely affect the goals we as Black people have set.

Now that the American people have elected you as our President, we all pray that your years in Washington will be most successful. I must respectfully say I am very much concerned over what I consider a lack of understanding in White America of the desires and ambitions of most Black Americans. This lack of understanding and some surprising statements by some members of the Cabinet give rise to the fear that unless something concrete is done, we should continue on the collision course that will bring a serious confrontation between the races.

I am sure you know, Mr. President, I am not interested in anything but equal rights and opportunities for my people. I am sure you must be aware from the strife in the streets that our youth is sincere and unafraid. They want equality and unless there is evidence from your administration that we will continue to move forward, those of us who are concerned, and believe me, Sir, I am among the legion of concerned you spoke of in your speech, will not have any effective role to play in what happens in the next few months. Yours is not an easy position. We Blacks are in a most difficult position. Only sincerity and dedication can prevent a holocaust.

I sincerely hope you will forget the fact that the Black community, as Mr. Finch said, hardly had a role to play in your election and do all you can to continue our move toward the mainstream. For Mr. President, Black people cannot afford a racial conflict; White people cannot afford one. If we are to survive as a nation, we must do it together. Black people will work for a one America if we are given hope. Without hope, the present feeling of despair will lead to worse problems.

This, Sir, is the most important role your administration must play, for a house divided unto itself cannot stand. Surely you see we are a divided nation searching our souls for answers. It can only come from sincere, dedicated leadership. I pray to God you have the capacity to provide that leadership.

Sincerely,
Jackie Robinson

RICHARD NIXON TO ROBINSON

February 14, 1969

Dear Jackie,

First, I want to thank you for having taken the time to write such a thoughtful letter. As I indicated in my press conference this past week, when asked about the attitude toward me of many Black Americans, all I can hope is that by my acts and those of the men whom I have chosen to help me set policies, I can earn the respect and then the friendship of Black America.

I want to express my desire for all of us to work for one America, and I enlist your help in building together a country that has for too long now been divided.

We must rebuild respect for the institutions of this country and for the process of government; but at the same time that respect will not be rebuilt until government is truly serving the needs and aspirations of all Americans.

Sincerely,
Dick Nixon

ROBINSON TO NELSON ROCKEFELLER

Robinson solicits financial backing for a planned community that would help poor southerners, especially African American families, become self-sustaining farmers. Rockefeller would accept Robinson's invitation and donate funds to support the community's development. The following letter represents Robinson's return to his own familial roots in rural Georgia, where his family had toiled on a farm owned by whites.

February 26, 1969

Dear Governor:

My attention has been drawn to a very interesting and exciting program for providing not only decent housing to low-income rural families, but also to provide a means of livelihood and a better way of life in a planned community.

This program is directed at the problem of families with a farm background in the rural south who today are being forced to flee to the cities because there is no viable alternative for them in their home counties. Although it is commonly believed that there is no hope for rural farm families because the "small farm is no longer viable," this program is making an adaptation from experience gained in Israel, where thousands of immigrants from Europe, Asia and Africa have been successfully resettled by means of a unique concept of building new rural communities which combine both intensive and extensive farming, and also diversified employment in related food processing industries or other light industry, even including electronics.

Initiated by a group of individuals long associated with organizations (National Sharecroppers Fund, SCLC, Southwest Georgia Project, etc.) working on problems of economic development in the South, the new organization is called New Communities, Inc. New Communities, Inc. has acquired an option on a 4800-acre tract of land in southwest Georgia and is now in the process of planning a "Rural New Town" for as many as eight hundred families. They would live there and work at intensive farming, which is their immediate skill; they would also, especially their younger people, begin learning new skills for light industrial development on the same land.

New Communities, Inc. expects to develop a prototype community which can be duplicated in many parts of the South and in other parts of the nation.

With firm offers of technical assistance from such agencies as the Jewish National Fund and Histadrut, they are now searching for major funding sources through government agencies such as OEO and HUD as well as the churches and foundations. A great deal of interest has been shown, but so far, not enough action. Within the Rockefeller Brothers Fund, for example, they have found general interest; but what is needed is affirmative support at a higher level.

What they are attempting fits very well into the program for Community Development Corporations which has been formulated into the

Community Self-Determination Act of 1968, approved by a wide variety of Congressmen and Senators, such as Senators Nelson and Percy, as well as Senator Tower, but not yet enacted into law. It is not a program based on welfare but on real economic private development and investment; I am sure it would be supported by the Nixon administration. As one writer (Ben Bagdikian writing in the August 1968 *Saturday Evening Post*) put it:

> The cost of establishing a family on a small farm today would be about $18,000 counting equipment, closer to $10,000 in the rural south. Those costs would be self-liquidating. The $18,000 is the equivalent of six years on New York City welfare—the $10,000 of three and one-half years—all of it now being paid to rural refugees, more of whom come from the cotton south than from any other rural area.

I urge you to lead the way in offering a helping hand to this program which could mean so much not only to the farm families, but to the cities, which cannot answer their own problems until the rural migration is stopped and *reversed*.

It seems whenever a real need arises I look to you. I hope you don't consider me presumptuous. I do so only because there are so few people with your capacity, both as a humanitarian and one who has the means.

Most sincerely,
Jackie Robinson

ROBINSON TO NELSON ROCKEFELLER

Shortly before writing this letter, Robinson encountered demonstrations protesting the construction of a new state building in Harlem. He had also read about widespread protests at Cornell University, where African American students, angered by such issues as insufficient representation on judicial councils and the absence of a quality program in African American studies, had brandished guns after taking over a student hall.

May 1, 1969

Dear Governor Rockefeller:

I am available at your convenience. I am pleased you understand why I must be as frank as I am.

When I see and hear the threats on 125th Street re the state office building; when I see and hear the concern of Black people regarding the conservative party; when I see and fear the possible conflict in the streets this coming summer, it is time we yell loud and clear.

We cannot afford, Governor, strife in the streets. I am sure you are concerned as we look at Cornell, and as we see the revolt already developing with our young.

It would appear to me a public relations project must be started to win over again people who want the state office building, but are not now vocal, and to focus attention on working together to solve our problems.

Continued success.

Sincerely,
Jackie Robinson

J. EDGAR HOOVER TO JOHN EHRLICHMAN

The following is a memorandum that FBI director J. Edgar Hoover sent to John D. Ehrlichman, counsel to President Nixon, after receiving a "name check request." At the very least, Ehrlichman's request suggests that the Nixon administration was strategizing about Robinson's public criticism of Nixon. Twenty days before Hoover sent this memo, Robinson, ever the dissident, criticized flag-waving U.S. patriots. "I wouldn't fly the flag on the Fourth of July or any other day," he told the New York Times. *"When I see a car with a flag pasted on it I figure the guy behind the wheel isn't my friend."*

July 24, 1969

JACKIE ROBINSON

Jackie Robinson, nationally-known former baseball player, who was born on January 31, 1919, at Cairo, Georgia, has not been the subject of an investigation by the FBI. However, our files reveal the following information concerning him.

The June 1, 1946, issue of "People's Voice" reported that Jackie Robinson, the first Negro to break into organized baseball, has accepted chairmanship of the New York State Organizing Committee for United Negro and Allied Veterans of America (UNAVA). The "People's Voice" has been cited by the California Committee on Un-American Activities as being communist initiated and controlled. The UNAVA has been cited as a communist front by the Internal Security Subcommittee of the Senate Judiciary Committee.

The November, 1946, issue of "Fraternal Outlook" contained an article concerning the opening of the Solidarity Center of the International Workers Order (IWO) in Harlem, New York. The name, Jackie Robinson, baseball player, was listed as one of the persons on the Advisory Board of this Center.

"Fraternal Outlook" is an official publication of the IWO, an organization cited pursuant to Executive Order 10450.

According to a news release on September 13, 1968, Jackie Robinson, former baseball star, while speaking at a news conference minutes before leaving to address a Black Panther meeting in Brooklyn, New York, was reported as having stated, "The Black Panther organization is one with an interest in seeking peace and reports otherwise are due to misinformed newsmen. Improper reporting has determined that they (the Black Panthers) are a militant group while the fact is they are seeking peace. DELETED.

DELETED

The Black Panther Party has been described as a black extremist, militant, violence-prone organization whose members have been involved in confrontations with law enforcement officers.

The fingerprint files of the Identification Division of the FBI contain no arrest data identifiable with captioned individual based upon background information submitted in connection with this name check request.

NOTE: Per request of John D. Ehrlichman, Counsel to the President

ROBINSON TO NELSON ROCKEFELLER

Concerned once again with the business side of civil rights, and with making money, Robinson and several others founded Jackie Robinson Associates—a group of business leaders committed to providing business loans and affordable housing for minorities. Robinson later developed the Jackie Robinson Construction Corporation, an interracial company with a focus on training minority contractors and the construction of affordable housing for people with low incomes. The following letter provides evidence of Robinson's use of political connections for his business interests.

November 14, 1969

Dear Governor:

In our meeting we discussed the possibility of forming a group to develop housing in minority areas within the state. I have had some discussion with our associates about this and we are of the opinion that Jackie Robinson Associates could handle the program well. I am therefore requesting that we have a meeting to determine how we can develop some of the areas we discussed.

I was very pleased to hear you say you want to move immediately. I believe we can play a role once again in your campaign and I would like very much to do so because of my respect and admiration for you. However, I am sure you know it is not going to be easy. We will need considerable work in Black areas and the sooner we can demonstrate your real concern, the easier the task.

I know I can rally support, but we will be asked about demonstration programs that will enable people in both parties to get behind you.

I know you recognize the shortness of time and hope we can move very soon.

With all good wishes and personal regards to Mrs. Rockefeller.

Sincerely,
Jackie Robinson

ROBINSON TO RICHARD NIXON

The following is a letter fragment that Robinson published in I Never Had It Made*—an autobiography he wrote with Alfred Duckett. While he offers his support for the progressives in Nixon's cabinet—William Rogers, Maurice Stans, Robert Finch, and George Romney—Robinson is sharply critical of Spiro Agnew, John Mitchell, and Strom Thurmond, referring to all three as "enemies" of African Americans.*

February 9, 1970

If you are sincere in wanting to win the respect of Black America, you must be willing to look at your own administration's attitude. There seem to be no key officials in your administration who have an understanding of what motivates black people. I find it difficult to believe there will be any, when it appears your most trusted advisers are Vice President Agnew, Attorney General Mitchell and Strom Thurmond. How can you expect trust from us when we feel that these men you have selected for high office are enemies? You would not support known anti-Semitics to placate Jewish feelings. Why appoint known segregationists to deal with black problems? If you could see a projection in terms of influence by others of your administration, men like Secretary of State Rogers, Secretary of Commerce Stans, HEW Secretary Finch and Housing Secretary Romney, many of our frustrations would dissipate. Confidence in and respect for you will be based upon the attitudes of those whom you trust.

I respectfully submit this, and hope that it is received in the same spirit as it is sent.

Sincerely,
Jackie Robinson

ROBINSON TO MAURICE STANS

Several months earlier Secretary of Commerce Maurice Stans traveled to Freedom National Bank to meet with Robinson and others about implementing Nixon's minority business initiatives. While he liked Stans, Robinson was critical of Nixon's efforts to help black businesses and the black community in general, and in an appearance before the Senate Small Business Committee's Subcommittee on Urban and Rural Development on January 20, Robinson testified that "the very poor relations between black Americans and the present Administration are causing a serious rift in this country." Robinson also stated that because of their mistrust of Nixon, many African American businessmen and -women chose not to pursue opportunities made possible by the Commerce Department's Office of Minority Business Enterprise. Nevertheless, Robinson believed that Stans was sincere in his efforts to advance minority businesses, and in this letter he even offers to become a consultant to the Nixon administration.

March 11, 1970

Dear Mr. Secretary,

Thank you very much for the pictures. They did remind me of a very pleasant visit. The more I observe you, the more impressed we are with your efforts and sincerity. I wish, however, more of this sincerity could be expressed by others in the administration, for we are very much concerned about the attitudes that are being expressed in the Black communities. Only positive action in my opinion can prevent a holocaust. I believe the best possible action at this particular point would be for the administration to use individuals that are trusted in the Black community. In my conversations with others when we visited, there was an indication that they felt I could be of service in this end. I believe that most people know I am dedicated to improving the conditions of underprivileged people. It is also widely known that I would not sell my people out for individual gain. If there would be any interest on a consulting basis, I believe a proper announcement could very well bring a better understanding and perhaps ease tensions that we see happening in the Maryland area. It is my belief that because of the many opportunities you have had to visit Black communities, to be able to see their concern, that you know exactly what is going on in the minds of most Black Americans. Because I believe you understand this, I urge you to get the President to use someone who may be able to work with you and others and perhaps turn the tide. This is a matter of deep concern and urgency. I hope you will consider the matter. Again my thanks for the pictures and the visit. I appreciate getting the opportunity of knowing you better.

Sincerely,
Jackie Robinson

MAURICE STANS TO ROBINSON

Stans refers to Abraham Venable, the first African American director of the Office of Minority Business Enterprise in the Department of Commerce. There is no available evidence to suggest that the Nixon administration ever employed Robinson as a consultant for the Department of Commerce or for any other part of the administration.

March 19, 1970

Dear Jackie:

Thank you for your thoughtful letter of March 11, 1970. I appreciate your candid comments, and your offer to help is most welcome.

There is no question that we can benefit from your advice and assistance. I understand that Mr. Venable will be meeting with you on other matters on Monday, March 23, 1970, and I have asked him to hand deliver this letter and discuss with you the ways in which you might contribute to the minority enterprise effort.

I will give his report my personal and immediate attention. I am encouraged in our difficult, but urgent, task by your willingness to lend assistance.

Sincerely,
Maurice H. Stans

ROBINSON TO THE EDITOR OF THE *MIAMI HERALD*

Curt Flood, an outfielder for the St. Louis Cardinals, dared to challenge "the reserve clause" found in Major League Baseball contracts. This clause bound players to their teams for life and effectively prevented what we now know as "free agency." Flood refused to report to the Philadelphia Phillies, to whom he had been traded following the 1969 season, and filed suit against Major League Baseball. Robinson offered testimony in federal court in support of Flood's case. "The reserve clause," he stated, "is one-sided in favor of the owners and should be modified to give the player some control over his destiny." Bill Braucher, a sportswriter and columnist for the Miami Herald, *criticized Robinson's appearance, and below is Robinson's response to the column.*

June 8, 1970

Dear Sir:

I hope I am not being presumptuous in writing to your letter to the editor column regarding an article written May 27. The article in my opinion was based on prejudice, bigotry and Bill Braucher's personal dislike for me, which of course does not bother me. When he uses this as a pretense for a column, my side should be aired.

Why should Bill Braucher be so upset because Curt Flood's attorneys asked that I testify at the hearings against the reserve clause? Why should he be so concerned because I expressed myself on politics, society, industry, the anti-missile system and practically any other subject, including baseball, of course?

He seems to feel I don't have a right to express my opinion, which, contrary to the popular opinion of many, Casey Stengel was not the great manager many writers make him out to be.

Because I answer questions asked of me certainly does not make me an expert. I know where my strengths are, and act according to the dictates of my conscience. In the past I have appeared before many legislative committees made up of distinguished members of the Congress, and will continue to do so when asked. It would seem to me that in these troubled times, when answers are being sought from all sources, none of us should be so bigoted that he would deny that person his or her right to freedom of speech.

Braucher's biggest concern seems to be that I end up "into the civil rights league." Well, Mr. Editor, this is one area where I do consider myself an expert. Being Black in these United States, having to contend with the Bill Brauchers for over 50 years, I know a little about bigots and bigotry.

Bill says, regarding the reserve clause, "maybe Robinson has a solution. If he does, however, I'm not sure I want to hear from him again." I have never spoken for his ears. One does not waste time on men as little as Bill Braucher. All one has to do is read this column carefully to know it was a narrow bigoted one that tells you of the level of his competence, not only as a writer but also as a man.

Sincerely,
Jackie Robinson

Robinson, most likely with the assistance of Alfred Duckett, pitches his autobiography to Michael Hamilburg, a literary and talent agent for the Mitchell J. Hamilburg Agency in Los Angeles. The following is a fragment of the letter.

October 10, 1970

Dear Mr. Hamilburg:

I believe that Al and I have pulled together sufficient material in the attached outline to give a good overview of the book you, he and I have been discussing—working title—I NEVER HAD IT MADE.

Almost a quarter century ago when I was chosen by Mr. Branch Rickey to be the first black man in major league baseball, I immediately became the target of three kinds of attention—hatred from some owners, players, managers, coaches, press personnel and some fans; encouraging good will from some press personnel, some fans and some players. Third species of attention was curiosity from a vast body of all kinds of people who were committed neither to my success or failure.

Almost a quarter century later, there is virtually, unanimously only one kind of attitude toward the many black players and stars of America's favorite sport. There is no major league team which does not have black players and the roar from the stands comes pouring forth, uninhibited by racism.

Within the span of these years, our country and the world have undergone many changes. So have I. I have engaged in three careers—business as vice-president for personnel of a restaurant chain and founding Board Chairman of the highly successful Freedom National Bank in Harlem—civil rights as volunteer, traveling fund-raiser for the NAACP and fundraiser and supporter of the late Dr. Martin Luther King and lastly—politics as a campaigner for Hubert Humphrey, Lyndon Johnson, Richard Nixon and Nelson Rockefeller.

Beautiful things and bad things have happened to me. I have been reinforced in some of my early convictions. I have changed my mind about others. I have been called blessed by some people of both races and damned by others of both races. I have been labeled militant, radical, conservative and even Uncle Tom. I have not got of life all I wished or deserved. But who does? I have been most fortunate. I owe a great deal to baseball but I gave a great deal to the game. Baseball has made magnificent strides and set the tempo for other facets of our society to do the same. But baseball is still quite imperfect as I shall prove in the chapter, "There Are No More Mr. Rickeys." I love baseball and—even though I do, in fact BECAUSE I do—I will continue to criticize it. I love this country. It has done a lot for me. In this country, I, grandson of a slave, son of a sharecropper, rose to the Hall of Fame. As I say, this country has done a lot for me and I have done in return, the best it has let me do for it. That is why I do not have to wave flags or have stickers on my car or wear patriotic cufflinks or armbands on my sleeve. I do not have to leave this country at the suggestion of some third generation European who wants to compare grandfathers—his who came here seeking freedom and immediately enslaved others for his own advancement—and mine who was brought here in chains in the stinking hold of a ship. This land is my land as much as it is his. And it is his, too. With the land, I've been told, Americans inherit the legacy of free speech, free expression, of the right to dissent. I always intend to indulge that freedom.

I once put my freedom into mothballs for a season, accepted humiliation and physical hurt and derision and threats to my family in order to do my bit to help make a lily white sport a truly American game. Many people approved of me for that kind of humility. For them, it was the appropriate posture for a black man. But when I straightened up my back so oppressors could no longer ride upon it, some of the same people said I was arrogant, argumentative and temperamental. What they call arrogant, I call confidence. What they call argumentative, I categorize as articulate. What they label temperamental, I cite as human.

I paid more than my dues for the right to call it like I see it. And I could care less if people like me, so long as they respect me. The only way I know how to deserve respect—even if one does not receive it—is to be honest enough with oneself, to be honest with others. This is the cardinal principle I have kept in mind in making plans for this book.

CALVIN MORRIS TO ROBINSON

Plagued by advanced diabetes, Robinson still continued to schedule trips to benefit the civil rights movement, and on January 23 he visited Operation Breadbasket in Chicago—an SCLC campaign to improve the economic conditions of poor blacks in that city. His rallying speech called for African Americans "to wake up and reclaim this land that belongs to us and take back the flag which has now become the personal property of the kind of bigot who says 'love it or leave it.'" Robinson also took the occasion to describe Jesse Jackson, who directed Operations Breadbasket at this time, as "a tall, young, brave, Black Moses who can take us some giant steps along the way to that Promised Land of which Dr. King spoke." As his own life drew to a close, Robinson actively supported a number of young African Americans emerging on the national scene—including Charles Rangel, whose endorsement from Robinson helped him to defeat Adam Clayton Powell, Jr. in the 1970 Democratic primary election to represent Harlem in the House of Representatives. Below is a letter of thanks from Calvin Morris, the associate director of Operation Breadbasket.

February 1, 1971

Dear Mr. Robinson:

We would like to express on behalf of Reverend Jackson and our entire staff how honored we were that you took time out from your very busy schedule to come speak to the people of Chicago, and particularly to the Breadbasket Community.

For many of us growing up in the time when there were few black male images, particularly black males with dignity and respect, you were as a shining beacon which we could aspire to become. I say this, not just as relative to sports, but rather because of the way you talked, walked, and carried yourself off the field. Because of your inspiration in the field of sports and elsewhere, many black youth were encouraged to hold fast to their dreams. Therefore, you awakened memories in the hearts of some and were a living example of history to the young.

All of us sincerely thank you again for coming and we send our deepest regards to Mrs. Robinson.

Sincerely yours,
Rev. Calvin S. Morris

ROBINSON TO CALVIN MORRIS

The following is the text of Robinson's handwritten reply, as found on the margins of Calvin Morris's letter.

No date [February 1971]

My only regret is that I am unable to do more. I have been moved many times but never more than by my participation with the breadbasket community. I left Chicago to attend a sports banquet. After my Chicago experience, the dinner was an empty affair. Imagine having to leave a Breadbasket affair where people were deeply involved in creating dignity and self-respect to attend a banquet honoring people because they were able to catch and hit a ball but not at all concerned about people. I thank all of you for an experience I shall never forget. Please continue your dedicated effort to lift us. I hope I can play a role, for I am deeply impressed with the role Jesse Jackson is playing and the image he has among people. His is a leadership role that must be protected.

E. J. BAVASI TO ROBINSON

E. J. "Buzzie" Bavasi, president of the San Diego Padres and the former general manager of the Dodgers, expresses his disagreement with Major League Baseball's decision to elect into the Hall of Fame only one player a year from the Negro leagues, and to keep tablets honoring the Negro-league players separate from those of the other inductees.

February 11, 1971

Dear Jackie:

I am writing the Commissioner today with regard to my reactions to his new policy pertaining to the Hall of Fame.

I, for one, feel that men such as Satchel Paige, Josh Gibson, etc., belong in the Hall of Fame. There should be no restrictions whatsoever. It seems to me that we are asking them to "sit in the back of the bus" again. Baseball itself has come a long way and I hate to see it do anything to affect the fine relationship we have with minority groups.

Perhaps I am wrong but in my simple way I have to feel that if Satchel and the other players are invited to share a house with Babe Ruth and Lou Gehrig, then they should not be asked to segregate themselves from the other members of the house.

Perhaps you do not feel this way, Jackie, but I feel this way very strongly. If you have a chance, I would like to hear your views on this subject.

With all best wishes, I am

Very truly yours,
Buzzie Bavasi

ROBINSON TO E. J. BAVASI

The following is Robinson's reply to Bavasi, as found on the bottom margin of the February 11 letter. Robinson refers to an unidentified "misunderstanding" in 1957, when Robinson announced his retirement from baseball after Bavasi and O'Malley traded him to the New York Giants.

No date [February 1971]

Dear Buzzie:

Your letter of the 11th was sincerely appreciated. I not only agree with your sentiments but have expressed myself on the subject. 1971 is not time to go backwards and, frankly, I personally would refuse the dubious honor. You know I feel strongly about this matter. I am pleased you are expressing yourself about the way you feel. Your action justifies the way I thought of you before the 1957 misunderstanding. I know baseball feels it's honestly doing its part to bring better understanding. I think it has failed miserably but your attitude and the action of Mike Burke of the Yankees is encouraging. I hope this is only the start, for there is so much more to be done.

ROBINSON TO NELSON ROCKEFELLER

Robinson campaigned for Rockefeller in the 1970 gubernatorial election, although not as formally as he had in previous years. In early 1971 Robinson even became a public critic of Rockefeller's plan to tighten restrictions on eligibility requirements for welfare.

March 18, 1971

The attached is a letter to the editor of the *New York Post*. This letter is my response to an article by Pete Hamill that appeared in the *Post* on March 1, 1971. Instead of sending the letter to the *Post*, I am sending it to you. I am sure that by this time you are aware of my concern over the entire welfare issue. The letter expresses this concern.

It is my hope that we can help bridge the communication gap and to that end I have a specific recommendation: There are many individuals within the Black and Puerto Rican community and others who, because of their faith in you and your fairness, want to give constructive help. However, they must hear directly from you. I recommend that a meeting between you and such individuals be arranged as expeditiously as possible in order to curtail any misinformation that may be spreading through our communities.

March 18, 1971

To the Editor
NEW YORK POST
210 South Street
New York, N.Y. 10002

Dear Sir:

Would like to try to answer Mr. Pete Hamill's column of March 1st relating to the welfare problem.

No one has agreed with Governor Rockefeller more than I. He has been, in my opinion, a Governor with insight and understanding. We have great faith in him and whenever there has been a crisis, underprivileged people could count not only on Nelson Rockefeller but the entire family. There can be no doubt about the Rockefeller Family's concern for the less fortunate. Is it any wonder then, when poor people feel the pressure of hunger and poverty, when the welfare of their loved ones are at stake, they turn to a friend? New York has been that friend over the years and the leadership in this area has come from the Governor's chair.

As much as I believe in Governor Rockefeller, as much respect and admiration as I have for him, I don't agree we should support his welfare proposals without making sure that he is taking into account the facts. Most people on welfare would be happy to get off if there were jobs that would enable them to support their families. Blacks and Puerto Ricans on welfare are unskilled, as are other welfare recipients, because in most cases they had been denied the opportunity to get a skill. Too often more money can be obtained from welfare than from an unskilled job. I have seen and talked with many unskilled welfare recipients and they would welcome the chance of working to provide for themselves.

Statistics show that over 60% of the people on welfare are children. We have all heard others say, "I am fed up with supporting other people's children." Perhaps we can solve this problem with more day care centers which would enable those who must stay home to care for the children, to go to work and maybe reduce the amount of money to dependent children.

None of us could honestly complain about the aged and disabled. They make up over 20% of those on welfare. How we handle this problem certainly needs a great deal of research.

Then those who must stay home to care for the sick and aged make up the next highest percentage of those on welfare. There are some 2 to 3% who take advantage of the welfare loopholes and I, like everyone else, hope we can clamp down on those. But can we honestly answer the call of the great numbers of people—and I am sure you have heard from them—who pray to get off welfare but ask: "Where are the jobs?"

I don't think our priorities are reached when we would deny people their needs while we spend billions searching for rocks on the moon. We must care more about people and when we do, I think we will find poor people caring more about themselves. I believe dignity should be our prime target. Cutting back on welfare only indicates that we are not truly concerned about the needy. If we do it without another program, the problems confronting us will become much greater. We cannot just eliminate any program without a thoroughly planned program to replace it.

We have heard people say: "Put welfare recipients on the streets cleaning them." Can you imagine the cry from the Sanitation Department? What we heard a few years back from them would be mild compared to what we would hear today.

This country is big enough and strong enough with enough funds to take care of people all over the world. Let's show those right here at home that we care enough about our own. And then perhaps we will be able to reach those who truly are troubled.

Sincerely,
Jackie Robinson

NELSON ROCKEFELLER TO ROBINSON

After graduating from Daytop Rehabilitation, Jackie, Jr. participated in antidrug campaigns with his father.

May 3, 1971

Dear Jackie:

Sam Singletary tells me that you and Jackie, Jr. appeared in a recent drug abuse conference sponsored by the Scotia-Glenville School District and community. I am certain you can never fully realize the impact the two of you had on the community. I thank you both for your courage and for your willingness to help others out of your own experience.

If I'm back in New York City on Thursday, I believe we have an afternoon appointment. It has been too long since I have seen you—I look forward to it.

With warm regard,

Sincerely,
Nelson

RICHARD NIXON TO ROBINSON

Jackie, Jr. died in a car accident on June 17, and less than a week later a long-scheduled "Afternoon of Jazz," attended by Jesse Jackson, Roberta Flack, and Bayard Rustin, among so many others, celebrated Jackie, Jr.'s life and raised money for Daytop Rehabilitation.

June 17, 1971

Dear Jackie:

I have just learned of the tragic death of your son, and I want you to know that my thoughts and prayers are with you and Mrs. Robinson at this difficult time.

I know that nothing said could relieve the pain that this loss has brought you, but I do want you to know that Mrs. Nixon and I will be praying that God may give you the strength and courage to persevere.

Sincerely,
Richard Nixon

ROBINSON TO WILLIAM BLACK

Robinson had left Chock Full O' Nuts on unhappy terms, and here he offers a letter of reconciliation to his former employer.

June 22, 1971

Dear Mr. Black,

Word has come to us regarding the gesture you made concerning the concert. I'm sure you know that since that time, we have lost our son. But because of his endearing efforts to make the jazz concert a success, we have decided to go ahead with it, and do the job he wanted to do.

What you are doing I shall never forget. I am sure you must know how much your bringing me in to the Chock Full O' Nuts family in the early years meant to me and my life. While we have been apart these last few years, your influence has been a factor in many of the things I've done since that time. And now that you have made our jazz concert a success, I am even more deeply indebted to you.

In the near future, I would like to meet with you at your convenience, and express my thanks in person.

Very truly yours,
Jackie Robinson

ROBINSON TO RICHARD NIXON

Robinson was the guest of honor at a testimonial dinner on December 6, 1971, and to help celebrate his recognition as "The Man of 25 Years in Sports," Nixon wrote a glowing statement about Robinson's athletic prowess. According to his autobiography, Robinson replied to Nixon's statement by sending him the following letter. Robinson refers to Henry Cashen, deputy assistant to the president for public liaison.

No date [December 1971]

Dear Mr. President:

Your understanding of the inadequacy of our present social structure to meet the needs of every citizen was well expressed. Truly, it is most important that we stand up like men, express ourselves, and, in the dictum of Mr. Cashen, realize that in our attempt to help others, our own image is observed and read by others.

This letter, these words, coming from you, are most important, and, I believe, they will help in the effort to get blacks to understand that it is totally unnecessary to get on their hands and knees in order to be accepted or recognized.

Because I felt strongly that it is not good policy for any minority to put all of their eggs in one political basket, many of us had decided it may be best to support you and your candidacy in the coming election. However, your Vice President, Mr. Agnew, makes it impossible for me, once again, to do so. I feel so strongly about his being anti-black and anti-progressive in race relations that I dread the fact of anything happening to you and Mr. Agnew becoming President of the United States.

As always, I am available to discuss the forward movement of black and white relations.

Again, my sincere thanks for your kind sentiments.

Sincerely,
Jackie Robinson

ROBINSON TO ANDRE BARUCH

Robinson refers to the Jackie Robinson Construction Corporation in this letter to his longtime friend and former Dodgers broadcaster Andre Baruch. Accompanying this letter in the Jackie Robinson Papers is the following note from Rachel Robinson: "The Jackie Robinson Construction Corp. received its first building contract in 1972 (State of New York—Whitney Young Manor in Yonkers, NY). Jackie Robinson passed after the groundbreaking. Rachel

Robinson took over the business and through a joint venture with Joel Halpern (Halpern Building Corp) founded the Jackie Robinson Development Corp. The Jackie Robinson Development Corp. completed six housing developments in Yonkers, Brooklyn and Harlem totaling 1,300 units." As he pursued his passion for affordable housing, Robinson also continued to work on his golf swing, and here he notes his pleasure at having been invited to join Baruch for a golf tournament in California.

February 14, 1972

Dear Andre,

As you see, we are in another business and it's very exciting. For really the first time we have a potential that is great, and my partners have about a billion dollars worth of building experience, and one has real strong financial backing. As things have not worked out in other ventures, I am trying to hold down my enthusiasm. However, with each passing day things look better. I hope the same is true in your new setup.

Sorry to hear of the new operation. Glad that is behind you.

The reason I asked about the cart is that there was no explanation. I was pleased at the invitation and in spite of not feeling quite up to par would not miss this opportunity. I hit some balls the other day for the first time in about seven months. It felt good. I only hope I don't disgrace myself, but it is fun and I am pleased the committee invited me. As you may know, blacks have the feeling only the "good blacks" get invited to tournaments. I will do my best to make the day successful . . .

My plan is to take an early Sunday flight in hopes of playing in the afternoon. If you are up to it, we may as well have two cripples on the course . . .

Looking forward to seeing you soon.

Jackie

ROBINSON TO RICHARD NIXON

Robinson continued to make his presence known in political circles, and in spite of the following prophetic letter about Nixon's call for a moratorium on busing, Robinson attended a spring dinner hosted by the Black Committee to Reelect the President.

March 21, 1972

Dear Mr. President:

As a proud Black American who feels Blacks have contributed greatly to whatever successes have been achieved as a nation, I am greatly concerned with your leadership at a time when understanding and courage is needed to head off what could be the worst racial turmoil we have witnessed.

Mr. President, whether we blacks helped to put you in office or not, you still are president of all the people, and you as president must realize that the idea that blacks want busing for racial balance is erroneous. This notion springs from white America. While it is important that as a nation we have understanding and racial equality, as a black, I could not care less about integration except that it is the only way to build a strong country. We want busing so our children can compete! You know, as all Americans must know, our kids will make it only on the quality of their education. Non-integrated schools, no matter what, are not equal in terms of educational opportunities.

To go backward in 1972 is certainly no credit to America, and history will show it was not to your credit to urge a nation to go down hill after the promise of a new day. Politically, this may be the smart move but if you are honest with yourself, you know you are polarizing this country to such an extent there can be no turning back from the position taken by young blacks that "we ain't afraid of dying, we're just barely living anyhow."

Because I want so much to be a part of and to love this nation as I once did, I hope you will take another look at where we are going and be the president who leads the nation to accept difficult but necessary action, rather than one who fosters division.

Very truly yours,
Jackie Robinson

ROBINSON TO ROLAND ELLIOTT

Nixon did not bother to reply to Robinson's March 21 letter—a decision that showed just how far apart the two had grown since the time when Nixon had first courted Robinson's endorsement. Roland Elliott, special assistant to the president, responded on Nixon's behalf, and below is Robinson's critical response.

April 20, 1972

Dear Mr. Elliot:

Thanks for your letter of the 14th. I am sorry the President does not understand my concern. Black America, it seems, comes up short as Presidents study or give time to fashion standards that are designed to help all Americans when in reality it is a smoke screen.

Black America has asked so little, but if you can't see the anger that comes from rejection, you are treading a dangerous course. We older blacks, unfortunately, were willing to wait. Today's young blacks are ready to explode! We had better take some definitive action or I am afraid the consequences could be nation shattering.

I hope you will listen to the cries of the black youth. We cannot afford additional conflict.

Sincerely,
Jackie Robinson

ROBINSON TO NELSON ROCKEFELLER

By the end of his life, Robinson had also become disillusioned with his favorite politician, Nelson Rockefeller. Although he does not detail his reasons here, Robinson was angry at Rockefeller's decision to order an assault on Attica State Prison during the September 1971 riots (twenty-three of the thirty-nine inmates killed were African Americans), and no doubt was troubled by the governor's defensive testimony before the investigating state commission, excerpts of which appeared in the May 1 issue of the New York Times. *Changes to welfare policies also continued to irritate Robinson, and it is highly likely that he was disturbed by Rockefeller's support for Nixon's proposed one-year moratorium on busing as a tool for integrating schools.*

May 2, 1972

Dear Governor Rockefeller:

It is with the greatest difficulty that I write this letter. It's difficult because the one man in public life in whom I had complete faith and confidence does not now measure up to his previous highly laudable stand. It has not been easy taking a stand over the years, but when one believes, as I do, you fight back. I cannot fight any longer, Governor, for I believe you have lost the sensitivity and understanding I felt was yours when I worked with you. Somehow, it seems to me, getting ahead politically is more important to you than what is right. Perhaps you honestly feel you are doing what is right, but it certainly is not the way Governor Rockefeller used to function.

Frankly, if I were asked to give reasons for my feelings, I could not pinpoint them. I am just confused and discouraged and feel a good friend has let me down.

Sincerely,
Jackie Robinson

NELSON ROCKEFELLER TO ROBINSON

May 8, 1972

Dear Jackie:

I have your letter of May second and I understand what you are saying. I am saddened by the circumstance that you felt it necessary to write in this vein, but I think I also understand the considerations which prompted you to write it.

You and I have been friends for many years and I hope it will be possible for us to continue to be friends regardless of changing circumstances. Certainly I shall never forget the ways in which you have helped me and worked with me for things in which we mutually believed—as I am sure you will also recall that the help has been mutual.

Times have changed, Jackie, and it would be easier for me if in fact I had "lost the sensitivity and understanding" that you felt I had. It would be a lot easier for me emotionally. I can only say to my old friend that I haven't changed—but conditions have changed.

Putting on the brakes, retrenching, calling a halt—these are actions alien to my nature. But I have learned from bitter experience that liberalism ceases to work at some point if it is not controlled by realism. We have come face to face with the fact that state and local governments are running out of money, abuses have occurred, and an inevitable taxpayer reaction has set in. I am simply trying to bring things back into balance and I hope that you will ponder the possibility that, in the circumstances, I may be able to hold things together—by virtue of experience and progressive outlook—better than a lot of others I can think of who might be sitting in this chair.

I am sorry indeed that it looks to you now as though I am more interested in getting ahead politically than in doing "what is right." As to "what is right," one can only exercise his best judgment after thoughtful and prayerful consideration—and in these times, what is right to one person is very, very wrong to another. But as to my interest in getting ahead politically—I can only ask, where? I cannot foresee any circumstances that would prompt me to run for office again. As for all those media rumors about Washington, I have asked for nothing and have been offered nothing and I don't want anything. So how can I be trying to "get ahead politically"—least of all at the expense of what I feel in my heart to be the right thing to do?

As I said at the outset, I understand what you are saying and I understand in particular your last paragraph, in which you say that you cannot pinpoint the reasons for your feelings. This, too, suggests the kind of times we are living in. All I can say is that I am doing my best in a very difficult period and I hope in time you will understand this. I hope we can sit down together and talk it over sometime soon. Just let me know if you want to.

As always,
Nelson

ROBINSON TO ROY WILKINS

At the first National Black Political Convention (NBPC) in Gary, Indiana, held in early March, young African American leaders eclipsed the old guard represented by Robinson and other mainstream civil rights leaders, and on May 16 Wilkins publicly announced that the NAACP had withdrawn its support from NBPC. Wilkins's disagreement with NBPC centered on the convention's adoption of anti-Israel and antibusing resolutions. With their difficult past behind him, Robinson applauds Wilkins's public battle with the younger black militants.

May 17, 1972

Dear Roy:

Just a note of appreciation for your stand against what I consider backward steps taken by the National Black Political Convention. In these days, which demand inspirational leadership to move forward in our struggle for equal opportunities, we cannot approve any activities that would relegate us to the posture and disposition of the past. Your forthright position was extremely encouraging, and I offer my full support for whatever it may be worth.

Congratulations again, Roy. These direct affirmations you have employed recently mean a great deal to Black America. I know you will continue your fine leadership.

With warm personal regards.

Sincerely,
Jackie Robinson

RICHARD NIXON TO ROBINSON

Nixon's last known letter to Robinson is this form letter he sent to all the baseball players he had selected for his "all-time baseball team."

September 29, 1972

Dear Jackie:

As you may know, I was recently asked to name my all-time baseball team. Intrigued by the challenge, I began to work on making my choices, only to discover this was a far more difficult task than I had anticipated.

However, thanks to the splendid help of David Eisenhower and a quiet afternoon at Camp David, I did come up with a list, although I found it quite impossible to limit myself to just nine ballplayers. Thus, David and I decided on two teams from each League to cover the years before and after the Second World War.

Because you are a member of our all-time teams, I thought you might like to have a specially printed copy of the complete roster.

Needless to say, it comes to you with the best wishes of two of your many fans.

Sincerely,
Richard Nixon

RICHARD NIXON TO PATRICK O'DONNELL

Patrick O'Donnell, special assistant to the president, drafted the following memorandum for political strategist Charles Colson on October 9: "I have been informed that NBC has filed a petition with the FCC for an interpretive ruling of Section 315 vis-à-vis a presentation by a 'prominent political figure and candidate' to Jackie Robinson at the final game of the World Series, probably October 16. This would, of course, be covered on national television. Although the petition does not mention who the candidate is, Al Snyder and I have explored the matter with NBC and learned that they have the President in mind. This might not be a bad event for him to do and I understand the Commission will rule that such use of air time will be in coverage of a news event and, therefore, not subject to the equal time provision of Section 315. Do you have any thought on the matter?" Nixon had a thought, and below is his reply, as written on the bottom of the memo.

October 9, 1972

Pat,

Colson thinks this might be a very good event!

Dick

By the following day, however, the White House decided against Nixon's participation in the event, and on October 15 Robinson threw out the ceremonial first ball of the second game of the 1972 World Series, marking the twenty-fifth anniversary of his role in shattering Major League Baseball's color barrier. In his televised speech, Robinson stated: "I am extremely proud and pleased to be here this afternoon but must admit I'm going to be tremendously more pleased and more proud when I look at that third base coaching line one day and see a black face managing in baseball." At this point Robinson, white-haired and unsteady on his feet, was virtually blind from diabetes.

Jackie Robinson died of a heart attack on October 24 at the age of fifty-three. The New York Times *obituary published the following day highlighted Robinson's competitive spirit: "His dominant characteristic, as an athlete and as a black man, was a competitive flame. Outspoken, controversial, combative, he created critics as well as loyalists. But he never deviated from his opinions." Telegrams poured into the Robinson home, and below are those sent by SCLC president Ralph Abernathy, Motown Records founder Berry Gordy, and baseball great Hank Aaron.*

October 25, 1972

Our nation in general and black people in particular have lost a pioneer, a champion, and a heroic fighter for justice and freedom in the person of Jackie Robinson. He was an inspiration to countless numbers of young black people; he opened the door through which many have entered; and proved to young people they could go even to the Hall of Fame, regardless of the color of their skin. Jackie Robinson belonged not only to the Brooklyn Dodgers but to all black and underprivileged people of America. He was a spirit not only at bat, but also in stealing bases. He stole his way into history, baseball's Hall of Fame, and now he has stolen another base—eternal rest in the ages for his tired and worn body, which he so generously gave in lifting others. Mrs. Abernathy and the entire family of the Southern Christian Leadership Conference join me in expressing our deepest and most sincere sympathy to you during these dark and difficult moments as we all say goodbye to Jackie Robinson.

Ralph Abernathy

He was and is truly black and beautiful and an inspiration to me. I will miss him but always remember him.

Berry Gordy

I share with you your grief upon the passing of a great American. Baseball and the Black athlete are the poorer because of his death. My own success in baseball has been in large measure because Jackie Robinson marked the trail well. May you and your family take consolation in knowing that he did so much for so many.

Hank Aaron

ABBREVIATIONS

ACOAP	Papers of the American Committee on Africa, Amistad Research Center, Tulane University, New Orleans, Louisiana
APRP	A. Philip Randolph Papers, Library of Congress, Washington, D.C.
ARP	Abraham Ribicoff Papers, University of Rochester, Rochester, New York
BGP	Barry Goldwater Papers, Arizona Historical Foundation, Tempe, Arizona
BRP	Branch Rickey Papers, Library of Congress, Washington, D.C.
BSCPP	Papers of the Brotherhood of Sleeping Car Porters, Library of Congress, Washington, D.C.
CBP	Chester Bowles Papers, Yale University, New Haven, Connecticut
COREP	Papers of the Congress of Racial Equality, 1941–1967, microfilm edition
DDEL	Dwight D. Eisenhower Library, Abilene, Kansas
DSP	Dorothy Schiff Papers, New York Public Library, New York, New York
FBIP	Papers of the Federal Bureau of Investigation, U.S. Department of Justice, Washington, D.C.
HHHP	Hubert H. Humphrey Papers, Minnesota Historical Society, St. Paul, Minnesota
JDP	John Dempsey Papers, Connecticut State Library, Hartford, Connecticut
JFKL	John F. Kennedy Library, Boston, Massachusetts
JRP	Jackie Robinson Papers, Library of Congress, Washington, D.C.
KAPLANP	Kivie Kaplan Papers, American Jewish Archives, Cincinnati, Ohio

KKP	Kenneth Keating Papers, University of Rochester, Rochester, New York
LBJL	Lyndon Baines Johnson Library, Austin, Texas
MLKP-GAMK	Martin Luther King, Jr. Papers, 1950–1968, Martin Luther King, Jr. Center for Nonviolent Social Change, Atlanta, Georgia. Letters in this collection are identified by their number in the Martin Luther King, Jr. Papers Project, Stanford University.
MLKP-MBU	Martin Luther King, Jr. Papers, 1954–1968, Boston University, Boston, Massachusetts. Letters in this collection are identified by their number in the Martin Luther King, Jr. Papers Project, Stanford University.
MSP	Maurice Stans Papers, Minnesota Historical Society, St. Paul, Minnesota
NAACPP	Papers of the NAACP, microfilm edition
NAR	Nelson A. Rockefeller Papers, Rockefeller Family Archives, Rockefeller Archive Center, Sleepy Hollow, New York
NBHFM	National Baseball Hall of Fame Museum, Cooperstown, New York
NTP	Norman Thomas Papers, New York Public Library, New York, New York
NYAN	*New York Amsterdam News*
NYT	*New York Times*
NYP	*New York Post*
OMR	Papers of the Office of the Messieurs Rockefeller, Rockefeller Family Archives, Rockefeller Archive Center, Sleepy Hollow, New York
RFKP	Robert F. Kennedy, Jr. Papers, John F. Kennedy Library, Boston, Massachusetts
RJBP	Ralph J. Bunche Papers, University of California at Los Angeles, Los Angeles, California
RMNL	Richard M. Nixon Library, Anaheim, California
RMNP	Richard M. Nixon Presidential Papers, National Archives and Records Administration, College Park, Maryland
RUSTINP	Bayard Rustin Papers, Library of Congress, Washington, D.C.
SCLCP	Records of the Southern Christian Leadership Conference, 1954–1970, microfilm edition
WTP	Walter N. Thayer Papers, Herbert Hoover Presidential Library, West Branch, Iowa

NOTES

1. FAITH IN DEMOCRACY: 1949–1956

Norman Thomas to Robinson, September 23, 1947

"I live": Letter from Bernice Franklin to Robinson, August 20, 1947, JRP, box 1, folder 29.

"turn the other cheek": See Arnold Rampersad, *Jackie Robinson: A Biography* (New York: Ballantine Books, 1997), pp. 126–27. I am indebted to Professor Rampersad's book for details about Robinson's civil rights legacy.

Lester Granger to Robinson, July 19, 1949

"It is unthinkable": Quoted in Martin Duberman, *Paul Robeson: A Biography* (New York: Ballantine Books, 1990), pp. 341–42.

"very silly": "Text of Jackie Robinson's Statement to House Unit," NYT, July 19, 1949, p. 14.

Robinson to Maxwell Rabb, November 15, 1954

"The Negroes today": See Alan Paton, "The Negro in America Today," *Colliers*, October 15, 1964, pp. 52–66 (http://historymatters.gmu.edu/d/6337/).

Robinson to William Keefe, July 23, 1956

"insolent": *Times-Picayune*, July 18, 1956.

Branch Rickey to Roy Wilkins, December 7, 1956

"Today marks the high point": "Acceptance Address by Jackie Robinson at Special Luncheon Honoring Him on Presentation of 41st Spingarn Medal," Hotel Roosevelt, New York, New York, December 8, 1956, JRP, box 4, folder 9.

2. FROM FAITH TO FRUSTRATION: 1957

Robinson to Martin Luther King, Jr., February 11, 1957

"The more I read": Quoted in Rampersad, *Jackie Robinson*, p. 287.

"Although my schedule": Letter from Martin Luther King, Jr. to Jackie Robinson, February 18, 1957, MLKP-MBU, 570218-015.

Robinson to Richard Nixon, March 19, 1957

"Nixon then proceeded": Document titled "Incident recalled by Harrison McCall and dictated by him," January 3, 1959, JRP, box 5, folder 11.

Robinson to Dwight Eisenhower, May 15, 1957

"brief hello": Memorandum from Maxwell Rabb to Mr. Shanley, May 9, 1957, DDEL, President's Personal File, box 897, folder 51-A.

Martin Luther King, Jr. to Robinson, June 12, 1957
"in the name": quoted in Taylor Branch, *Parting the Waters: America in the King Years, 1954–1963* (New York: Touchstone, 1988), p. 186.

Robinson to Richard Nixon, June 25, 1957
"Today Nixon says": Herbert H. Lehman, "The Truth About Civil Rights Radio Address," October 28, 1956 (www.columbia.edu/cu/lweb/indiv/lehsuite/civil_rights_radio.html).

Robinson to Maxwell Rabb, July 19, 1957
"I hope": "The President's Statement," NYT, July 17, 1957, p. 14.
"I personally believe": "Transcript of the President's News Conference," NYT, July 18, 1957, p. 12.

Robinson to Richard Nixon, August 2, 1957
"a vote against the right to vote": William S. White, "Senate, 51 to 42, Attaches Jury Trials to Rights Bill in Defeat for President," NYT, August 2, 1957, p. 1.

Robinson to Dwight Eisenhower, September 13, 1957
"patience": W. H. Lawrence, "President Urges Patience in Crisis," NYT, September 11, 1957, p. 25.

Robinson to Louis Seaton, November 4, 1957
"When we moved": Louis Kraar and Lester Tanzer, "Industry Integration," *Wall Street Journal*, October 24, 1957, p. 1.

Robinson to Richard Nixon, December 24, 1957
"cooling off": W. H. Lawrence, "U.S. Won't Seek New Rights Bill," NYT, December 10, 1957, p. 24.

3. AGAINST PATIENCE: 1958

Robinson to Maxwell Rabb, no date [April 1958]
"[Your] suggestion about helping": Letter from Maxwell Rabb to Jackie Robinson, May 8, 1958, DDEL, General Files, box 1297, folder 186 R.

Robinson to Dwight Eisenhower, May 13, 1958
"there are no revolutionary cures": Felix Belair, Jr., "Eisenhower Bids Negroes Be Patient About Rights," NYT, May 13, 1958, p. 1.

4. PROFILES IN QUESTION: 1959

Robinson to Frederic Morrow, April 15, 1959
"The basic failure": "Negro Vote Vital, G.O.P. Women Told," NYT, April 15, 1959, p. 23.

Robinson to John Kennedy, May 25, 1959
"the records": NYP, May 8, 1959, p. 92. The column was titled "Jackie Robinson."

Robinson to Chester Bowles, July 14, 1959
"I think Kennedy": "Alabama Governor Endorses Kennedy," NYT, June 17, 1959, p. 38.

Robinson to Chester Bowles, August 26, 1959
"In my conversations": NYP, December 14, 1959, p. 68.

5. SELLING NIXON: 1960

Robinson to Ray Robinson, January 4, 1960
"And if it should come": NYP, December 30, 1959, p. 40.

Robinson to Richard Nixon, January 29, 1960

"I submit that Negroes": NYP, January 20, 1960, p. 80.

"Every act of discrimination": "Nixon Finds Reds Now on Defensive," NYT, December 24, 1953, p. 3.

Hubert Humphrey to Robinson, February 16, 1960

"From the very first": NYP, February 22, 1960, p. 36.

"I want right here": NYP, March 16, 1960, p. 88.

Robinson to Readers, March 25, 1960

"shutting up": Clayton Knowles, "Truman Believes Reds Lead Sit-Ins," NYT, April 19, 1960, p. 21.

"Truman's patronizing gradualism": NYP, March 25, 1960, p. 96.

Richard Nixon to Robinson, April 13, 1960

"Jackie has been chock full o' zeal": "Keeping *Posted* with Jackie," *Time*, April 11, 1960, p. 93.

John Kennedy to Robinson, May 25, 1960

"it is quite clear": NYP, June 3, 1960, p. 96.

Richard Nixon to Robinson, June 3, 1960

"impressions": NYP, May 23, 1960, p. 72.

"Contrary to some published reports": NYP, June 10, 1960, p. 87.

Robinson to Richard Nixon, June 9, 1960

"to be instituted": Robinson quoting from "Text of Eisenhower's Special Message to Congress on Mutual Security Program," NYT, February 17, 1960, p. 10.

"University of Friendship of People": The *Moscow News* reported in February that the Soviet Union would open the Peoples' Friendship University in Moscow in September 1960 (*Moscow News*, February 27, 1960, p. 5, cited in J. Gregory Oswald, "Soviet News and Notes," *Hispanic American Review* 41, no. 1 [February 1961]: 125).

Richard Nixon to Robinson, June 14, 1960

"see no reason": NYP, June 10, 1960, p. 96.

John Kennedy to Robinson, July 1, 1960

"limited experience": NYP, July 6, 1960, p. 84.

Hugh Scott to Robinson, July 12, 1960

"proven segregationist": NYP, July 15, 1960, p. 60.

"a cold, calculating political machine": NYP, July 18, 1960, p. 44.

Richard Nixon to Robinson, November 4, 1960

"Jackie Robinson": "A Note on Jackie Robinson," NYP, September 7, 1960, p. 96.

"grandstanding": Robinson quoting Nixon; see Rampersad, *Jackie Robinson*, p. 351.

Robinson to Nelson Rockefeller, November 15, 1960

"And speaking of Rockefeller": NYP, July 29, 1960, p. 60.

Robinson to Albert Hermann, November 18, 1960

"for the magnificent contribution": Letter from Albert Hermann to Robinson, November 14, 1960, JRP, box 5, folder 6.

"Personally, it is": Letter from Albert Hermann to Robinson, November 23, 1960, JRP, box 5, folder 19.

6. WRONG ABOUT KENNEDY?: 1961

Robinson to Robert Kennedy, May 11, 1961
"We will not stand by": "Text of Attorney General Kennedy's Civil Rights Speech at University of Georgia," NYT, May 7, 1961, p. 62.

Robinson to Richard Nixon, May 25, 1961
"just stupid": *Jet*, May 25, 1961, p. 9.

Robinson to James Eastland, June 1, 1961
"Communist": Tom Wicker, "Move to Applaud Marshals Fails," NYT, May 26, 1961, p. 20.

John Kennedy to Robinson, September 6, 1961
"in high spirits": Memorandum from Harris Wofford to Dick Goodwin, September 5, 1961, JFKL, White House Staff Files, Harris Wofford Papers, box 8, folder: Robinson, Jackie, July 28–September 5, 1961.

Robinson to Richard Nixon, December 8, 1961
"We're not going": Quoted in Pearl T. Robinson, "Whither the Future of Blacks in the Republican Party?" *Political Science Quarterly* 97, no. 2 (Summer 1982): 214. Part of the quotation can also be found in "Goldwater Solicits G.O.P Votes for Southern Segregationists," NYT, November 19, 1961, p. 70.

7. FROM THE HALL OF FAME TO HALLOWED ASHES: 1962

Nelson Rockefeller to Robinson, September 19, 1962
"The Negro people": NYAN, September 22, 1962, p. 11.

Robinson to Robert Kennedy, October 30, 1962
"In my opinion": NYAN, October 27, 1962, p. 11.
"We will not win": Irving Spiegel, "Robert Kennedy Links Cuban and Rights Crises," NYT, October 29, 1962, p. 10.

Robinson to Richard Nixon, November 12, 1962
"You won't have Nixon": "Transcript of Nixon's News Conference on His Defeat by Brown in Race for Governor of California," NYT, November 8, 1962, p. 18.

Robinson to African Leaders, December 29, 1962
"resolute action": NYAN, December 1, 1962, p. 11.
"The average African": "Travel Is So Narrowing," *Time*, December 14, 1962, p. 22.

8. BACK OUR BROTHERS—EXCEPT ADAM AND MALCOLM: 1963

Robinson to Adam Clayton Powell, Jr., March 30, 1963
"We must seize control": "Powell Attacks NAACP Set-Up," NYT, April 1, 1963, p. 16.

Letters to the Editor of the *New York Amsterdam News*, April 6, 1963
"If Jackie is": Quotations in this section are from NYAN, April 6, 1963, p. 25.
"if 'sticking together' ": NYAN, April 20, 1963, p. 11.

Robinson to Richard Nixon, May 4, 1963
"We need men": Letter from Jackie Robinson to Richard Nixon, February 8, 1962, RMNL, general correspondence, series 320, box 649; JRP, box 5, folder 11.
"completely ignored": NYAN, February 16, 1963, p. 6.

Robinson to John Kennedy, May 7, 1963
"The fact is": NYAN, May 18, 1963, p. 11.
"America's greatness": "Ghana Paper Comments on Birmingham Incidents," NYT, May 5, 1963, p. 82.

Robinson to John Kennedy, June 12, 1963
"examine his conscience": For this and other quotations from Kennedy's June 11 speech, see "Transcript of the President's Address," NYT, June 12, 1963, p. 20.

Nelson Rockefeller to Robinson, July 25, 1963
"We call": NYAN, June 15, 1963, p. 11.

O. L. Weller to Robinson, August 17, 1963
"white man's party": Jackie Robinson, "The G.O.P: For White Men Only?" *Saturday Evening Post*, August 10–17, 1963, p. 10.

Robinson to A. Philip Randolph, August 23, 1963
"I have never been so proud": NYAN, September 7, 1963, p. 11.

Ralph Bunche to Robinson, November 20, 1963
"a black form": "Bunche Upbraids Race Extremists," NYT, October 24, 1963, p. 24.
"we have not heard": Robinson quoting Powell; see NYAN, November 16, 1963, p. 11.

Malcolm X to Robinson, November 30, 1963
"When we have heard": NYAN, November 16, 1963, p. 11.

9. THE CAMPAIGN AGAINST BIGOTRY: 1964

Branch Rickey to Robinson, February 21, 1964
"The Republican Party": NYAN, November 9, 1963, p. 11.
"is why I believe": NYAN, November 30, 1963, p. 11.
"fine man": Quoted in Rampersad, *Jackie Robinson*, p. 351.

Hubert Humphrey to Robinson, April 24, 1964
"illegal disturbances": Quoted in E. W. Kenworthy, "Rights Bill Heads Caution Negroes," NYT, April 16, 1964, p. 1.

Barry Goldwater to Robinson, July 25, 1964
"I never could": NYAN, July 4, 1964, p. 19.

Robinson to Barry Goldwater, no date [August 1964]
"states' rights": E. W. Kenworthy, "Campaign—Goldwater's Strategy Takes Shape," NYT, August 2, 1964, p. 131.

Robinson to Hubert Humphrey, August 14, 1964
"We have talked": "Transcript of President Johnson's Address before the Joint Session of Congress," NYT, November 28, 1963, p. 20.

Robinson to Nelson Rockefeller, October 7, 1964
"As for the Republican Party": NYAN, November 14, 1964, p. 9.

Robinson to A. Philip Randolph, December 30, 1964
"serious deficiency of banking facilities": Untitled document, JRP, box 7, folder 4.
"We need to fight": NYAN, January 2, 1965, p. 7.

10. A ROCKEFELLER REPUBLICAN: 1965–1966

Robinson to Nelson Rockefeller, February 1, 1965
"If the Republican Party": Jackie Robinson, "Does the Republican Party Need an Anti-Poverty Program?" January 26, 1965, speech at the National Conference on Poverty in the Southwest, Tucson, Arizona, NAR Personal, RG 4, series P, box 16, folder 392.

Robinson to Nelson Rockefeller, February 22, 1965
"generous expressions": Letter from Nelson Rockefeller to Jackie Robinson, February 11, 1965, NAR Personal, RG 4, series P, box 16, folder 392.

Robinson to Hubert Humphrey, March 10, 1965
"good attitude": John D. Pomfret, "U.S. Hopes Federal Intervention in Selma Will Be Unnecessary," NYT, March 10, 1965, p. 23.

Hubert Humphrey to Robinson, March 29, 1965
"But even if we pass this bill": "Transcript of the Johnson Address on Voting Rights to Joint Session of Congress," NYT, March 16, 1965, p. 30.

Robinson to Kenneth Keating, April 27, 1965
"On another subject": Letter from Kenneth Keating to Jackie Robinson, April 16, 1965, KKP, series 7, box 8, folder 14.

Robinson to Walter O'Malley, July 2, 1965
"It was thoughtful": Letter from Walter O'Malley to Jackie Robinson, July 15, 1965, at www.walteromalley.com.

Hubert Humphrey to Robinson, September 27, 1965
"To Fulfill These Rights": Tom Wicker, "Johnson Pledges to Help Negroes to Full Equality," NYT, June 5, 1965, p. 1.

Robinson to Jacob Javits, November 22, 1965
"Senator Jacob K. Javits": Warren Weaver, "Javits Cautions Governor on '66," NYT, November 20, 1965, p. 1.

Robinson to Nelson Rockefeller, January 12, 1966
"fine record": NYAN, January 8, 1965, p. 11.

Robinson to John Lindsay, February 10, 1966
"one of the high priests": NYAN, February 12, 1966, p. 13.

Robinson to Ray Bliss, May 23, 1966
"The victory of Ronald Reagan": NYAN, June 18, 1966, p. 15.

Adam Clayton Powell, Jr. to Robinson, November 10, 1966
"when we use": NYAN, October 22, 1966, p. 7.

Robinson to Nelson Rockefeller, no date [December 1966]
"In my book": NYAN, November 19, 1966, p. 9.

11. SHARP ATTACKS, SURPRISING DEFENSES: 1967

Roy Wilkins to Robinson, February 8, 1967
"a kind of dictatorship": NYAN, January 14, 1967, p. 14.

Robinson to Nelson Rockefeller, March 6, 1967
"what the Congress": NYAN, January 21, 1967, p. 17.

Robinson to Nelson Rockefeller, March 9, 1967
"castigated his party": James F. Clarity, "Jackie Robinson Condemns Party over Meredith," NYT, March 9, 1967, p. 1.

Robinson to Lyndon Johnson, April 18, 1967
"Let us hear": NYAN, April 8, 1967, p. 17.

Clifford Alexander, Jr. to Robinson, April 20, 1967

"I think it may be": Memorandum from Clifford Alexander, Jr. to Lyndon B. Johnson, April 18, 1967, LBJL, White House Central Files, HU, box 4, folder: HU 2, 2/4/67–5/31/67.

"While it is true": Memorandum from Clifford Alexander, Jr. to Bess Abell, November 22, 1965, LBJL, White House Central Files, name file, box 206, folder: Robinson, Jackie (Baseball Player).

Robinson to Martin Luther King, Jr., May 13, 1967

"is the third president": NYAN, October 21, 1967, p. 17.

Robinson to the Editor of the *New York Times*, July 30, 1967

"the other side of the story": See "Black Racism," NYT, July 24, 1967, p. 26.

Robinson to Alton Marshall, October 2, 1967

"Anyway, because of Tom Yawkey": "He's No Friend of Tom Yawkey," UPI, September 20, 1967, published in *Patriot-Ledger*, Quincy, Massachusetts, September 21, 1967. Filed at NAR Gubernatorial, RG 15, series 34.4, box 42, folder 1129.

Robinson to Nelson Rockefeller, October 24, 1967

"We are angry": Untitled document, October 23, 1967, p. 1. Filed at NAR Gubernatorial, RG 15, series 34.4, box 42, folder 1129.

Robinson to Nelson Rockefeller, October 31, 1967

"It would be a sin": NYAN, March 18, 1967, p. 17.

"If the GOP should nominate": NYAN, September 22, 1967, p. 17.

Robinson to George Hinman, November 13, 1967

"reprehensible and a little more difficult": Charlotte Buchen, "Jackie Robinson Shares Dais with Barry at NPAA Dinner," *Arizona Republic*, November 12, 1967, p. 5. Filed at NAR Gubernatorial, RG 15, series 34.10, box 102, folder 3341.

Robinson to Nelson Rockefeller, December 7, 1967

"The more I see of you": Letter from Jackie Robinson to Nelson Rockefeller, December 6, 1967, NAR Personal, RG 4, series P, box 16, folder 392.

12. THE POLITICS OF BLACK PRIDE: 1968

Robinson to the Editor of the *New York Times*, January 27, 1968

"You send the best": "Eartha Kitt Denounces War Policy to Mrs. Johnson," NYT, January 19, 1968, p. 1.

"This is the heart": "From the Heart of Eartha Kitt," NYT, January 20, 1968, p. 23.

Robinson to Barry Goldwater, February 27, 1968

"I must confess": NYAN, March 23, 1968, p. 13.

Robinson to Nelson Rockefeller, March 27, 1968

"I'm not a candidate": "Rockefeller Says He'd Accept Draft," NYT, February 25, 1968, p. 31.

"order before progress": When accepting the Republican nomination for president, for example, Nixon stated: "The American Revolution was and is dedicated to progress. But our founders recognized that the first requisite of progress is order" ("Transcripts of Acceptance Speeches by Nixon and Agnew to the G.O.P. Convention," NYT, August 9, 1968, p. 20).

Hubert Humphrey to Robinson, April 5, 1968

"the greatest leader": NYAN, April 13, 1968, p. 21.

Hubert Humphrey to Robinson, July 10, 1968
"some commendable contributions": NYAN, June 8, 1968, p. 15.

Barry Goldwater to Robinson, August 22, 1968
"Now he's sold out": "Jackie Robinson Splits with G.O.P. over Nixon Choice," NYT, August 12, 1968, p. 1.

Robinson to Barry Goldwater, September 5, 1968
"I am proud": NYAN, September 7, 1968, p. 13.

Robinson to Nelson Rockefeller, September 9, 1968
"When an individual": Robert B. Semple, Jr., "Nixon Stresses Commitment to Israel," NYT, September 9, 1968, pp. 1, 43.

13. MOVING FORWARD IN OUR STRUGGLE: 1969–1972

Robinson to Richard Nixon, January 22, 1969
"To go forward": "Nixon's Promise to Search for Peace," NYT, January 21, 1969, p. 21.

Robinson to Nelson Rockefeller, February 26, 1969
"The cost of establishing a family": Ben H. Bagdikian, "It Has Come to This," *Saturday Evening Post,* August 10, 1968, p. 82.

J. Edgar Hoover to John Ehrlichman, July 24, 1969
"I wouldn't fly the flag": Jon Nordheimer, "Flag on July 4," NYT, July 4, 1969, p. 23.

Robinson to Maurice Stans, March 11, 1970
"the very poor relations": Paul Delaney, "Jackie Robinson Scores Nixon on Black Capitalism Problems," NYT, January 21, 1970, p. 27.

Robinson to the Editor of the *Miami Herald,* June 8, 1970
"The reserve clause": Quoted in Rampersad, *Jackie Robinson,* p. 455.
"into the civil rights league": *Miami Herald,* May 27, 1970.

Calvin Morris to Robinson, February 1, 1971
"to wake up": "Remarks of Mr. Jackie Robinson at SCLC Operation Breadbasket Saturday Morning Meeting," January 23, 1971, Chicago, Illinois, JRP, speeches file, p. 3.
"a tall, young, brave, Black Moses": Ibid., p. 4.

Robinson to Andre Baruch, February 14, 1972
"The Jackie Robinson Construction Corp.": Rachel Robinson, "Note to File," JRP, box 8, folder 11.

Richard Nixon to Patrick O'Donnell, October 9, 1972
"I have been informed": Memorandum from Patrick O'Donnell to Charles Colson, October 9, 1972, RMNP, White House Central File, RE 2, box 3.
"I am extremely proud": Quoted in Rampersad, *Jackie Robinson,* p. 459.

Telegrams, October 25, 1972
"His dominant characteristic": Dave Anderson, "Jackie Robinson, First Black in Major Leagues, Dies," NYT, October 25, 1972, p. 56.

LOCATION OF LETTERS

1. FAITH IN DEMOCRACY: 1946–1956

Robinson to Ralph Norton, March 12, 1946, JRP, box 1, folder 19.
Norman Thomas to Robinson, September 23, 1947, NTP, box 31.
Robinson to Admirer, October 15, 1947, JRP, box 1, folder 28.
Lester Granger to Robinson, July 19, 1949, JRP, box 3, folder 7.
Robinson to Branch Rickey, no date [November 1950], BRP, box 24, folder 13.
Branch Rickey to Robinson, December 31, 1950, BRP, box 24, folder 13.
John D. Rockefeller III to Robinson, January 18, 1951, OMR, series: Welfare Interests—Youth, box 33, folder 344.
"The Travelers" to Robinson, no date [received May 20, 1951], NBHFM, courtesy of Rachel Robinson.
"Dodger Hater" to Robinson, September 15, 1953, FBIP, file: Jackie Robinson.
Robinson to Dwight Eisenhower, November 25, 1953, DDEL, President's Personal File, box 798, folder 47.
Dwight Eisenhower to Robinson, November 30, 1953, DDEL, President's Personal File, box 798, folder 47.
Robinson to Maxwell Rabb, November 15, 1954, DDEL, Alphabetical File, box 2643, folder: Robinson, Jackie.
Robinson to Averell Harriman, December 6, 1955, JRP, box 5, folder 3.
Robinson to Caroline Wallerstein, January 3, 1956, JRP, box 15, folder 14.
Robinson to William Keefe, July 23, 1956, JRP, box 1, folder 24.
Herbert Lehman to Robinson, August 21, 1956, JRP, box 5, folder 2.
Branch Rickey to Roy Wilkins, December 7, 1956, JRP, box 4, folder 9.
Harold Howland to Robinson, December 14, 1956, JRP, box 10, folder 15.

2. FROM FAITH TO FRUSTRATION: 1957

Brooks Lawrence to Robinson, no date [postmarked January 18, 1957], JRP, box 3, folder 3.
Robinson to Martin Luther King, Jr., February 11, 1957, MLKP-MBU, 570211-016.
Gloster Current to Roy Wilkins, March 18, 1957, NAACPP, supplement to part 16, reel 10, frame 14; JRP, box 4, folder 22.
Robinson to Richard Nixon, March 19, 1957, RMNL, general correspondence, series 320, box 649; JRP, box 4, folder 22.
Richard Nixon to Robinson, March 22, 1957, RMNL, general correspondence, series 320, box 649.

Robinson to Martin Luther King, Jr., April 24, 1957, NAACPP, part 24, series C.
Robinson to Dwight Eisenhower, May 15, 1957, DDEL, President's Personal File, box 897, folder 51-A.
Robinson to Maxwell Rabb, May 15, 1957, DDEL, President's Personal File, box 34, folder 1-Q.
Dwight Eisenhower to Robinson, May 21, 1957, DDEL, President's Personal File, box 897, folder 51-A.
Martin Luther King, Jr. to Robinson, June 12, 1957, MLK-MBU, 570621-014.
Robinson to Richard Nixon, June 25, 1957, RMNL, general correspondence, series 320, box 649.
Richard Nixon to Robinson, July 12, 1957, RMNL, general correspondence, series 320, box 649.
Robinson to Maxwell Rabb, July 19, 1957, JRP, box 4, folder 22.
Robinson to Richard Nixon, August 2, 1957, RMNL, general correspondence, series 320, box 649.
Richard Nixon to Robinson, August 8, 1957, RMNL, general correspondence, series 320, box 649.
Robinson to Frederic Morrow, August 12, 1957, DDEL, Official File, box 732, folder 142-A-5-A.
Richard Nixon to Robinson, August 13, 1957, RMNL, general correspondence, series 320, box 649.
Robinson to Richard Nixon, August 28, 1957, RMNL, general correspondence, series 320, box 649.
Averell Harriman to Robinson, September 8, 1957, JRP, box 5, folder 3.
Robinson to Dwight Eisenhower, September 13, 1957, JRP, box 5, folder 13.
Robinson to Dwight Eisenhower, September 25, 1957, DDEL, Official File, box 732, folder 142-A-5-A.
Robinson to Louis Seaton, November 4, 1957, NAACPP, supplement to part 13, reel 7, frames 204–5.
Robinson to Walter Reuther, November 7, 1957, NAACPP, supplement to part 13, reel 7, frame 203.
Robinson to Richard Nixon, December 24, 1957, RMNL, general correspondence, series 320, box 649; JRP, box 5, folder 11.

3. AGAINST PATIENCE: 1958

Robinson to Chester Bowles, January 15, 1958, CBP, box 153, folder 556.
Richard Nixon to Robinson, January 23, 1958, RMNL, general correspondence, series 320, box 649; JRP, box 5, folder 9.
Robinson to Richard Nixon, February 5, 1958, RMNL, general correspondence, series 320, box 649; JRP, box 5, folder 9.
Chester Bowles to Robinson, February 10, 1958, CBP, box 153, folder 556; JRP, box 5, folder 1.
Richard Nixon to Robinson, March 12, 1958, RMNL, general correspondence, series 320, box 649; JRP, box 5, folder 9.
Chester Bowles to Robinson, April 7, 1958, CBP, box 153, folder 556; JRP, box 5, folder 1.
Robinson to Maxwell Rabb, no date [April 1958], DDEL, General File, box 1297, folder 186-R.
Robinson to Chester Bowles, May 1, 1958, CBP, box 153, folder 556; JRP, box 5, folder 1.
Robinson to Dwight Eisenhower, May 13, 1958, DDEL, Official File, box 731, folder 142-A.
Dwight Eisenhower to Robinson, June 4, 1958, DDEL, Official File, box 731, folder 142-A.

Robinson to Dwight Eisenhower, June 10, 1958, DDEL, Official File, box 731, folder 142-A.
Roy Wilkins to Robinson, July 22, 1958, NAACPP, supplement to part 5, reel 9, frame 456.
Robinson to James Hagerty, October 15, 1958, DDEL, General File, box 1222, folder 156-F.

4. PROFILES IN QUESTION: 1959

Robinson to Frederic Morrow, April 15, 1959, JRP, box 5, folder 9.
Robinson to John Kennedy, May 25, 1959, JFKL, Pre-Presidential Papers, General Files (1953–1960), 1958–1960 President's Office Files, box 536, file: Civil Rights.
John Kennedy to Robinson, June 18, 1959, JFKL, Pre-Presidential Papers, Senate Files, Correspondence Copy Files (1953–1960), 1960 File, 1 M-R, box 470, folder: ROA–ROC.
Robinson to Chester Bowles, July 14, 1959, CBP, box 215, folder 264.
Chester Bowles to Robinson, August 20, 1959, CBP, box 215, folder 264.
Robinson to Chester Bowles, August 26, 1959, CBP, box 215, folder 264.
Chester Bowles to Robinson, August 31, 1959, CBP, box 215, folder 264.
Robinson to Chester Bowles, October 6, 1959, CBP, box 215, folder 264.
Gloster Current to Robert Carter, October 28, 1959, NAACPP, part 24, reel 23, frames 297–98.
Robinson to Chester Bowles, November 12, 1959, CBP, box 215, folder 264.
Chester Bowles to Robinson, December 3, 1959, CBP, box 215, folder 264.
Robinson to Abraham Ribicoff, December 7, 1959, ARP, RG 05, Office of the Governor, box 630, outgoing correspondence.
Thurgood Marshall to Robinson, December 11, 1959, NAACPP, part 22, reel 4, frames 676–77.

5. SELLING NIXON: 1960

Robinson to Ray Robinson, January 4, 1960, JRP, box 5, folder 19.
Richard Nixon to Robinson, January 16, 1960, RMNL, general correspondence, series 320, box 649; JRP, box 5, folder 11.
Robinson to Richard Nixon, January 29, 1960, RMNL, general correspondence, series 320, box 649; JRP, box 5, folder 11.
Hubert Humphrey to Robinson, February 16, 1960, JRP, box 5, folder 6.
Robinson to Readers, March 25, 1960, NYP, March 25, 1960, p. 96.
Rose Mary Woods to Richard Nixon, March 30, 1960, JRP, box 5, folder 11.
Richard Nixon to Robert Finch, April 10, 1960, JRP, box 5, folder 11.
Richard Nixon to Robinson, April 13, 1960, RMNL, general correspondence, series 320, box 649; JRP, box 5, folder 11.
James Robinson to Robinson, April 22, 1960, COREP, series 4, frame 7.
Robinson to Richard Nixon, April 25, 1960, RMNL, general correspondence, series 320, box 649; JRP, box 5, folder 11.
Robinson to Martin Luther King, Jr., May 5, 1960, MLKP-MBU, 600505-006.
Robinson to Roy Wilkins, May 10, 1960, NAACPP, supplement to part 16, reel 10, frame 100; JRP, box 4, folder 23.
Rose Mary Woods to Richard Nixon, May 10, 1960, RMNL, general correspondence, series 320, box 649; JRP, box 5, folder 11.
Robinson to Richard Nixon, May 11, 1960, RMNL, general correspondence, series 320, box 649; JRP, box 5, folder 11.
John Kennedy to Robinson, May 25, 1960, JFKL, Pre-Presidential Papers, box 470, folder 112.

Richard Nixon to Robinson, June 3, 1960, RMNL, general correspondence, series 320, box 649; JRP, box 5, folder 11.
Robinson to Richard Nixon, June 9, 1960, RMNL, general correspondence, series 320, box 649; JRP, box 3, folder 10.
Richard Nixon to Robinson, June 14, 1960, RMNL, general correspondence, series 320, box 649; JRP, box 5, folder 11.
Adam Clayton Powell, Jr. to Robinson, June 15, 1960, JRP, box 5, folder 11.
Martin Luther King, Jr. to Robinson, June 19, 1960, MLKP-MBU, 600619-001.
Robinson to Martin Luther King, Jr., June 29, 1960, MLKP-MBU, 600629-002.
Hubert Humphrey to Robinson, July 1, 1960, JRP, box 5, folder 4.
John Kennedy to Robinson, July 1, 1960, NBHFM.
Billie Fleming to Robinson, July 7, 1960, NAACPP, supplement to part 16, reel 10, frames 110–11; JRP, box 4, folder 22.
Robinson to Richard Nixon, July 11, 1960, RMNL, general correspondence, series 320, box 649; JRP, box 3, folder 10.
Hugh Scott to Robinson, July 12, 1960, JRP, box 3, folder 10.
Richard Nixon to Robinson, November 4, 1960, JRP, box 5, folder 11.
James Wechsler to Robinson, November 8, 1960, JRP, box 10, folder 18.
Robinson to Nelson Rockefeller, November 15, 1960, JRP, box 5, folder 25.
Robinson to Albert Hermann, November 18, 1960, JRP, box 5, folder 19.
Hubert Humphrey to Robinson, December 21, 1960, JRP, box 5, folder 6.

6. WRONG ABOUT KENNEDY?: 1961

Robinson to Richard Nixon, January 18, 1961, RMNL, general correspondence, series 320, box 649; JRP, box 5, folder 11.
Richard Nixon to Robinson, January 19, 1961, JRP, box 5, folder 9.
Robinson to John Kennedy, February 9, 1961, JFKL, Harris Wofford Papers, alphabetical box 8, file: Robinson, Jackie, 7/28/61–9/5/61; JRP, box 5, folder 14.
Robinson to Richard Nixon, March 3, 1961, RMNL, general correspondence, series 320, box 649; JRP, box 5, folder 11.
Hubert Humphrey to Robinson, April 20, 1961, JRP, box 5, folder 4.
Robinson to Robert Kennedy, May 11, 1961, *Chicago Daily News*, May 11, 1961.
Robinson to Caroline Wallerstein, May 16, 1961, JRP, box 15, folder 14.
Robinson to Robert Kennedy, May 25, 1961, RFKP, attorney general's correspondence, box 49, file: Robins-Robling; JRP, box 5, folder 15.
Robinson to Richard Nixon, May 25, 1961, RMNL, general correspondence, series 320, box 649; JRP, box 5, folder 11.
Robinson to James Eastland, June 1, 1961, COREP, series 4: 7.
Robert Kennedy to Robinson, June 2, 1961, JRP, box 5, folder 15; RFKP, attorney general's correspondence, box 49, file: Robins-Robling.
Richard Nixon to Robinson, June 5, 1961, RMNL, general correspondence, series 320, box 649; JRP, box 5, folder 11.
Hubert Humphrey to Robinson, June 19, 1961, JRP, box 5, folder 6.
Robinson to Everett Hutchinson, June 21, 1961, NAACPP, part 24, series A, reel 26, frame 699.
John Kennedy to Robinson, September 6, 1961, JFKL, White House Central Name Files, box 2355, file: Jackie Robinson; JRP, box 5, folder 14.
Richard Nixon to Robinson, November 8, 1961, RMNL, general correspondence, series 320, box 649; JRP, box 5, folder 11.
Robinson to Nelson Rockefeller, December 7, 1961, NAR Personal, RG 4, series J.2, box 52, folder 326.

Robinson to Richard Nixon, December 8, 1961, RMNL, general correspondence, series 320, box 649; JRP, box 5, folder 11.

7. FROM THE HALL OF FAME TO HALLOWED ASHES: 1962

Bill White to Robinson, January 20, 1962, NAACPP, part 25, series D, reel 3, frame 896.
Richard Nixon to Robinson, January 29, 1962, JRP, box 5, folder 11.
Robinson to Richard Nixon, February 8, 1962, RMNL, general correspondence, series 320, box 649; JRP, box 5, folder 11.
Roy Wilkins to Robinson, March 23, 1962, NAACPP, part 25, series B, reel 3.
Robinson to Paul Zuber, April 21, 1962, JRP, box 4, folder 6; NAACPP, supplement to part 16, reel 10, frames 125–26.
Robinson to John Kennedy, May 5, 1962, NYAN, May 5, 1962, p. 9.
Martin Luther King, Jr. to Robinson, May 14, 1962, MLKP-GAMK, 620514-004.
Ralph Abernathy to Robinson, June 7, 1962, SCLCP, part 2, reel 15, frame 780.
Robinson to William Black, July 16, 1962, JRP, box 6, folder 9.
Roy Wilkins to Robinson, July 16, 1962, JRP, box 4, folder 23; NAACPP, supplement to part 16, reel 10, frames 217–18.
"Hate White" Movement to Robinson, July 18, 1962, JRP, box 3, folder 23.
Robinson to Roy Wilkins, July 20, 1962, JRP, box 4, folder 23.
Robinson to Branch Rickey, July 24, 1962, BRP, box 24, folder 14.
Robinson to Walter O'Malley, July 25, 1962, JRP, box 1, folder 17.
Nelson Rockefeller to Robinson, September 19, 1962, NAR Personal, RG 4, series P, box 16, folder 392.
Ralph Abernathy to Robinson, October 5, 1962, SCLCP, part 2, reel 15, frame 888.
Robinson to Ralph Abernathy, October 8, 1962, SCLCP, part 2, reel 15, frame 895.
L. K. Jackson to Robinson, October 8, 1962, SCLCP, part 2, reel 15. frame 898.
Robinson to Martin Luther King, Jr., October 9, 1962, MLKP-GAMK, 621009-001.
Robinson to Robert Kennedy, October 30, 1962, RFKP, attorney general's correspondence, box 49, file: Robins-Robling; JRP, box 5, folder 15.
Robinson to Richard Nixon, November 12, 1962, RMNL, general correspondence, series 320, box 649; JRP, box 5, folder 11.
Robert Kennedy to Robinson, November 13, 1962, JRP, box 5, folder 15; RFKP, attorney general's correspondence, box 49, file: Robins-Robling.
Robinson to African Leaders, December 29, 1962, JRP, box 10, folder 19.

8. BACK OUR BROTHERS—EXCEPT ADAM AND MALCOLM: 1963

Robinson to Adam Clayton Powell, Jr., March 30, 1963, JRP, box 4, folder 6; NAACPP, supplement to part 16, reel 10, frames 234–36.
Letters to the Editor of the *New York Amsterdam News*, April 6, 1963, NYAN, April 6, 1963, p. 25.
Robinson to Richard Nixon, May 4, 1963, NYAN, May 4, 1963, p. 11.
Robinson to John Kennedy, May 7, 1963, JRP, box 5, folder 14.
Robinson to the Editor of the *New York Daily News*, May 23, 1963, published in NYAN, May 23, 1963, p. 11.
Lee White to Robinson, May 27, 1963, JRP, box 5, folder 14.
Robinson to John Kennedy, June 22, 1963, NYAN, June 22, 1963, p. 11.
Robinson to John Kennedy, June 15, 1963, JRP, box 5, folder 14.
Hugh Morrow to Nelson Rockefeller, June 27, 1963, NAR Personal, RG 4, series L, box 201, folder 2021.

Nelson Rockefeller to Robinson, July 25, 1963, NAR Personal, RG 4, series P, box 16, folder 392.
Robinson to William Black, August 14, 1963, JRP, box 6, folder 16.
O. L. Weller to Robinson, August 17, 1963, JRP, box 5, folder 21.
Robinson to O. L. Weller, no date [August 1963], JRP, box 5, folder 21.
Robinson to A. Philip Randolph, August 23, 1963, RUSTINP, reel 7; for same telegram to Roy Wilkins, see NAACPP, supplement to part 16, reel 10, frames 243–44.
Martin Luther King, Jr. to Rachel Robinson, October 24, 1963, MLKP-GAMK, 631024-010.
Ralph Bunche to Robinson, November 20, 1963, RJBP, box 127, folder 33; NYAN, November 30, 1963, p. 1.
Malcolm X to Robinson, November 30, 1963, NYAN, November 30, 1963, p. 1.
Robinson to Malcolm X, December 14, 1963, JRP, box 4, folder 35.

9. THE CAMPAIGN AGAINST BIGOTRY: 1964

Branch Rickey to Robinson, February 21, 1964, BRP, box 24, folder 15.
Robinson to Walter Thayer, no date [February 1964], WTP, People File, Rich–Roch.
Robinson to A. Philip Randolph, March 28, 1964, NYAN, March 28, 1964, p. 11.
Hubert Humphrey to Robinson, April 24, 1964, HHHP, Senatorial Files, Control Files, 1964, 150.C3.6 (F); JRP, box 5, folder 6.
Robinson to Nelson Rockefeller, July 2, 1964, NAR Personal, RG 4, Series J.2, box 52, folder 326.
Barry Goldwater to Robinson, July 25, 1964, JRP, box 5, folder 20.
Robinson to Barry Goldwater, no date [August 1964], JRP, box 5, folder 20.
Hubert Humphrey to Robinson, August 5, 1964, HHHP, Senatorial Files, Control Files, 1964, 150.C3.6 (F); JRP, box 5, folder 6.
Robinson to Hubert Humphrey, August 14, 1964, HHHP, Senatorial Files, Control Files, 1964, 150.A.13.1 (B).
Robinson to Hubert Humphrey, August 26, 1964, HHHP, Senatorial Files, Control Files, 1964, 150.D.9.1 (B).
Robinson to Nelson Rockefeller, October 7, 1964, NAR Personal, RG 4, series L, box 207, folder 2078.
Martin Luther King, Jr. to Robinson, October 7, 1964, MLKJP-GAMK, 641007-003.
Robinson to John Dempsey, October 25, 1964, JDP.
Robinson to John Dempsey, November 4, 1964, JDP.
Robinson to A. Philip Randolph, December 30, 1964, BSCPP, box 26.

10. A ROCKEFELLER REPUBLICAN: 1965–1966

Nelson Rockefeller to Robinson, January 4, 1965, JRP, box 5, folder 25.
Robinson to Nelson Rockefeller, February 1, 1965, NAR Personal, RG 4, series P, box 16, folder 392.
Robinson to Lyndon Johnson, February 4, 1965, LBJL, White House Central Files, SO, box 3, folder: Ex SO 2, 12/1/64–4/14/65.
Robinson to Nelson Rockefeller, February 22, 1965, NAR Personal, RG 4, series J.2, box 52, folder 326.
Robinson to Lyndon Johnson, March 9, 1965, LBJL, White House Central Files, Name File, box 29, folder: Robinson, Jackie (Baseball Player).
Robinson to Hubert Humphrey, March 10, 1965, HHHP, Vice Presidential Files, Civil and Human Rights Files, 150.E.7.8 (F).

Hubert Humphrey to Robinson, March 29, 1965, HHHP, Vice Presidential Files, Civil and Human Rights Files, 150.E.4.9 (B); JRP, box 5, folder 6.
Robinson to Branch Rickey, no date [received April 12, 1965], BRP, box 24, folder 15.
Robinson to Kenneth Keating, April 27, 1965, KKP, series 7, box 8, folder 14.
Nelson Rockefeller to Robinson, May 3, 1965, JRP, box 5, folder 25.
Robinson to Walter O'Malley, July 2, 1965, accessed at http://www.walteromalley.com/docu_gallery.php?gallery=2&set=5.
Robinson to Hubert Humphrey, September 21, 1965, HHHP, Vice Presidential Files, Control Files, 1965, 150.E.7.9 (B).
Hubert Humphrey to Robinson, September 27, 1965, HHHP, Vice Presidential Files, Control Files, 1965, 150.E.4.9 (B); JRP, box 5, folder 6.
Hubert Humphrey to Robinson, October 14, 1965, HHHP, Vice Presidential Files, Control Files, 1965, 150.E.4.9 (B); JRP, box 5, folder 6.
Robinson to Jacob Javits, November 22, 1965, NAR Personal, RG 4, series P, box 16, folder 392.
Nelson Rockefeller to Robinson, December 2, 1965, JRP, box 5, folder 25.
Robinson to Kivie Kaplan, no date [1966], KAPLANP.
Robinson to Nelson Rockefeller, January 12, 1966, NAR Personal, RG 4, series P, box 16, folder 392.
Nelson Rockefeller to Robinson, February 8, 1966, JRP, box 6, folder 1.
Robinson to John Lindsay, February 10, 1966, NAR Personal, RG 4, series P, box 16, folder 392.
Robinson to Nelson Rockefeller, May 13, 1966, NAR Gubernatorial, RG 15, series 34.10, box 102, folder 3341.
Robinson to Ray Bliss, May 23, 1966, NAR Personal, RG 4, series J.2, box 52, folder 326.
Nelson Rockefeller to Robinson, June 22, 1966, JRP, box 6, folder 1.
Robinson to Nelson Rockefeller, August 16, 1966, NAR Gubernatorial, RG 15, series 34.10, box 102, folder 3341.
Robinson to Barry Gray, August 17, 1966, JRP, box 4, folder 23.
Robinson to Nelson Rockefeller, September 19, 1966, NAR Gubernatorial, RG 15, series 34.10, box 102, folder 3341.
Nelson Rockefeller to Robinson, September 23, 1966, NAR Gubernatorial, RG 15, series 34.10, box 102, folder 3341.
Adam Clayton Powell, Jr. to Robinson, November 10, 1966, NAR Gubernatorial, RG 15, series 34.10, box 102, folder 3341.
Robinson to Adam Clayton Powell, Jr., no date [November 1966], NAR Gubernatorial, RG 15, series 34.10, box 102, folder 3341.
Robinson to Nelson Rockefeller, December 14, 1966, NAR Gubernatorial, RG 15, series 34.10, box 102, folder 3341.
Robinson to Nelson Rockefeller, no date [December 1966], NAR Personal, RG 4, series P, box 16, folder 392.

11. SHARP ATTACKS, SURPRISING DEFENSES: 1967

Robinson to Nelson Rockefeller, January 11, 1967, NAR Gubernatorial, RG 15, series 34.10, box 102, folder 3341.
Roy Wilkins to Robinson, February 8, 1967, JRP, box 4, folder 23.
Robinson to Roy Wilkins, February 15, 1967, JRP, box 4, folder 23.
Roy Wilkins to Robinson, February 17, 1967, JRP, box 4, folder 23.
Robinson to Roy Wilkins, February 20, 1967, JRP, box 4, folder 23.
Robinson to Nelson Rockefeller, March 6, 1967, NAR Gubernatorial, RG 15, series 34.10, box 102, folder 3341.

Robinson to Nelson Rockefeller, March 9, 1967, NAR Gubernatorial, RG 15, series 34.10, box 102, folder 3341.
Robinson to George Fowler, March 15, 1967, NAR Personal, RG 4, series P, box 5, folder 145.
Robinson to Avery Brundage, March 21, 1967, ACOAP, box 25, folder 48.
Robinson to Lyndon Johnson, April 18, 1967, LBJL, White House Central Files, HU, box 4, folder: HU 2, 2/4/67–5/31/67.
Clifford Alexander, Jr. to Robinson, April 20, 1967, LBJL, White House Central Files, HU, box 4, folder: HU 2, 2/4/67–5/31/67.
Hubert Humphrey to Robinson, April 29, 1967, HHHP, Vice Presidential Files, Control Files, 1967, 150.F.2.7 (B).
Robinson to Martin Luther King, Jr., May 13, 1967, NYAN, May 13, 1967, p. 17.
Robinson to the Editor of the *New York Times*, July 30, 1967, NYT, July 30, 1967, p. E9.
Robinson to Alton Marshall, October 2, 1967, NAR Gubernatorial, RG 15, series 34.4, box 42, folder 1129.
Robinson to Nelson Rockefeller, October 24, 1967, NAR Gubernatorial, RG 15, series 34.4, box 42, folder 1129.
Robinson to Nelson Rockefeller, October 31, 1967, NAR Gubernatorial, RG 15, series 35.3, box 18, folder 224.
Robinson to George Hinman, November 13, 1967, NAR Gubernatorial, RG 15, series 34.10, box 102, folder 3341.
Robinson to Barry Goldwater, November 21, 1967, BGP, series I, personal correspondence, folder 1967–1968.
Robinson to Hubert Humphrey, November 28, 1967, HHHP, Vice Presidential Files, Control Files, 1967.
Barry Goldwater to Robinson, November 30, 1967, BGP, series I, personal correspondence, folder 1967–1968.
Robinson to Nelson Rockefeller, December 7, 1967, NAR Personal, RG 4, series P, box 16, folder 393.

12. THE POLITICS OF BLACK PRIDE: 1968

Robinson to Nelson Rockefeller, January 18, 1968, NAR Gubernatorial, RG 15, series 34.4, box 42, folder 1129.
Robinson to the Editor of the *New York Times*, January 27, 1968, NYT, January 27, 1968, p. 28.
Robinson to Nelson Rockefeller, February 26, 1968, NAR Personal, RG 4, series J.2, box 52, folder 326.
Barry Goldwater to Robinson, February 26, 1968, NAR Personal, RG 4, series J.2, box 52, folder 326.
Robinson to Barry Goldwater, February 27, 1968, BGP, series I, personal correspondence, folder 1967–1968.
Robinson to Clarence Townes, Jr., February 29, 1968, JRP, box 5, folder 24.
Robinson to Nelson Rockefeller, March 8, 1968, NAR Gubernatorial, RG 15, series 34.4, box 42, folder 1129.
Robinson to Barry Goldwater, March 26, 1968, BGP, series I, personal correspondence, folder 1967–1968.
Robinson to Nelson Rockefeller, March 27, 1968, NAR Personal, RG 4, series P, box 16, folder 393.
Hubert Humphrey to Robinson, April 5, 1968, HHHP, Vice Presidential Files, Control Files, 1968, 150.F.3.1 (B).
Robinson to Hubert Humphrey, May 3, 1968, HHHP, Vice Presidential Files, Control Files, 1968, 63.G.14.6 (F); JRP, box 5, folder 6.

Robinson to Robert Douglass, May 17, 1968, NAR, Gubernatorial, RG 15, series 35.1, box 3, folder 65.
Hubert Humphrey to Robinson, July 10, 1968, HHHP, Vice Presidential Files, Control Files, 1968, 150.F.3.1 (B).
Barry Goldwater to Robinson, August 22, 1968, BGP, series I, personal correspondence, folder 1967–1968.
Robinson to Barry Goldwater, September 5, 1968, NAR Personal, RG 4, series P, box 16, folder 392.
Robinson to Nelson Rockefeller, September 9, 1968, NAR Personal, RG 4, series P, box 16, folder 392.
Barry Goldwater to Robinson, September 16, 1968, BGP, series I, personal correspondence, folder 1967–1968.
Hubert Humphrey to Robinson, December 14, 1968, HHHP, Vice Presidential Files, Control Files, 1968, 150.F.3.1 (B).

13. MOVING FORWARD IN OUR STRUGGLE: 1969–1972

Robinson to Dorothy Schiff, January 9, 1969, DSP, box 63, folder: Robinson, Jackie.
Robinson to Richard Nixon, January 22, 1969, RMNP, White House Central Files, (HU) 2, EX HU-2, box 1.
Richard Nixon to Robinson, February 14, 1969, RMNP, White House Central Files, (HU) 2, EX HU-2, box 1.
Robinson to Nelson Rockefeller, February 26, 1969, NAR Personal, RG 4, series L, box 184, folder 1847.
Robinson to Nelson Rockefeller, May 1, 1969, NAR Personal, RG 4, series P, box 16, folder 392.
J. Edgar Hoover to John Ehrlichman, July 24, 1969, FBIP, file: Jackie Robinson.
Robinson to Nelson Rockefeller, November 14, 1969, NAR Personal, RG 4, series P, box 16, folder 392.
Robinson to Richard Nixon, February 9, 1970, Jackie Robinson (as told to Alfred Duckett), *I Never Had It Made: An Autobiography of Jackie Robinson* (New York: G. P. Putnam's Sons, 1972; reprint, New York: Ecco, 1995), pp. 239–40.
Robinson to Maurice Stans, March 11, 1970, MSP, box 9, 144.H.12.4 (F).
Maurice Stans to Robinson, March 19, 1970, JRP, box 7, folder 15.
Robinson to the Editor of the *Miami Herald*, June 8, 1970, JRP, box 10, folder 19.
Robinson to Michael Hamilburg, October 10, 1970, JRP, box 11, folder 6.
Calvin Morris to Robinson, February 1, 1971, JRP, box 4, folder 23.
Robinson to Calvin Morris, no date [February 1971], JRP, box 4, folder 23.
E. J. Bavasi to Robinson, February 11, 1971, JRP, box 1, folder 20.
Robinson to E. J. Bavasi, no date [February 1971], JRP, box 1, folder 20.
Robinson to Nelson Rockefeller, March 18, 1971, JRP, box 5, folder 25.
Nelson Rockefeller to Robinson, May 3, 1971, JRP, box 5, folder 25.
Richard Nixon to Robinson, June 17, 1971, JRP, box 5, folder 9.
Robinson to William Black, June 22, 1971, JRP, box 16, folder 13.
Robinson to Richard Nixon, no date [December 1971], Robinson, *I Never Had It Made*, pp. 242–43.
Robinson to Andre Baruch, February 14, 1972, JRP, box 1, folder 18.
Robinson to Richard Nixon, March 21, 1972, RMNP, White House Central File, GEN, HU 2, box 7.
Robinson to Roland Elliott, April 20, 1972, RMNP, White House Central File, GEN, HU 2-1, box 12.
Robinson to Nelson Rockefeller, May 2, 1972, NAR Personal, RG 4, series P, box 16, folder 392.

Nelson Rockefeller to Robinson, May 8, 1972, NAR Personal, RG 4, series P, box 16, folder 392.

Robinson to Roy Wilkins, May 17, 1972, NAACPP, part 30, series A, frame 537.

Richard Nixon to Robinson, September 29, 1972, RMNP, White House Central File, RE 2, box 3.

Richard Nixon to Patrick O'Donnell, October 9, 1972, RMNP, White House Central File, RE 2, box 3.

Telegrams: Ralph Abernathy, Berry Gordy, and Hank Aaron, October 25, 1972, JRP, boxes 15 and 16.

PERMISSIONS CREDITS

I am grateful for permission to publish or reprint letters, telegrams, or articles by the following:

Henry Aaron, by permission of Henry Aaron.

Ralph Abernathy, by permission of Juanita J. Abernathy. Credit: Reverend Dr. Ralph David Abernathy.

E. J. Bavasi, by permission of E. J. Bavasi.

Chester Bowles, by permission of Chester Bowles Papers, Manuscripts and Archives, Yale University Library.

Ralph Bunche, reprinted by permission of the Ralph J. Bunche Papers (Collection 2051, Box 127), Department of Special Collections, Charles E. Young Research Library, UCLA.

Gloster Current, by permission of Rebecca E. Current.

Billie Fleming, by permission of Robert M. Fleming.

Barry Goldwater, by permission of the Personal and Political Papers of Senator Barry M. Goldwater, Series I: Personal Correspondence, Arizona Historical Foundation.

Berry Gordy, by permission of Berry Gordy.

Hubert Humphrey, by permission of the Minnesota Historical Society.

L. K. Jackson, by permission of S. Yvonne Jackson McCall.

Martin Luther King, Jr., reprinted by arrangement with the Heirs to the Estate of Martin Luther King, Jr., c/o Writers House as agent for the proprietor, New York, NY. Copyright by Martin Luther King, Jr. Copyright renewed by Coretta Scott King.

Brooks Lawrence, by permission of Anthony Lawrence.

Herbert Lehman, by permission of Herbert H. Lehman Suite and Papers, Rare Book and Manuscript Library, Columbia University in the City of New York.

Peter Lisagor, by permission of the *Chicago Sun-Times.*

Malcolm X, reprinted by permission of the estate of Malcolm X, licensed by CMG Worldwide.

Calvin Morris, by permission of Calvin S. Morris.

Hugh Morrow, by permission of the Rockefeller Archive Center.

Adam Clayton Powell, Jr., by permission of Adam C. Powell III.

Branch Rickey, by permission of Elizabeth R. Wolfe.

Jackie Robinson, by permission of Rachel Robinson, © 2007 Rachel Robinson licensed by CMG Worldwide, www.JackieRobinson.com.

Jackie Robinson (select "Home Plate" columns), by permission of the *New York Amsterdam News* Archives.

James Robinson, by permission of James R. Robinson.

John D. Rockefeller III, by permission of the Rockefeller Archive Center.

Nelson Rockefeller, by permission of the Rockefeller Archive Center.

Hugh Scott, by permission of the University of Virginia, © Rector and Visitors of the University of Virginia.

Patricia Stephens (letter embedded in "Home Plate"), by permission of Patricia Stephens Due. Credit: Patricia Stephens Due and Tananarive Due, coauthors of *Freedom in the Family: A Mother-Daughter Memoir of the Fight for Civil Rights*. Excerpts of the *New York Post* were reprinted as courtesy of the *New York Post*.

Norman Thomas, by permission of the New York Public Library.

James Wechsler, by permission of Nancy F. Wechsler.

Bill White, by permission of Bill White.

ACKNOWLEDGMENTS

"And now, with your indulgence, I would like to ask my wife to come and share this great honor with me. It is hers fully as much as it is mine. I could keep you here all afternoon telling you about her faith in me, her quiet devotion, her wise counsel—above all, the confidence which she instilled and endlessly renewed in me." Jackie Robinson spoke these words of gratitude as he accepted the Spingarn Medal of the NAACP in 1956, and while I can only imagine the depths of his feelings for Rachel Robinson, I can easily join him in recognizing her as a woman of remarkable generosity. *First Class Citizenship* is in our hands primarily because of Rachel Robinson's willingness to share her husband's rich legacy with the rest of us, and I offer her my deepest thanks.

This book includes letters written by many individuals other than Jackie Robinson, and I am indebted to those who have kindly offered permission to publish material they own or manage. This esteemed list includes Hank Aaron, Juanita Abernathy, the Arizona Historical Foundation, Buzzie Bavasi, the *Chicago Sun-Times*, Columbia University, Rebecca Current, Patricia Stephens Due, Lindsay Edelstein of the *New York Post*, Robert Fleming, Berry Gordy, the estate of Martin Luther King, Jr. (in care of Writers House, especially Michele Rubin and Talia Shalev), Anthony Lawrence, the estate of Malcolm X (in care of CMG Worldwide, especially Pete Enfield), S. Yvonne Jackson McCall, the Minnesota Historical Society, Calvin Morris, the New York Public Library, Adam C. Powell III, the Rector and Visitors of the University of Virginia, the Regents of the University of California, James Robinson, the Rockefeller Archive Center, Elinor Tatum of the *New York Amsterdam News*, Nancy Wechsler, Bill White, Elizabeth Wolfe, and Yale University. The inimitable, colorful, and well-connected Buzzie Bavasi also answered more than a few of our research questions.

Countless others have supported this project along the way, and among the most important is Linda Loewenthal of the David Black Literary Agency. Linda responded within minutes of my initial inquiry, and she's been a steady presence ever since, expertly guiding the project through maddening highs and lows far beyond our control. My respect for Linda's collaborative shepherding is immense, and I consider her to be an agent among agents.

I thought that Linda's enthusiasm for *First Class Citizenship* was impossible to match, but along came Paul Golob, the exceptional editor of Times Books and, perhaps even more significant, the son of a devoted Brooklyn Dodgers fan. Paul strengthened the manuscript with analytical and editorial abilities of the highest order, and working with him has been the intellectual highpoint of the project. Many thanks to Paul and his staff at Times Books, especially Christopher O'Connell, Pearl Wu, Jessica Firger, and David Wallace-Wells, for their professionalism, collegiality, and first-rank skills.

Sharon Herr, my dear friend and trusted colleague, offered the administrative support that made it possible for me to meet deadly deadlines. I asked Sharon to take charge of the permissions process not just because of her remarkable attention to detail but also because she has a gracious presence that makes it easy for people to love her. She worked that charm on me long ago, and I remain appreciative to her and her husband, Bob. These two remarkable friends offered me their house, including the refrigerator and pantry and sunroom, while I was compiling and editing the manuscript.

My gratitude extends to a team of research assistants, including Marilyn Farnell, Johnny Trotter, Brian McGovern, Maria Paz Gutierrez Esguerra, Jason Theobald, Diana Claitor, Andrea Gates, and Walt Wilson. There is no group better equipped to uncover hidden treasures and, of course, to provide careful documentation along the way.

Equally deserving of my thanks are the many librarians and archivists who shared their time and expertise. I am indebted especially to Paul Wormser of the National Archives in Laguna Niguel, California, for encouraging me to take a look at the Jackie Robinson file in Richard Nixon's pre-presidential papers (now deposited at the Nixon Library in Anaheim). Invaluable assistance also came from Mary Ann Quinn of the Rockefeller Archive Center; Samuel Rushay of the Nixon Project at the National Archives in College Park, Maryland; the entire reference staff of the Manuscripts Division of the Library of Congress; Steven Nielsen of the Minnesota Historical Society; Linda Whitaker and Susan Irwin of the Arizona Historical Foundation; Anne McFarland of the National Baseball Hall of Fame; and William Stingone, Wayne Furman, Susan Waide, and Laura Ruttum, all of the New York Public Library. I am also grateful to Randy

Sowell of the Harry S. Truman Library, Dwight Strandberg of the Dwight D. Eisenhower Library, Stephen Plotkin of the John F. Kennedy Library, Barbara Cline and Adam Alsobrook of the Lyndon Baines Johnson Library, Meghan Lee of the Richard M. Nixon Library, Stacy Davis of the Gerald R. Ford Library, and the staff at the Herbert Hoover Library.

Thanks, too, to Mildred Bond Roxborough of the NAACP, Diane Kaplan of Yale University, Susan Hamson and Tara Craig of Columbia University, Nancy Shawcross of the University of Pennsylvania, Louis Jackson of the King Papers Project at Stanford University, Kelly Haigh and Genie Guerard of University of California at Los Angeles, Patrizia Stone of the Kheel Center at Cornell University, Mary Huth of the University of Rochester, Edward Gaynor of the University of Virginia, Shannon Burrell of the Amistad Center at Tulane University, Mel Smith of the Connecticut State Library, Betsy Pittman and Thomas Wilsted of the Thomas J. Dodd Research Center at the University of Connecticut, Kevlin Haire of the Ohio State University, Leigh McWhite of the University of Mississippi, Kristen Nyitray of Stony Brook University, Dale Stieber of Occidental College, Teresa Hebron of the University of Michigan, Elaine Ardia of Bates College, William LeFevre of Wayne State University, Sylvia Morra of Elizabethtown College, Bridgette Kelly of the United Church of Christ Archives, the staff at the Chicago History Museum, the staff at the American Jewish Archives, Kerrie Cotton Williams of Auburn Avenue Research Library, and Mike Allen of Massimo Zanetti Beverage USA.

A word of appreciation is also due to the writers whose extensive knowledge about Jackie Robinson has served this project so well, especially Sharon Robinson, Jonathan Eig, Arnold Rampersad, David Falkner, and Jules Tygiel.

Elizabethtown College, my home institution, granted me the space and time I needed to complete the task at hand, and no one has been more supportive of my work than Jeffery Long, the new chair of the religious studies department and an excellent scholar in Hindu studies. Bernadette Schock and Lesley Finney of the development office steered me toward Janice Black, president and CEO of the Foundation for Enhancing Communities, who arranged for a grant to support my travel and research in the early days of the project. Sean Melvin, the imposing chair of our business department, provided expert legal counsel when I had questions about the headache-inducing relationship between scholarship and copyright law. And Karen Hodges was kind enough, unsurprisingly, to let me use her expensive camera.

Thanks to the students who have endured and encouraged my interest in Jackie Robinson; the students in my seminar on religion and politics—Steven, Melissa, Pierce, Megan, Joshua, and Melanie—have been stellar. Thanks, too, to the owners of the neighborhood coffeehouse where I often write: Susan and Al Pera of Cornerstone Coffeehouse in Camp Hill. It's not coffee talking when I say that theirs is the most hospitable coffeehouse in our corner of the world.

Because of the book's recent demands, my parents and in-laws, especially Connie Long and Lis Hagen-Frederiksen, have spent more hours than usual in our home, and I thank them from the depths of my heart for helping me and Karin raise our incredible sons, Jackson Griffith and Nathaniel Finn. Jack and Nate are sheer delights, and they deserve my hugs and kisses for climbing on my lap and asking me to use our laptop computer for galactic games and peek-a-boo with furry monsters.

A final note to Karin, the love of my life. May I give back to you all the patience, support, and encouragement that you have offered me so freely throughout the preparation of this book. If Jack and Nate see anything in my life that's worth imitating, I hope it's all the love and respect and passion that I have for you.

INDEX

Note: JR stands for Jackie Robinson throughout the index

ABOUT THE EDITOR

MICHAEL G. LONG is an associate professor of religious studies at Elizabethtown College and is the author of several books on religion and politics in midcentury America, including *Against Us, but for Us: Martin Luther King, Jr. and the State* and *Billy Graham and the Beloved Community: America's Evangelist and the Dream of Martin Luther King, Jr.* He lives in Camp Hill, Pennsylvania.